HUNGARY 1944-1945

The Forgotten Tragedy

Aspekt non-fiction no 1

Perry Pierik

HUNGARY 1944-1945
The Forgotten Tragedy

★

The Last German Offensives of the
Second World War

★

The Destruction of Europe's last remaining
Jewish Community

★

1998 Aspekt

Pierik, Perry

Hungary 1944-1945 : the Forgotten Tragedy : the Last German Offensives of the Second World War,The Destruction of Europe's last remaining Jewish Community / Perry Pierik ;[transl. [from the Dutch: D.E. Butterman-Dorey]. -
Foto backside book: Xander Colee
Nieuwegein : Aspekt. - Ill., foto's. - (Aspekt non-fiction; 1)
Vert. van: Hongarije 1944-1945 : de vergeten tragedie : de laatste Duitse offensieven van de Tweede Wereldoorlog, de ondergang van de laatste joodse gemeenschap in Europa. -
Nieuwegein : Aspekt, 1995. - (Ciceroreeks ; nr. 2). - Met lit. opg., reg.
ISBN 90-75323-10-7

© Perry Pierik

Aspekt b.v.
P.O. Box 7081
3430 JB Nieuwegein/The Netherlands 1996
Aspekt@knoware.nl

First published 1996
Second edition 1998

All rights reserved. No reproduction, copy or transmission of this publication may be made without written permission.

Contents

Foreword to the second edition	7
Introduction: Hungary, the final part of Hitler's political destruction campaign	11
The Klessheim conspiracy	17
The burning oil of Ploesti	35
The secret power of Ferenc Szálasi	59
The annihilation of Hungarian Jews	77
Wacht an der Donau	111
Budapest is sacrificed	127
The 'Konrad' prelude	151
Frühlingserwachen: Hitler's spring offensive	201
Retreat to the Reichsschutzstellung	223
Vienna, the oil of Zisterdorf and the myth of the Alpenfestung	239
The Hungarian tragedy	273
Sources	283
Bibliography	285
Archive material	297
V. Verbal and written official statements/available correspondence	299
Abbreviations	301
The ranks of the SS and their equivalents in the British Army (1940)	303
Name index	305

Foreword to the second edition

Every so often it is claimed that the Second World War is now definitely a thing of the past but, in spite of this claim there are still, apparently, many aspects of the war that lend themselves to monographic study. As this second edition would indicate, research into the last phases of the war in Hungary is one such area. It is indeed encouraging to see that all over the world this book has been well received by contemporary enthusiasts and historians. Obviously one should first mention, in this connection, Hungary itself where the book received a good review in the leading daily newspaper *Magyar Nemzet*. In journals, too, the book was given a good press. We hope that this second edition will reach an even wider audience so that, with the end of the century in sight, people will be able to thoroughly come to terms with this past, the Hungarian tragedy included.

It has not been necessary to make any textual changes in this book. A year and a half after publication the issues dealt with remain, in broad outline, the same. Furthermore, no new detailed studies of military operations in Hungary between 1944 and 1945 have since appeared in English, German or Hungarian, neither has any new integral research into the persecution of the Jews been produced that might serve to alter the view given here of the Hungarian Holocaust. However, I understand that a new study is at present being done into the way in which Hungarian Christians reacted to the Hungarian Holocaust and into the ways in which they endeavoured to ease people's suffering. Such a study might throw new light on the Hungarian 'bystander' problem examined by Raul Hilberg. A further interesting piece of research to have emerged has been that of Dr. Claudia Steur on the 'Judenreferat', Theodor Dannecker, which has supplied new information on the men who helped to make Adolf Eichmann's deportations possible. The speculations surrounding Raoul Wallenberg also persist. The 40/1996 issue of *Der Spiegel* published a highly speculative article claiming that Wallenberg was in fact a double agent. On examining this article we can only conclude that the facts are too unfounded to support the hypothesis. The interest surrounding Raoul Wallenberg was only heightened by his mysterious disappearance at the end of the Second World War and people remain intrigued. On the Internet there are a number of pages that concentrate on Wallenberg and/or the Wallenberg empire. The Hilversum historian and publisher, Martin Ros, in his Dutch publication *Jakhalsen van het Derde Rijk (Jackals of the Third Reich)* which has since also been translated into German and published by Klett Gotta, throws new light on the last days of the Arrow Cross movement.

Those who lived through the Hungarian tragedy are growing older and older and are gradually dying off. The eye-witness and historian, Dr. Palotas, has died since this book was published. He was in Budapest throughout the fifty-two day long siege and was able to tell me about the atrocities there in graphic detail. Mr. Horst Lange, the only 711.I.D. soldier I was able to trace, who told me all about the incredible taking of Esztergom and of the fighting in the Pilis Heights has, sadly, also passed away. Karl Ullrich, the last commandant of the 5.SS Pz.D. 'Wiking' which, as a division of the IV.SS Pz. corps, played an important part during the 'Konrad' operations has also died. The 'Wiking' 01., Günter Jahnke, from whose diary I frequently cited, spoke at his funeral.

Since the book has come out, in Dutch and English, a number of new facts have come to my attention and so I hope, in the near future, to publish all this in a collection of short essays. For instance, also since the Dutch publication of my book *Van Leningrad tot Berlijn (From Leningrad to Berlin)*, on Dutch Waffen-SS volunteers on the eastern front, the family of a Dutch volunteer have contacted me to let me know that their missing relative was killed during the siege of Budapest. It turned out that this Dutch soldier had served in the 'Florian Geyer' SS cavalry division. Up until then I had been unaware that Dutchmen had served in this division. From another Dutch 'Ehemalige' I learned certain new facts about heavy fighting that had taken place around Rechnitz and the

'Reichsschutzstellung' in the border region between Hungary and Austria (then part of the German Reich) and also that a task force composed in an extremely irregular way, the 'Schweitzer' combat group, had taken part in the fighting there. The unit was composed of troops of different nationalities who had recently recovered from their war wounds. There were Scandinavians from the Waffen-SS division 'Nordland', Dutch Waffen-SS volunteers from the 'Nederland' division, Norwegians from the 'Norge' battalion (formerly with 'Wiking'), German senior officials and Hungarian Waffen-SS men from the combat group 'Ney'. The bloody character of this combat group deployed in the early days of April 1945 shows, once again, how very grim the fighting was on the south front towards the end of the war. The amazing diversity of the troops brought together in this combat unit once again confirms the opinion posited in this book to the effect that Hitler really had sent his last reserves to Hungary where his Waffen-SS 'political soldiers' took a leading role.

Just one remark, finally, about the chapter 'The Burning Oil of Ploesti which describes events on the front prior to the siege of Budapest and the 'Konrad' operations. A number of people have pointed out that the descriptions given in that chapter of the fighting in the Crimean and Romania are particularly brief. My reason for concentrating on the period between the end of December 1944 and the beginning of April 1945 was because that is the time when, to my mind, the true nature of the forgotten Hungarian tragedy comes most sharply into focus. That was where the most important German counter offensives were launched in which the oil fields to the south of Lake Balaton were of crucial importance. The other two central issues, the siege of Budapest and the persecution of the Jews, are dealt with together in one chapter. For descriptions of the fighting that took place in the Crimean and on Romanian soil my sources, contrary to those used for the events from December onwards, were chiefly secondary. What remains rather obscure in these sources is the information relating to the German-

Romanian losses in the Crimean. Though dealt with in only a couple of sentences it would seem worth pointing out that the statistics represent the highest possible mortality rate and that, in all probability therefore, the losses were lower. The problem with these figures is that notably the number of Romanian fatalities remains unclear. Perhaps, in the future, new archive research will help us to form a better picture of the situation but, in the interests of clarity, it seems only right to mention these points here.

With the going to press of this second edition I would like to express the wish that, perhaps at long last, the forgotten Hungarian tragedy will become a little less forgotten. As we stand on the threshold of a new millennium it might be good to first shake the dust of this century from our shoes before venturing forwards. The witnesses of the dramatic events described in this book are slowly disappearing from the stage. It is now the task of the people and academics of today to take over where they have left off. I hope that this book will contribute to that process.

Perry Pierik
Spring 1998

Introduction

When Adolf Hitler died in the catacombs of his Berlin bunker in 1945, a kind of political banditry once described by Hitler himself as a 'Politik des Kühnen Wagnisses' came to an end. It was a long time before historians really understood something about the man who had instigated the Second World War, a war which was above all else Hitler's war.
It was not until the sixties that people began to realize that Hitler had not just been an angry opportunist with a flair for detecting his enemy's weak points. Up until then most people's image of Hitler had largely been formed by the writings of Hermann Rauschning who described the rise of National Socialism as a nihilistic revolution. Rauschning saw Hitler as a man without objectives, who was only interested in gaining power. In his opinion Hitler did not have a proper world view. The ideas generated by him were seen as nothing more than tactical instruments of power. Well-known Hitler biographers, such as Allan Bullock, adhered to this view. Georg Lukacz claimed that Hitler did not have a 'comprehensive ideology'.
In 1969, the German historian Eberhard Jaeckel effectively banished such views for all time with the publication of his book 'Hitlers Weltanschauung, Entwurf einer Herrschaft'. A close study of Hitler's books, letters, speeches and political testament had revealed to him that Hitler's thoughts and political dealings throughout the years did reflect great consistency. Hitler was, in fact someone who stubbornly held on to his original notions, ideas that had been developed earlier on. His book 'Mein Kampf', in retrospect an extremely frank confession of his opinions, perfectly illustrates this point. It prompted Jaeckel to call it the world's greatest unread bestseller. Hitler published three books at different times in his life so it is possible to examine the consistency of his various theories. The pattern becomes ever clearer. This way of examining his works was adopted by a new generation of Hitler biographers. Helmuth Heiber was one of the first to

claim that Hitler and National Socialism was one and the same thing. Sebastian Haffner spoke of the emergence of so-called 'Hitlerism', Hitler being the Lenin and Marx of National Socialism. National Socialism was the private dream of a man who had once been a simple soldier, who was a failed artist, who went on to become Führer of the German Reich and whose ideas were to dictate the politics of a powerful Germany in the heart of Europe. All that was now left for historians to do was to unravel Hitler's political ideologies.

The core of Hitler's ideology was (and historians now agree on this) that the history of mankind is not determined by factors such as social class and religion but rather by matters such as nationality and race. As far as foreign political aims go the chief objective of any nation is simply to have the capacity to fight for its existence, or to use Hitler's term, its 'Lebensraum' (living space). To attain this goal it was necessary for Hitler to have total control over domestic affairs.

Haffner was right when he pointed out that such aims were close to the general power politics of all superpowers. What was new about Hitler's ideas was that fighting was seen as an end in itself. Hitler's struggle for Lebensraum was simultaneously an impetus to go into combat. In his view such eternal strife was central to existence and would preserve the purity of the race. The kind of securing of Lebensraum that Hitler had in mind would be a perpetual process. In the east of the 'Continental Empire' that was to be established (colonies overseas were of less interest to Hitler) a 'burning' frontier would be created where SS corps would live in permanent conflict with the 'barbaric' peoples of the east.

The second point of departure between Hitler and other geopolitical thinkers of his day was that he regarded the conflict ahead as purely racial. He was eminently intuitive in his approach. Nowhere in his writings or speeches does Hitler exactly define what he means by race. What was clearly evident though was that he regarded Jews as the outcasts of the world and Slavic peoples as 'Untermenschen' who deserved to be suppressed. This brings us back to Hitler's concept of Lebensraum. In his vision of the future for Germany Hitler saw a 'Continental Empire' free of Jews in which Slavs would be servants to German overlords in what would be a newly regulated racial ('völkische') state. In his 'Anmerkungen zu Hitler' Haffner concluded, on the basis of this information, that since Hitler's ideas gave rise to nothing creative he could not correctly be called a statesman. His ideas only led to catastrophe: 'Hitler had got it wrong in an incredibly big way'. Hitler had made the big mistake of judging a country's importance by its geographical size when what really counts is the technological level at which a country operates. With his deep-rooted anti-Semitic feelings he quickly turned the entire Jewish community against him even though in the 1914-1918 war Jews had been predominantly pro-German.

Hitler's notions were so radical that most of his critics, before and after the war, believed him to be insane. 'The man does not exist', Kurt Tucholsky maintained, 'he is nothing more than all the commotion he creates.' If only that had been true. Hitler was not only a man with extremely radical ideas, he also implemented these ideas and found a nation that was prepared to follow him! It was through his various achievements that Hitler was able to win the support of the German people. One need only think of Germany's remarkable economic recovery after 1933.

Hitler's political notions were intelligent, effective and successful, especially in the early years but the eventual outcome of his objectives was disastrously destructive and it was with great counter-productive force that things finally turned against Germany. In order to realize his plans Hitler had to reject the existing institutions and norms and values of people of his day. He left the League of Nations and altered Germany's economic status within Europe. Hitler wanted the country to become an autarkical state independent of the outside world for all its raw materials. In this respect Hitler's notions incorporated the lessons learnt in the 1914-1918 war. It had been the growing scarcity of raw materials and food supplies that had seriously crippled imperial Germany in the '14-'18 trench war. The terror of the British blockade that had been set up around Germany and had led to the starvation of 600,000 Germans was imprinted on many people's memories. By changing the status-quo (Lebensraum) Hitler wanted to ensure that such a thing would never be able to happen again.

There were many politicians, military people and even civilians who were able to go along with and support this geopolitical standpoint. Hitler's racial views, though, and the huge scale of the perpetual battle that he envisaged, were either less clear or else too unpleasant for people to envisage. People turned away from these notions or found comfort in the words of Tucholsky.

So it was that the myth surrounding Nazism arose. After the war many Germans, historians included, regretted that Germany had been in the grip of a 'dunkles Rätsel'. Hitler was an ill-fated person who had popped up from nowhere, who had precipitated his country's downfall and had dragged it down with him like a helpless victim. This theme gave rise to a 'Historikerstreit' in which the book 'Griff nach der Weltmacht ' written by the historian Fritz Fischer played an important role. In his book 'Hitler war kein Betriebsunfall', published in 1991, he again protests about the 'Verharmlosung' of German historiography.

The Hungarian situation of 1944 and 1945 was no dark secret. It was a continuation of the consistent policy determining factors of Hitler's politics identified by Jaeckel: to exterminate Jews and gain Lebensraum.

What happened in Hungary was the logical continuation of a German political theory formed long before. In view of the fact that up until this stage Hungary had remained relatively unaffected by the war one may say that what happened there was a great tragedy. At five minutes to twelve, just before the Third Reich fell, Hungary was reduced to a burning ruin. The country's Jewish community, the last remaining community of its kind in Europe, fell under the command of Adolf Eichmann. At this stage in the war, everybody knew what happened to Jews who were handed over to Nazis. Despite many pleas and attempts to mediate - especially from Jews and people who were neutral - the last inevitable stage of the Holocaust began. It was an extremely bloody phase of the war. Eichmann afterwards referred to the extermination of the Hungarian Jews as' least problematic of all the exterminations'.

In the process of protecting the Hungarian oil fields and while using the country as a springboard for the lost oil fields of Ploesti (Ploiesti) in Romania, the whole of Hungary had been converted into one of the bloodiest battlefields of the Second World War. In Hitler's concept of Lebensraum oil had always been of paramount importance. Therefore Hitler became obsessive about these last natural oil reserves of the Third Reich with his familiar stubborness. It was this obsessiveness that largely decreed his strategic manoeuvres towards the end of the war.

Post-war historiographers focussed on the activities in the Ardennes and Berlin but while these battles were continuing the German army's élite was fighting a forgotten battle on Hungarian soil. 'These are the worst battles since Stalingrad', the local Soviet commanders complained to their superiors in Stavka. In three leading offensives: the 'Konrad' operations followed by the big March offensive 'Frühlingserwachen', Hitler made one final attempt to gain ultimate power with the result that the battles fought in Budapest turned out to be bloodier than those of the final battle for Berlin.

'Hungary 1944-1945, the Forgotten Tragedy' describes the plight of the last Jewish community in Europe, the way in which people were herded like cattle, the hopes and the desperation of all the Jews who were deported. One sees how, with the end of the war and the loss of the war in sight, the SS gradually appeared to be more willing to negotiate but how ultimately they deployed the extermination machine as viciously as ever before. The death marches to Hegyeshalom will be described and the opportunity that the Horthy regime and the Arrow Cross movement of Szálasi provided for the extermination of their own Jewish people. We see how Hitler's obsession with the oil reserves in Hungary mushroomed into a military strategic plan. An account is given of how, in the Gerecse and Pilis Heights, units of the best armed SS divisions initiated an offensive on New Year's Day 1945 as though it was May 1940. Parallels will be drawn between the operations that took place in the Ardennes, the Alsace and in Hungary and it will be shown how the Vistula (Wistra/Weichsel) and Oder (Odra) fronts were systematically undermined by Hungarian plans. A description is given of the last major German offensive of the Second World War, operation 'Frühlingserwachen' and of how, in the days when defeat was near, tension increased between the regular army and the SS. The commencement of the Russian Vienna offensive is sketched and the 6.SS Pz. army's attempt to escape imminent obliteration. Finally, the Soviet offensive in the direction of Vienna, the Reich's second capital, is traced and the final 'Alpenfestung' battle that never took place. By the time the last shots were fired, hundreds of thousands of people had been killed.

The Klessheim conspiracy

March 1944: proudly the red Soviet flag flies from official buildings in Leningrad once more. On the south front the troops of the Red Army had crossed the river Dniester and were approaching the Romanian frontier. In France there was conspicuous activity in the air. In anticipation of D-Day French railway lines were being bombed by RAF Bomber Command. By February 1944, plans for operation Overlord had been finalized. In Italy, soldiers of the 6th American army unit fought at Anzio and Nettuno. Airborne bomb attacks had reduced the beautiful monastery at Monte Cassino to ruins. By January, in the parts of Italy that had been liberated, legal proceedings had started against former members of the Grand Council. Large Italian cities, like Turin, were being afflicted by strikes and the first transportation of Jews from Athens to Auschwitz was just getting under way. At the same time, there was much activity in Salzburg, a city nestling deep in the heart of the Third Reich which was coming under increasing pressure on all sides.

On 18th March, there was much activity in Salzburg, the city that was to become famous by the anti-Nazi film 'The Sound of Music', made after the war. The only sound to be heard that day, though, was the sound of Allied bombers flying overhead with their fatal cargoes that were destined for the 'Reich' and the sound of black SS transport vehicles which, in the interests of security, had diverted all their activity to the city. Klessheim, the castle of archduke Ludwig Viktor (situated not far from Salzburg) was where all the activity was concentrated. In this ancient fortress, a masterly plan was being prepared.
The whole German Nazi top had been summoned to Klessheim. Hitler had called together his leading advisors, such as Wilhelm Keitel 'Chef des OKW', Alfred Jodl 'Chef des Wehrmachtführungsstabes', Reichsführer-SS Heinrich Himmler and 'Reichsleiter' Martin Bormann. What had occasioned this top-level meeting was the fact

that Joachim von Ribbentrop, the German Minister of Foreign Affairs, had written a letter of warning to Hitler in February 1944. He had heard that Hungary's Kallay administration was seeking contact with the Allies. On February 12th, Hitler received a letter from Miklos Horthy, Hungarian regent and admiral without fleet in which the Führer was asked to allow nine light Hungarian divisions to return to Hungary from the eastern front. In mid March, Hitler received word that the Kallay administration had issued orders to sabotage German military freight trains destined for the armies of Von Manstein and Kleist. This and other incidents reinforced the notion that the Hungarian allies were becoming increasingly unreliable. For Hitler it was the last straw. Horthy was invited to Klessheim for talks ostensibly aimed at 'resolving' their differences.

As far as Hitler was concerned the 'solutions' were all one-way solutions. He had decided to deal severely with the Hungarian' rebels'. The invitation extended to Horthy was all part of an extremely refined coup plan designed to make the Hungarians fall back in line. Just like Hitler's early political and military successes it was designed to be a quick operation causing little bloodshed. Hitler's reasoning was both logical and cold-blooded. In suggesting to Horthy that he wanted to discuss and resolve the military problems he put Horthy in the difficult position of being unable to refuse to cooperate. Subsequently Horthy, probably accompanied by several higher Hungarian military officers, would be enticed out of Hungary thus effectively 'beheading' the country politically and militarily for a time. German forces would then enter and occupy the country attacking from four different directions.

The day before Horthy arrived at Klessheim castle, Hitler went over the details of the plans with Jodl, Ribbentrop, Keitel and Himmler. The military plan to occupy Hungary, code-named 'Unternehmen Margarethe', had originally been thought out in September 1943. At that time Hitler was having to contend with disloyalty in Italy. Hitler decided that he was not going to experience a failure like this a second time. Operations 'Margarethe' I and II were, therefore, plans for the possible occupation of Romania and Hungary countries which, because of the shifting front lines both from southern (Italy) and eastern (the Ukraine) directions could no longer be fully depended upon.

The Romanian dictator, General Ion Antonescu, was the kind of person Hitler liked, a 'Gneisenau' and war-horse whose loyalty he could depend on. When it came to Hungary Hitler was more suspicious. Horthy, a feudal aristocrat with Habsburg traits, was the type of person with whom Hitler automatically clashed. The Habsburg realm - of which his father was a product - was something Hitler had always loathed and the loathing was mutual. Hitler was a typical parvenu, a corporal who made a stand against an admiral. Field Marshal Von Weichs wrote in his diary in 1944 'Hitler hated Horthy' and that just about summed up the situation.

Horthy had risen to power after the communists and social democrats in Hungary had failed to establish a Soviet-style republic. On 21st March, 1919 in the chaos following the end of the First World War and with the disintegration of the Habsburg state the revolutionaries had grasped their chance. Following the German example (between November 1918 and May 1919 an experimental Soviet-style republic had existed in Munich) and inspired by the communist revolution in Russia it was proclaimed that a Soviet-style republic now existed in Hungary. Because of the power vacuum that arose after the collapse of the Dual Monarchy, it was easy for the revolutionaries to seize power. When the Red Army failed to provide support, the coup was brought to a bloody end by Hungarian reactionaries who had the support of armies in neighbouring countries. The Soviet-style republic of Bela Kun, nicknamed the bloodhound, fell ingloriously and was followed by brutal white terror.

During that period, Horthy came to the fore as Hungary's strong leader. On 1st March, 1920 he was appointed Regent of Hungary. Though this administration remained loyal to the monarch for a time, allegiance soon switched to the alternative authoritarian regime with its decidedly feudal characteristics. Horthy could depend on the support of conservative and liberal factions of the Hungarian political spectrum and, by manipulating the elections, he managed to remain in power for many years. The small Christian and agricultural parties were forced to remain in opposition. Horthy's Hungary, therefore, knew no parliamentary democracy.

The foreign political aims of Hungary were entirely founded on a revision of the Treaty of Trianon. Just as with the Germans in Versailles, the Dual Monarchy was punished in France for the part it had played in the First World War. The Dual Monarchy disintegrated and Hungary lost 63% of its citizens and 73% of its territory. Though these areas were inhabited by Hungarian minorities tensions increased to such an extent that revising the Trianon treaty was something that remained permanently on the top of the political agenda.

For opportunist reasons Hungary had been pro-German. By latching on to expansionistic German politics Horthy hoped to be able to realize his revisions and to an extent this goal was achieved. In 1939, Hungary regained territory from Czechoslovakia. In 1940 Romanian land went to Budapest and in 1941 parts of Yugoslavia went to Hungary. The price for executing such political policies was, that Hungary quickly found itself securely in the German camp and when war broke out again it was difficult for Hungary to extricate itself from German domination. When it came to participating militarily in the campaign against the Soviet Union (operation 'Barbarossa'), a heavy price was paid on the front. It was clear that Horthy did not mind sharing victory with Hitler but he did not particularly want to share Hitler's defeats. At Klessheim, he hoped to be able to successfully implement his policy to distance Hungary from Berlin.

Hitler had thoroughly thought out his plans for occupying Hungary and had prepared for his meeting with Horthy well for very good reasons. He had a high opinion of Horthy as a political negotiator. The eminent grey-haired man had a long career to draw on after all. In previous meetings with Hitler, Horthy had proven to be an exceptionally skilled negotiator. In April 1943, Hitler had been particularly heavy-handed with Horthy. He had threatened him on pain of death to agree to all sorts of decisions and Horthy had returned the following day as promised. Cunningly, Horthy walked up to Hitler and whispered in his ear: 'I am rather hard of hearing, so I'm afraid that yesterday I must have missed at least half of the conversation.' This effectively threw Hitler into a desperate rage. Though politically and militarily the weaker party Horthy had then managed to corner Hitler but that was not going to happen a second time.

Obviously, Horthy realized that this time he was not going to get away with things as easily. The relationship between the two men had been deteriorating visibly for years and in March 1944 it was to reach its tragic low point. Horthy had first met Hitler in August 1936 and, like all politicians of his day, he was fascinated by this 'Gefreiter' who had seemingly emerged from nowhere and within no time was determining the entire political course of Central Europe. When Hitler started engineering plans with Austria, Horthy decided that it was high time to personally get to know this newcomer to the international political arena.

In his memoirs Horthy recalled how this first meeting with Hitler gave rise to mixed feelings. The Hungarian press had critically followed the rise of national socialism. In the Budapest newspapers, journalists had openly questioned the authenticity of the fire in the Reichstag's buildings in 1933. After this fire, Hitler had obtained an emergency order permitting him to rule outside of parliament and these emergency measures had never been revoked - ostensibly in the interests of avoiding a communist coup. In the Hungarian press one severely doubted the Nazi version of the fire story which put all the blame on the communists. Another thing that the admiral found distasteful was the night of the 'Long Knives' against the SA, this was something that he called 'revenge-justice'. Despite all this Horthy was motivated by a certain kind of curiosity to get to know the 'Führer' personally but to avoid political upheaval he decided to make it a private visit.

The meeting took place in Obersalzberg in August 1936. Like many others before him Horthy was bowled over by Hitler's perfectly orchestrated reception. Horthy was shown to an enormous settee in Hitler's study and was then made to listen to a three-hour long monologue. The rugged granite inclines of the Alps visible through the window of the study filtered into the room and somehow served to endorse all that Hitler said. Hitler, who was rhetorically at his best in these years, reminisced on the Hungarian tragedies of the First World War pointing out that no nation had been harder hit than Hungary. He reminded Horthy of how much land and how many citizens had been lost to neighbouring countries because of the Trianon treaty. Hitler likened this injustice to the Versailles dictate from which he had freed Germany. Hitler had won Horthy over, the Hungarian's suspicion disappeared and, as Horthy later wrote in his memoirs, 'I had no reason to contradict him'.

Horthy became more and more impressed by Hitler's incredible memory. The man was able to quote endless passages from all sorts of works and Horthy slowly became convinced that Hitler was a highly intelligent being who, autodidactically, with no formal higher education to back him up, had managed to assimilate an amazing amount of knowledge.

The two men parted on friendly terms. Later, when the war was over, Horthy confessed 'I was not the first person to be taken in by Hitler'. For the time being however everything seemed to be all right. On the anniversary of Horthy's celebrated arrival in Budapest after the quelling of the Bela Kun revolution Horthy received an enthusiastic telegram from Hitler. In those days the two men were still civil towards each other, but that was not to remain so for very long. In 1938 when Horthy saw Hitler again, this time on an official visit, Horthy's opinion of the man changed. At first, the whole meeting seemed to be friendly enough. Horthy's wife received a bunch of her

The European fear of communism. Soviet-style republic in Hungary, a large landowner is hanged. The culprits pose in front of the camera.

To a large extent the political instability in Hungary derived from the Treaty of Trianon which had effectively deprived Hungary of a great proportion of its territory and people.

*Admiral Horthy visiting the 'Germania' shipyard in Kiel.
Horthy was curious to meet Germany's new strong man. The 'Night of
the Long Knives' had made him wary of Hitler. When Hitler told Horthy
that he would not hesitate 'to destroy Prague' Horthy realized what kind
of a man he really was.*

favourite flowers from Hitler even though they were difficult to obtain at that time of the year. At the Germania shipyard in Kiel, Mrs Horthy was invited to launch the warship 'Prinz Eugen' which turned out to be a lucky vessel. The 'Prinz Eugen' was one of the few German warships to come out of the war undamaged. After the war though its fortune changed. The British gave the 'Prinz Eugen' to the Americans who used it in nuclear testing off Bikini island in 1946. A year later the ship's burnt out hull was sunk not far from Kwajalein.

After the ship had been launched, Hitler took Horthy on one side and, without further ceremony, proceeded to unfold his plans for the future. Horthy could not help noticing that Hitler clearly saw himself as the future ruler of all of Europe. Hitler also intimated that Czechoslovakia would be his first target. Horthy was somewhat taken aback by the way in which Hitler formulated his ideas. It was Hitler's contention that the Czechs would have to be 'wiped out' and if need be, the city of Prague 'obliterated'. Horthy was dumbstruck. 'The atmosphere which had been friendly enough up until then suddenly turned cool' noted the regent in his post-war memoirs. Anyone who could speak so lightly about possibibly destroying what was undoubtedly one of the most beautiful cities in the world, frightened him. As Horthy later realized his fears were not unfounded. Only seven years after this second meeting with Hitler, Budapest was reduced to a burning ruin, the whole city being sacrificed as part of Hitler's grand destruction plan to which he adhered with unmitigating resolve.

There was little that could be called courteous about the meeting that took place in the Alps in March 1944. To prevent Horthy from once again playing at being deaf Hitler had seen to it that the room was filled with microphones and tape recorders. To make sure that the regent kept his word Hitler saw to it that every sound Horthy made was recorded for posterity. Horthy's train arrived in Salzberg on 18th March. It was immediately clear that the Germans had played their cards right.

Horthy was not alone, he had brought with him his top advisors: Csatay, the Hungarian Minister of Defence, Szombathelyi, the army's Chief of Staff and Chyczy, the Minister for Foreign Affairs. Many of the Hungarian top functionaries were thus temporarily removed from their country making Hungary an easy prey.

Horthy had prepared himself for an unpleasant surprise and Kallay, Hungarian Premier, and the cabinet minister Csatay had been opposed to Horthy's trip to Klessheim all along. Horthy, who still secretly hoped that he might be able to convince Hitler of the necessity of precipitating a Hungarian military withdrawal, had managed to allay their fears. He and Chyczy had convinced themselves that such a visit might help to reduce tension. They based their predictions on the outcome of recent visits paid to Hitler by Tiso and Antonescu. In neither case had punitive sanctions been imposed by the Germans. All the same Horthy felt uneasy when, on 17th March, the train destined for Salzburg pulled out of Budapest station. 'A good seaman never sets sail on a Friday' he muttered to himself. His intuition was correct.

Horthy was met at Salzburg station by Hitler, Keitel and Von Ribbentrop. At first normal protocol was observed. It was not very long, though, before Hitler intimated that he wanted to speak with Horthy in private. Only the interpreter, Paul Schmidt, was present but only for the first part of the meeting between the two leaders. Horthy asked, after a short time, if Schmidt might be dismissed. As no others witnessed the meeting the only source we can draw on is Horthy's memoirs. Hitler accused Horthy of sabotage and of collaborating with the Allied Forces and made it quite clear that after what had happened in Italy such behaviour was intolerable. Horthy firmly repudiated all the accusations which only caused Hitler to issue more threats and demand Kallay's resignation. With his bushy eyebrows and square chin the Hungarian politician Kallay was a striking personality. A fierce supporter of the age-old Hungarian struggle for freedom and sovereignity he was the embodiment of the Hungarian desire for independence. As far as Horthy was concerned Hitler had gone too far with his threats. 'If everything has already been decided' he retorted 'my presence is no longer necessary' and with that he stood up and left the room. Hitler had not responded to Horthy's request to withdraw the Hungarian units. The regent, who was fed up with the war and who had already lost his son Stephan on the Eastern Front, had said all needed to be said.

That was when Hitler chose to use the tricks he had been keeping up his sleeve. Suddenly, all the air-raid sirens went off at Klessheim. Apparently all telephone connections had been broken. Of course, none of this was true but in this way Hitler was able to delay Horthy's return to Budapest. Meanwhile, without the regent's knowledge, numerous German divisions were rapidly filtering into Hungary, moving in response to operation 'Margarethe'. Unable to travel or to communicate Horthy was stranded at Klessheim. With hypocritical politeness Hitler invited his guest to lunch and Horthy reluctantly accepted.

It was a macabre scene, Horthy eating with Hitler while fearing the worst for his country and Hitler eating nervously from his vegetarian salad while waiting for news from the Hungarian front. Reichsführer-SS, Heinrich Himmler, was also present at that meal. Himmler headed the SS imperium which, over the years, had started to become more and more of a state within a state. He had power over the country's whole police and intelligence network. His say in economic affairs and his military power had also expanded tremendously during the war years. Above all else, Himmler was in command of the programme to eradicate all European Jews. While Horthy was exchanging pleasantries with the Reichsführer-SS Adolf Eichmann's convoy, the big motor behind all the European Jewish deportation movements, was invading Hungary as part of operation 'Margarethe' under the protection of the German armed forces. They proceeded to execute what Eichmann later called the smoothest Jewish deportation operation of his entire career.

While the men sat together at table in what was a strained atmosphere, Hitler addressed Keitel. In a loud voice so that Horthy could hear him Hitler asked: 'Can the invasion be stopped?' Keitel immediately turned to Hitler and replied: 'No my Führer, the troops are already on the move.' It was nine in the evening when Hitler finally accompanied Horthy to his train. Horthy was utterly devastated. He had played the game and lost. After the meal, he had signed a protocol that had been drawn up by the Nazis in which he had agreed to German demands regarding Hungary. In the agreement there was no doubt about where Horthy's Hungary stood in the European struggle for power. Hungary had been and was to remain in the German camp. A pro-German government would be appointed to replace the Kallay administration and Hungarian troops would only be allowed to operate according to German OKW plans.

The Germans were so confident of their diplomatic success with Horthy that they thought it unnecessary to employ all the units planned for operation 'Margarethe'. The original plan had been for parachutists to land near Budapest but for psychological reasons the Germans decided it would be best not to occupy the Hungarian capital just yet. Hitler did not want to upset the ordinary man in the street unnecessarily.

The defeated Hungarian delegation was accompanied on its return journey by two uninvited guests: Winckelmann, the Chief of Police and Dr. Edmund Veesenmayer, 'Reichsbevöllmächtigter Ungarn' (Commandant responsible for Hungary). Together, these officials who travelled back with Horthy constituted two important components of the German repression plan. By now Horthy knew that on arriving in Hungary he would find his country occupied by German troops. In Budapest, he would be greeted by a German 'guard of honour'.

Though all this was dramatic enough Horthy could not possibly have envisaged what was still to come. Within a year the whole country would be economically crippled and its entire Jewish community wiped out. Budapest would be one big ruin and five of the biggest and most destructive battles of modern military history would have been fought on Hungarian soil: battles described by the Red Army as the worst since those fought in Stalingrad.

Operation 'Margaretha', the military occupation of Hungary went very well for Germany. It was one of the last military actions to go as smoothly as those of the early war years. The Germans were supreme, the adversary surrendered without opposition.

The operation began with the so-called Hungarian bombing of a German train travelling from Vienna to Budapest. The Hungarians hurried forward with apologies for a crime they had not committed and the alleged bombing served to 'justify' the ensuing German invasion. The same tactics had been used by the Hungarians in 1941 when they had started war with the Soviet Union in the hope of gaining some of the spoils of war that were supposed to be had in the east. This same ploy was now being used by the Germans against the Hungarians.

The only problem the Germans had was with the logistics of the operation. For them it was difficult to get together the armed units they needed now that their country was being approached on all sides in the all-out attack that was being mounted by Germany's enemies. Troops were summoned from all corners of the 'Reich' and diverted to Hungary. This included Ob.Southeast troops drawn from the Yugoslavian front that had been fighting against Tito's partisans. Several units, such as the 16.SS Pz.Gren. D. 'Reichsführer-SS', were taken from Italy where parts of the division were caught up near Nettuno. From the west came the Pz.Lehr division together with other units and 'landesschutzen'-batallions.

Another problem was that the units gathered around Hungary were continually aware that they might at any given moment be diverted to the moving eastern front. The generals on the southern front put in many requests for reinforcements when they heard that new units were on their way. The Führer's headquarters was under continual pressure. It was obvious that 'Margarethe' could only be supported by so many divisions for a short time and that afterwards most of the units would have to be sent off to the front - often immediately.

Despite these problems the operation went 'without a hitch', as the diary OKW recorded. All of Hitler's demands relating to the Kallay administration were met without difficulty. On 23rd March, a pro-German government was officially installed in Budapest. Kallay's term of office had lasted for exactly one year. The German military attaché in Budapest, General Von Greiffenberg was ordered to summon together pro-German Hungarian officers for the pending reorganization of the Hungarian defence system.

The initiation of operation 'Margarethe' was the prelude to Germany's destructive Hungarian political programme. Hitler wasted no time. On the same evening that Horthy left for Budapest and German tanks crushed Hungarian sovereignty, Hitler called for Karl Otto Saur instructing him to put all Hungarian resources to good use in the interests of the German war effort.

Saur, Chief of Staff of the German War Office, right-hand man to Albert Speer (and later Speer's successor) was a typical example of someone who was close to Hitler. He had the ability to continually pander to Hitler's needs and to support all his grand, but sometimes completely absurd plans. The following example of something which occurred in May 1943 illustrates how totally lacking in personality Saur was. Just outside Hitler's East Prussian headquarters, a demonstration was given of what could be done with a 180 ton (!) super tank. It had been designed at Hitler's request and the model was made of wood. The presentation was attended by professor Porsche, the tank genius Heinz Guderian and General Zeitler whom were extremely pessimistic about the possibilities in battle with this hideous thing. When praise was not forthcoming Hitler was quickly disappointed. At that moment, Saur spoke up. He started singing the praises of the enormous hulk of a tank. It would revolutionize warfare. An excited discussion then ensued between Saur and Hitler that was so divorced from reality and bedded in the realms of fantasy that the experts were flabbergasted. By the end of their heated debate, Hitler and Saur were both absolutely convinced that this was just the tip of the iceberg. Both contended that the ideal tank of the future would weigh 1,500 ton (!) and that it could be transported to the front by train and in sections. The tank would be welded together on site before going on to pulverize the enemy. One of the tank specialists present could not contain himself any longer. He pointed out that such a 'monstrosity' would produce such a cloud of smoke that one would be able to ignite it with a single hand-grenade. Hitler was irritated, he turned on him and said that the hypertrophic armoured vehicle would therefore have to be equipped with automatic weapons so that nobody could approach it. Saur was again in agreement with the Führer. 'If anyone deserved to be put on trial' Albert Speer wrote in his Spandau diary of the Nuremberg trials 'then it was that grovelling man Saur.'

The task that Hitler had in mind for Saur was to get him to immediately make use of the opportunities created by operation 'Margarethe' in order to set in motion Germany's economic exploitation of Hungarian resources. Hungary was a valuable asset to the Germans in March 1944 and in the following months its importance would only increase.
The country had at that time a population of over ten million people many of whom were employed in agriculture; 50.8% of the working population was employed in the agrarian sector. At a time when food was becoming scarce, the Germans were glad to be able to tap this new source. There were five million sheep and pigs and almost 900,000 horses in the country. Reichsführer-SS Himmler already had his eye on these horses. They would be useful to him in building up his SS cavalry divisions. It did not take long for Himmler to think up even more mercenary demands. Having seen that the country had a sizable Jewish community he decided that

he could motorize his divisions by exchanging Jews for trucks. The details of this plan will be explained later.

Hungary was also rich in raw materials. The oil fields at Nagykanizsa had recently started producing more oil. In 1939 after the Standard Oil Company had bored new holes, production had risen to 200,000 tons per annum, enough to supply a third of the domestic oil requirement. In subsequent years, production had soared rising above the domestic requirement of 600,000 tons per year. The greater part of the excess oil was exported to Germany. In 1943 alone, 310,000 tons of oil went to Germany.

As the war progressed, Hungarian oil became ever more important to the Germans. Eventually the Hungarian oil fields would even come to influence Hitler's strategic dealings and military planning. In March 1944 though this problem did not yet exist. Germany still had the luxury of being able to import its oil from the Romanian oil fields in Ploesti though rumours about a Romanian pact with the Allied Forces and knowledge that the Red Army was approaching were making Hitler increasingly nervous.

Apart from its oil reserves Hungary was also rich in bauxite, an important raw material for the aircraft industry. From 1936 onwards, bauxite production increased going from 329,000 to over 500,000 tons in 1937 and the ensuing years. Hungary was producing approximately 14% of the world's bauxite. During the war years, the growth in production was nothing short of explosive. In 1942, Hungary produced over 1,000,000 tons of bauxite no less than 926,123 tons of which were destined for the German market.

Operation 'Margarethe' allowed the German War Office to gain a firmer hold on the Hungarian economy and thus to forcefully increase production until their requirements were met. It was not just Speer and German industrialists who saw chances in Hungary, Heinrich Himmler's SS imperium also had an interest in Hungarian business. The moment 'Margarethe' was initiated the German secret service came into operation. In the night of 18th and 19th March no less than 3076 prominent Jewish citizens were arrested, many of whom were leading Hungarian industrialists.

The SS was interested in the vital role of these Jews in the Hungarian economy. In the private sector their share in business was disproportionate to that of other citizens. According to census statistics of the thirties the circa 445,000 Jews constituted merely 5% of the population yet they owned 53% of all Hungary's private companies. As Germany's dominion over Hungary increased so Himmler was able to expand his SS imperium, at the expense of the Jewish people. Major businesses were taken over. Himmler's interest was not only in what the Jews owned but also in their community which, like a last European refuge had, up until then, remained untouched by the Holocaust. While in the rest of Hitler's European 'stronghold' Jews had been rounded up, deported and finally executed the Hungarian Jews quietly awaited their destiny. All this changed, though, when Adolf Eichmann set foot on Hungarian soil on the night of 18th March.

The Burning Oil of Ploesti

Operation 'Margarethe' marked the beginning of Hitler's political plan. The political and military changes of 1944 accelerated Germany's rapid involvement in Hungarian affairs. At first, Hitler seemed to be euphoric about his success with the recalcitrant Horthy and with the Kallay administration. On 20th March, Hitler gathered together a number of his generals and made one of his historic speeches.
To summarize, Hitler's estimation of the German military situation at that point was as follows. He contended that the decisive moment would concur with the success or failure of the western Allied landings. It was, therefore, vitally important to immediately intercept such forays and push the Allied Forces back into the sea. Hitler was convinced that Churchill was 'an old and sick man' and that he would, therefore, be incapable of carrying off such a plan. Operation 'Overlord' would thus fizzle out into a sort of Dieppe situation (i.e. the 1942 failed 'practice landing' of the Allies). So in practice the western front would remain free of attacks for a number of years to come (!) Germany would, therefore, be able to put all its efforts into the war in the east. In the meantime, Hitler wanted to fortify the Atlantic coastline where the so-called 'Atlantic Wall' that would run from the Spanish border to Norway would act as a sea defence.
Hitler's concerns about the western front were certainly grounded. While he was making his 20th March speech the western Allies had just started heavily bombing French road and rail networks from the air. This Allied air offensive, chiefly mounted by the RAF's Bomber Command squadron, would continue until June 1944 when operation 'Overlord', the Allied landing on the Normandy coast, was to commence. Already on 23rd December 1943, General Eisenhower had been appointed to act as coordinator of this massive combined maritime operation that hovered above the coast of Hitler's 'European Fortress' like a dark cloud.

Meanwhile, in the east, political and military matters were not going as Hitler wished. Since 1943, Hitler had been contemplating invading and occupying Romania, in much the same way that he planned to occupy Hungary. Obviously it was not so easy to make such moves where allies were concerned as this would clearly stir up anti-German feeling and that was something Berlin could well do without. On the other hand, Romania was very important to Germany.

Hitler was chiefly interested in Romania's oil fields which had become immensely valuable to him since the loss of the Ukrainian oil fields in 1944. Together with the German synthetic oil industry, the oil obtained from these fields guaranteed that the German army was able to meet all the demands that were required of it in the 'All-front war' that was continuing. As the Allies were stronger in the air, the German synthetic oil industry was coming under increasing pressure. When the Allies - invading from Italy - also started bearing down on the Romanian oil fields, the Germans were left with a major crisis on their hands.

The western Allied Powers first bombed the Romanian oil field at Ploesti on 1st August 1943. In one respect, the Germans were surprised that it had taken them so long to perform such strategically important air attacks but when it did happen the Germans were hard hit. German oil production, raffination and transportation was under serious threat. On 5th April 1944, another attack was carried out followed by renewed air shelling on 24th and 26th April and on 5th and 6th May 1944 and further bombings in July. Though the Allies suffered heavy losses the bombings were very successful. After 24th April, Romania was exporting 50% less fuel than in the past. In the 5th May bombings 25,000 tons of valuable oil went up in flames.
The Allied Forces had made sure to concentrate their attacks on oil fields and refineries and on the oil station at Ploesti. The refinery and the oil station at Bucharest were

1 May 1944 - 31 December 1944

also listed as vital strategic targets. All the railway connections that were important to Ploesti were systematically attacked. Campina, Kronstadt, Giurgiu and Vienna were bombed as was the oil pipeline to Giurgiu. Even the Bucharest-Tecuci railway line that was still under construction was bombed. Mines were dropped in the Danube to make sure that oil could not be transported by water and to prevent the already heavily hit railway network from being even further incapacitated. The small amount of rail transportation that took place after that had to go via Bulgaria. The mines in the Danube also seriously disrupted all transportation of supplies to the eastern front which the soldiers stationed on the Dniester and the Germans at the garrison in the Crimea depended upon.

Even though the oil fields in and around Ploesti constituted one of the best defended areas of the German imperium - they were protected by hundreds of anti-aircraft guns, mist blowers and searchlights - the enemies had still managed to completely cripple the German economy. But it was more than a blow to the German economy: the vulnerability of the whole German military-industrial machine had been laid bare. When the Second World War began in 1939, German strategic raw material resources had really been too meagre to support a war. This irresponsibilty of the past was starting to affect the Germans now that shortages were becoming acute. In 1944 the amount of aircraft oil produced each month was barely five percent of what the Luftwaffe needed.

The Germans did all they could to avoid a crisis. First they tried to improve upon organization in the region so that the aid programmes would be more effective. General Gerstenberg was appointed commandant of the Romanian oil and petroleum producing area in July 1944. It was his responsibility to organize anti-aircraft attacks and to deploy German and Romanian fighter planes. General Gercke was put in charge of transportation and was given the awesome task of seeing to it that all the damaged sections of railway track were repaired. His already difficult task was made even harder by

Antonescu's unrealistic demands upon an economy that was already heavily strained. He demanded 400 armoured locomotives for the Romanian railway network and kilometres of sleepers and track. Hitler also appointed someone to clear the Danube of mines. Admiral-General Marschall was the man who the Führer made special officer for the Danube. Major D.G. Dereser was appointed special officer of the OKW on 'fuel matters'.

German efforts to protect the oil reserves were hampered by many factors, not least by a general scarcity of materials. German industry had been severely maimed by all the Allied air-raids and it was difficult for damages to be repaired or for spare parts to be supplied. In addition, Romanian cooperation was not all that it might have been. The Germans often sarcastically referred to their Romanian allies as 'our gypsies' and they were not very impressed by the fighter-bombers manufactured by the Romanians. For their part the Romanians found the Germans rather aloof. What they also found suspicious was that the Germans employed many East European labourers - invariably Ukrainians - to carry out repair jobs at Ploesti. The Germans had their reasons for this. They found the Romanian workers rather jittery: at the slightest hint of an attack they would immediately down tools and run, which naturally slowed down the production and repair processes. The Ukrainians, by contrast, who were used to SS-Brigadeführer Hoffmeyer's strict regime kept working under all conditions.

Despite all these efforts, it was impossible to prevent the crisis. 'What is the point of having new fighter-bombers and tanks if we do not even have any fuel to put in them' Albert Speer complained. At the Nuremberg trials, he stated that as far as he could see the Second World War had in effect already been lost in 1944 for 'production-technical' reasons. Jodl too emphasized the importance of the Romanian oil fields. 'We cannot be fatally affected anywhere', he maintained 'except in the Romanian oil area'. This was just the spot where the Hitler's German Reich was attacked and taken by surprise, just as Horthy had been taken by surprise in Klessheim ...

Romania, the military practising ground for Hungary, was not subjected to an operation like 'Margarethe' simply because Hitler had confidence in Ion Antonescu, the Romanian leader. 'Antonescu is the only Romanian who understands what this war is about' someone once wrote of the Romanian leader in 'Das Reich', Goebbels' favourite paper. Hitler completely agreed with this point of view. To his mind Antonescu was a man of action and that was something Hitler respected enormously.

Just like Hitler the Romanian dictator was a veteran of the First World War. Antonescu was a product of the Iron Guard, a mysterious ultra nationalistic Romanian organization with a marked anti-Semitic bent. Antonescu had been one of the founding fathers of this dubious extreme right political group. 'We wait for the day when Romania will be nationalistic, possessed and chauvinistic, armed and strong, merciless and revengeful' was what one of the founders of the Iron Guard had written concerning their political aims. Under Antonescu anti-Semitic pogroms had been put into practice. In Bukovina and Bessarabia (Moldavia), the Jews were chased over the Dniester and killed in their thousands. In January 1941, in a spontaneous pogrom, in which the Iron Guard had a central role, Jews in and around Bucharest were slaughtered.

Romania was actually the only country in Europe where the Germans hardly had to lift a finger to instigate the Holocaust. Antonescu was rather two-faced about his part in the Holocaust that took place on his own soil. On the one hand, he was a product of the Iron Guard, but on the other hand, he sought to distance himself from their violence and anti-Semitic attitude. When, in September 1940, the Romanian leader was threatened by a coup Hitler took sides with Antonescu. He was too popular with his people to be lost altogether. Moreover Antonescu was a man who understood Hitler's political ideas and that was something valuable in the Balkans where the political situation was so complex. Nazi Germany provided refuge for members of the Iron Guard who fled their country after the coup had failed.

Romania, like certain other Balkan countries, was a difficult country to govern. Too small to dominate and too big to be completely ignored, it was a country that had always hovered between, on the one hand, grand chauvinistic notions and, on the other hand a status quo that was hard to retain. In typical Balkan style the country was composed of a mixture of minority groups with different ethnic backgrounds. In addition, Romania had to contend with agricultural poverty, beginning industrialization and an intricate past. Finally, the country was trapped between two European superpowers: Russia and Germany.

Romania went through a difficult period at the beginning of this century. First, there was the Balkan War which, almost imperceptibly, spilled over into the First World War. After this and when the Dual Monarchy fell apart there was a power vacuum in the region which was accompanied by the perpetual fear that Hungary would amend the Treaty of Trianon and demand to have Transylvania which was inhabited by many Hungarians. To ensure that its status quo be retained - which was the chief aim of King Carol II the constitutional Romanian monarch - contact was sought with Russia and Germany, with small nearby powers (Poland) and with various western nations. King Carol II soon realized that he need not expect any help from countries in the west. In April 1939, Paris and London had vouched for Romania's integrity but when, in September of that same year, Germany invaded Poland it became only too clear that such treaties were mere paper pacts. In the Molotov-Ribbentrop Pact signed in August 1939, only a month earlier, Bucharest had clearly indicated that in the Balkans matters would be decided by Germany and Russia.

Hitler was the cleverest of the two parties. By offering the Romanian-Russian border area of Bessarabia to Moscow in secret negotiations, he effectively affronted Bucharest and compelled it to turn to Germany. On 20th June 1940 Stalin issued an ultimatum in which he demanded that Bessarabia and North Bukovina be immediately handed over to Russia. There was little else Bucharest could do than submit to such political blackmail. Once the Crown Council had conceded to the Russians on 27th June (Romania had little choice in the matter) the regime of King Carol II became totally undermined. The King abdicated in favour of young prince Michael which meant that effectively Ion Antonescu was free to usurp power and strengthen the bond with Berlin. The ordinary man in the street did not realize that Moscow had only been able to make its claims with German endorsement.

By 1944, even the ordinary man did realize that Romania was definitely on the losing side. At Stalingrad, most of the Romanian divisions that had travelled east with the German Wehrmacht had been bitterly defeated so that when the Red Army neared Romanian soil, reaching the Dniester on 26th March 1944, Romanian unrest increased. Now that Germany had lost the Ukraine, it was obvious to the whole world that the expedition eastwards had been catastrophic. Even the most fervent Nazis were also eventually convinced that this was so.

When the Ukrainian governor Erich Koch withdrew from the area he had been governing he realised that 'another time Germany would have to do it very differently'. Alfred Frauenfeld, the governor stationed in the Crimea, another area that was threatened by the advancing Red Army, shared this opinion adding: 'our enemy could not have caused more damage than Koch's detrimental policies'. He was alluding to Koch's perverse racial notions and the antipathy that this had aroused among the Ukrainian people towards the German occupier. The Ukraine was left to waste, it was a ransacked and ruined country. With giant steps the war machine headed for the heart of the Balkans.

After the Ukraine it was the Crimea, traditionally viewed as the gate to the Balkans, that was in most immediate danger. This danger was only intensified by the presence of all the mines that had been dropped in the Danube. Hitler who always clung desperately to any land that had

Field Marshal Antonescu walking alonside of the German Field Marshal Von Manstein during an inspection of the front in the Crimea. Hitler admired Antonescu whom he thought of as a real 'Gneisenau'. When Romania fell and Germany lost the oil fields at Ploesti this came as a great disappointment.

Hans Friessner arriving at the Hungarian front.
Up until December 1944 he was in command of the South Ukrainian Army Group which later came to be known as Army Group South.

The Hungarian puszta aflame!
Towards the end of 1944 there was heavy defensive fighting to the east of Budapest. Around Debrecen there raged a battle between tanks which continued for many days.
The German armed forces did amazingly well but were ultimately overpowered by the superior strength of the Red Army.

The Horthys pose for a family portrait.
The anti-German uprising of October 1944 was, for the greatest part, plotted within the family circle. By now there were few people Horthy could trust.

been gained refused to surrender the Crimea even though the situation on the front there was deteriorating rapidly. He contended that, also in the eyes of neutral countries like Turkey, such remission would be a sign of weakness. Hitler was therefore very bitter when soon afterwards, on 10th April, the port of Odessa fell into the hands of the Red Army. Odessa was the equivalent - twin port - to Sevastopol on the peninsula. The armies in the Crimea were isolated and shortly afterwards the 10. Romanian Infantry division, an event followed in fear and trepidation from Bucharest, was ruthlessly trodden under foot when no less than 26 Russian divisions descended on Sevastopol. General Jaenecke, the man who was responsible for defending the Crimea, saw what was about to happen and advised his superiors to evacuate the area immediately.

Hitler responded to this by inviting his senior officers to his headquarters. The confrontation between Hitler and his generals went as it always did. Either the generals were enthusiastic and shared Hitler's optimistic view of things or they remained pessimistic but did not dare to speak up. On this occasion Jaenecke fell into the second category. He said nothing but, the following day, he sent a five page long letter to Hitler in which he described the hopelessness of the situation in Sevastopol as he saw it. Jaenecke was promptly replaced by General Karl Allmendinger, one of his corps commandants, but he too was unable to turn the tide. Finally on 5th May the Cape of Chersonesus was evacuated and people were moved to Constanta in Romania. It was a disaster though. By the end of the battle nearly 100,000 German and Romanian armed soldiers had been killed and, as a result of the Russian marine and air-forces having been brought in, a further 42,000 men had been killed at sea. Hitler was furious about this new defeat. 'I never want to see these soldiers at the front again', he stated and commanded that the survivors should be employed on the manufacturing and economic side of the war effort since they 'were no longer of any military worth.' Jaenecke and

Allmendinger were never again put in command of any division.

The short-lived euphoria that had surrounded 'Margarethe' was over. In the months to come, the loyalty of German allies and of German officers was put to the test in the arduous series of defeats and disappointments that were to follow. The biggest defeat was suffered on the western front. Barely a month after the fall of Sevastopol, Hitler was shaken by the news that the Allied Forces had landed on the coast of his Euopean 'Festung': an event he had feared throughout 1944. Operation 'Overlord' took place on 6th June of that year. The first repercussions of the attack were certainly not optimistic for Germany. The German units stationed in Normandy did not succeed in pushing back the Allied troops. It was not to be a new Dieppe. Of course, Hitler quickly found a few people to blame. On 2nd July, Von Rundstedt was ordered off the battle field. He was replaced by General Von Kluge but he too was unable to do the impossible and influence the situation in any way. On 19th August Hitler received news that Von Kluge had committed suicide. On 20th July, a group of officers under Colonel Claus von Stauffenberg had tried to assassinate Hitler in a bomb attack in Wolfsschanze, East Prussia. The Führer had been very close to death. Subsequently, his distrust in the army increased. This was good news for the Reichsführer-SS Himmler and his SS troops who, after this date, were never absent from any major offensive. The murder attempt only intensified Hitler's stubbornness and fear of plotting behind his back. More than ever before he was inclined to develop his own ideas and stick rigidly to previously made plans. 'The blue-bloodied pigs should be wiped out' wrote Robert Ley, leader of the 'Deutscher Arbeitsfront' (DAF) in 'Der Angrif', in an attack on aristocrats who were over-represented in the German forces.

The day after Von Kluge's suicide Charles de Gaulle, the Free French leader, once again set foot on French soil. Eleven days later, the Allied Forces crossed the river

Somme and proceeded towards Paris. As if this were not enough, on 23rd and 24th June the Soviets commenced their big summer offensive which took the Red Army as far as the gates of Warsaw. On 1st August, Armja Krajowa, the Polish army, rebelled in the Polish capital. The city battle that ensued was one of the most macabre of the entire Second World War. Under the leadership of the SS General, Von dem Bach Zelewski, the uprising was suppressed with great violence. Some eighty percent of the city was reduced to ruins. The Poles were viciously slaughtered while the end of the war was in sight.

Within the walls of the Third Reich things were starting to seethe and boil. In the Balkans Romania was about to fall and the strategic oil fields of Ploesti were to be lost. Though Antonescu had always supported Hitler's campaign in the east even he had become convinced that Germany would no longer win the war. In Antonescu's political situation it was impossible to reach a compromise with Moscow. The only way that Romania could get out of the war was by making some kind of a deal with the western Allies. In the back of his mind Antonescu hoped to be able to save his country while not betraying Germany. He imagined that it might be possible to unite the western Allies with Germany and Romania in a fight against communism.

Bucharest had first sought contact with the Allies in the west in the autumn of 1943. The contact had been made through the Romanian embassy in Ankara. The Romanian negotiator, ex-minister Maniu had quickly discovered that negotiations were not going smoothly. The U.S. had hardly any interest in the Balkans and Great Britain, which showed slightly more interest, found that Greece had higher priority. When the Red Army reached the Dniester in March 1944 Antonescu decided that the time was again ripe for a diplomatic offensive. This time the talks took place in Cairo and more concrete plans were made. On 12th April the Allied Powers put forward with their demands. Romania would have to break all ties with Germany immediately and make its armed forces available for the battle against Berlin. Romania would also have to release all prisoners of war, compensate for war damages the Soviet Union and permanently dissociate itself from North Bukovina and Bessarabia.

Antonescu was bitterly disenchanted with all these demands. It was out of the question for him to agree to them. What happened after that marked a strange phase in Romanian politics. As though numbed Antonescu stuck to his original course. He saw no possible way out and said repeatedly that perhaps it would be best if he were to resign from office. On 5th August 1944, Hitler and Antonescu met for the last time, this time at Rastenburg in East Prussia. Hitler succeeded in cheering up the disappointed Romanian dictator by talking to him for hours on end about new super weapons that would revolutionize the situation on the battlefield. Hitler said that the Ukraine and the Crimea had been lost 'because of traitors'. Antonescu assured Hitler that Romania would remain faithful to Germany till the bitter end and Hitler believed him. Antonescu departed but as his car drove slowly away Hitler suddenly ran after him. The vehicle stopped and Antonescu looked at Hitler in surprise. 'Don't go to the royal palace!' he yelled. Hitler had suddenly received some kind of intuition. The Führer had always distrusted King Michael, just as he distrusted all monarchs.

Hitler's intuitions were right. In Romania German interests were in danger in two respects. In August 1944 the commandant of the German front, General Hans Friessner, realized that the Red Army was on the point of mounting a huge offensive in the treeless steppe of Bessarabia. Friessner, whose resolute manner on the north front had been noticed by Hitler, was a straightforward officer who kept political and military affairs strictly separate. He was, therefore, not noticeably critical about National Socialism though he was himself from a conservative background. During one military meeting Friessner had boasted to Hitler of his men's heroic fighting in battle. Deeply moved Hitler had grasped

The molten 'black gold' of Hungary that so interested Hitler. The German synthetic oil industry plants were systematically bombed, the Romanian oil fields at Ploesti had been lost and so, in Hitler's mind, the Hungarian oil fields were now of paramount importance.

The fuel industry was the Achilles heel of the German war machine. In 1944 Albert Speer proclaimed: 'In production-technical terms we have already lost the war'. Germany was faced not only with the problem of shortage of fuel but also with the problem of transporting supplies over railway networks that were badly damaged due to all the air attacks.

both Friessner's hands and shaken them firmly. 'This is the best military account I have ever heard', he blurted out. The Führer was convinced that Friessner would save the Romanian front.

The prospects for this battle were anything but rosy. Friessner was not only concerned about the logistic relationships and the length of the front - Hitler had forbidden the shorter route back (Plan Bär) - but he was also suspicious of the Romanian soldiers who appeared increasingly defeatist and/or indifferent to the war.

What the general had sensed was right and there was reason for the soldiers' attitude. Unhappy about Antonescu's negotiating impasse a big political coalition had formed in Bucharest of parties who wanted to get rid of their dictator and go along with the agreement demands made in Cairo. In practice, this amounted to a coup against Antonescu and Hitler's Germany. Antonescu seemed oblivious to these threats. The German political representatives in Romania had also failed to warn Hitler as they should have done. As has been mentioned, on 5th August, Hitler listened to his political instincts when he ran after Antonescu to warn him of impending danger. Hitler actually received little disconcerting news from Bucharest. More to the point, on the day of the coup the German authorities stationed in Bucharest reported to Führer headquarters that 'everything was quiet'.

Friessner put this strange state of affairs down to the fact that the Germans 'were not open about matters'. What he meant was that bringing bad news was often interpreted as defeatism and with the Führer no one ever wanted to be a bringer of bad news. Hitler, therefore, only received fragments of news. On top of that, certain information simply got lost in the mazes of the bureaucratic pyramid that characterized the totalitarian construction of the Third Reich. 'That is the danger if all decisions are taken by one person', Friessner professed after the war.

The General had other problems on his mind though connected with the Army Group (Heeresgruppe) Südukraine, later commonly known as the Army Group South. In August, it became clearer by the day that the 2.

Ukrainian Front (Malinovsky) and the 3. Ukrainian Front (Tolbukhin) were on the verge of opening up an offensive. Theoretically, the front on the east of Romanian offered a number of advantages. The rivers the Dniester, Pruth and Sereth flowed diagonally across the line from which the 3. Ukrainian front was pressing down on Romania from the direction of Odessa and Tiraspol. By contrast, the 2. Ukrainian front that was threatening the German lines from the north-east direction was less hampered by natural obstacles. At his headquarters in Slanic, Friessner talked over the situation with spokesmen from the two German armies within his unit: the 8. army and the 6. army. It was generally expected that the Red Army would start its offensive on 20th August.

The general assumption was correct. On Sunday 20th August, the Red Army offensive started with a one and a half-hour long artillery bombardment of the German-Romanian ranks. At the city of Jassy on the Dniester the 2. Ukrainian front was threating to break through. The Red Army had concentrated its fire on the Romanian army divisions and the Romanians who Friessner noted in his memoirs had no 'staying power' had fled en masse. The 5. and 7. Romanian cavalry divisions had fled before even sighting a single Red Army soldier. It quickly became obvious that only a fast retreat of the combat forces would prevent the front from collapsing altogether.

Hardly a day later, it became apparent that even this had been too optimistic. The breakthrough was so complete that the Germans were forced to retreat fighting. This precipitated blockades on the few bridges that still existed and officers had to do their utmost to prevent panic in the ranks. In not retreating sooner from this long front and moving to the shorter front that was easier to defend the Germans had made a big mistake. That was the price that had to be paid for Hitler's obstinacy.

In the night of 22nd and 23rd August, Friessner sped to Ion Antonescu. He was afraid that, because of the soldiers' widespread lack of interest in the fighting, the Romanian forces were on the brink of total defeat. Antonescu who, according to Friessner was 'a man of

stature and military insight', was upset to see how badly his troops were faring. 'We must hold on to what we've got', was Antonescu's opinion 'otherwise the whole of the Balkans will be thrown open.' Friessner agreed with him. 'We're in the same boat together on a stormy sea. If one of us steps out now we'll not only endanger our own nation but also the whole of Europe.'
After these momentous words, Friessner and Antonescu parted. It was the first and last time they met. Antonescu then did what Hitler had warned him not to do on 5th August. He hastened to the king to report the latest developments. In the palace, he was met by conspirators who arrested him. Antonescu was locked up in the royal strong-room where King Carol II used to keep his collection of stamps and disappeared from the political arena.

At 22.00 hours on 23rd August King Michael summoned the Romanian soldiers to lay down their weapons. The soldiers at the rapidly disintegrating front received the message via the radio and the chaos was complete. Friessner immediately got on to the German authorities in Bucharest who confirmed that there was a revolt going on. The German military authorities were, of course, in the first place concerned about the situation at the front. In view of the catalogue of disastrous events that had happened since the Soviet offensive had started on 20th August, the Romanian desertion from the German camp could hardly have come at a worse time. Friessner immediately ordered commandant Dumitrescu, the most senior and authoritative general, to come to his headquarters. Against his better judgement Friessner implored Dumitrescu to support the Army Group Südukraine in their struggle against the Red Army and to ignore instructions from Bucharest. Dumitrescu's simple reply said all: 'I cannot break my oath of allegiance to the king.' Friessner had no answer to this kind of soldier's logic but Dumitrescu's stance did not lessen his anger. After the war, he called his memoirs 'Verratene

Schlachten' (battle betrayals). They were betrayals that, as we shall see, were not restricted to Bucharest.

'Why didn't he for goodness' sake listen to me', Hitler moaned when he heard about the coup against Antonescu at the royal palace in Bucharest. Hitler was at his wit's end. Not only did the breaking through of the front on the Dniester constitute a military catastrophe in which two German armies were in danger of being destroyed, but the political and economic shambles precipitated by the sudden desertion of the Romanians was also not to be underestimated. At 23.00, Friessner had Hitler himself on the telephone. The instructions were to instantly 'get rid of' the traitors. For Friessner who was busy trying to save a collapsing front, this was virtually an impossible task. The only units available, and conceivably deployable, in the hinterland were those defending the oil fields at Ploesti and the accompanying air squadron of the Luftflotte IV.

In the circumstances, the resulting distribution of troops was very unfair. In fresh talks Hitler again insisted on military action against the rebelling Romanians so the anti-aircraft units stationed at Ploesti assembled to attack Bucharest. Friessner had held back fearing that such action would arouse hostility between the one-time allies. The commanders of the air artillery combat group were SS-Brigadeführer Hoffmeyer and General Gerstenberg. The whole operation was a failure. The units were poorly equipped for land battle; the cumbersome cannons did not lend themselves to mobile warfare.

Disappointed and revengeful, Hitler then ordered Friessner to bomb Bucharest from the air as quickly as possible. From a military point of view such a move would create nothing but trouble so Friessner decided to stall these instructions by first carrying out a 'study' into the repercussions of such an action. Hitler was not in the mood for being played with. A short time later, Friessner heard that German dive bombers of the Luftflotte IV had bombed Bucharest. Hitler had gone straight to Göring with his request and Göring had carried out orders immediately. Since the German Luchtwaffe had been forced into the defensive, notably in the west, and Göring's image was, therefore, suffering badly he was glad to be able to appease his Führer in this way.

The bombardments precipitated no political change and brought no relief to the German army. Worse yet, the Romanians who until then had been fairly neutral with their former German allies now turned against the Army Group Südukraine. On 25th August, word was received in Berlin that Romania had declared war on Germany. As the German troops withdrew moving in the direction of the Carpathian Pass and the Romanian-Hungarian border, Friessner was forced to repress his anger about everything that had happened. Hitler who continued to involve himself in every detail of the war had said that various cities, such as Braila and Focsami, must be designated 'strongholds'. Friessner believed that such defences were an utter waste of manpower and ordnance. What he did not know was that this was only the beginning of much bigger military blunders and political sacrifices such as those that would characterize the situation in Hungary in the last year of the war. Many men in the German navy lost their lives in the delta of the Danube. 'Tirpitz' the coastal battery that the Germans took pride in had to be blown up by their own troops. Even the U-boat base on the Black Sea was lost for all time. The 8. army retreated ever faster towards Kolozsvár (Cluj/Klaussenburg). The 6. army retreated towards the Buzau pass. On top of everything else, the hostility in the Balkans soon spread to Bulgaria which, following Romania's example, also turned against the Germans declaring in Berlin on 5th September that Bulgaria was at war with Germany.

Friessner flew in his Fiesseler-Storch from one disaster spot to another. He landed on the road between Focsani and Ploesti and witnessed the defeat of the retreating but still fighting Winkler combat group. A handful of German tanks and infantrymen were standing their ground against the Red Army for as long as they could while behind them long cavalcades were retreating westwards.

The sky above their heads was dark from the oil burning in the big storage tanks at Ploesti which had been completely flattened and was no longer able to support the German 'war machine'. Now that Ploesti had fallen, Hitler's Germany only had the oil fields of Nagykanizsa in Hungary and the smaller fields at Zisterdorf in Austria. These regions would be central in Hitler's geopolitical planning of the next months.

The secret power of Ferenc Szálasi

After the fall of Bucharest and Ploesti the fighting quickly switched to the Hungarian-Romanian border area. This area, known in Latin as Transylvania, to the Romanians as Ardeal, to the Hungarians as Erdély and to the Germans as Siebenbürgen has been fought over from time immemorial: many a battle has been fought on its soil. Transylvania is a typical frontier area. It lies in the shadow of the Carpathian mountains and the Transylvanian Alps (South Carpathia) and has thus formed a natural barrier between tribes and peoples throughout the ages. In the distant past, it was not only its strategic positioning but also the gold reserves and its fertile soil that made the area so attractive. Today, around six million Romanians live there, making them the biggest population group of the area, but in 1944 there was an ongoing dispute between Romania and Hungary about who the land belonged to. So, on the very spot where the Huns and Goths had once waged war, new and heavy battles were fought once again in 1944, 'defensive battles' as the Germans called them.
The battle for Transylvania was fought in September 1944. After the fall of Ploesti Red Army units invaded the area via passes in the Carpathian mountains with no less than 31 infantry (Schützen) divisions and a number of corps. Friessner did his utmost to keep the situation under control. German reinforcements like the 'Gruppe Siebenbürgen' commanded by SS-Obergruppenführer Arthur Phleps and troops from the 8. SS Kav.D 'Florian Geyer' were brought to the front as quickly as possible. The German-Hungarian army, stricken by shortages of ammunition and fuel and heavily hit by the intense fighting, managed to withdraw fairly successfully. Surprisingly, the front did remain reasonably intact which said not only something about discipline on the German side of the front but also about Red Army stamina. After having been heavily hit in Romania they badly needed a break from all the fighting. In his

memoirs, Friessner called the retreat 'a complete defensive success' for the German army. In the confrontation the Red Army had lost nearly 200 tanks, around 150 pieces of artillery and 2,000 men had been made prisoners of war. In reality this was nothing compared to the success of the Red Army. In a short time, the Third Reich had been robbed of its last large fuel reserves, and with the fall of Romania, of one of its last allies. After losing Transylvania with its land area of 62,000 square kilometres the Red Army had arrived at the gates of the Hungarian buffer state.

Because of the Soviet advance, the German 8. Army, commanded by Otto Wöhler, had been pushed to the extreme northern flank of Friessner's front line. To defend Hungary Friessner was having to depend more and more on the German 6. Army (Fretter-Pico) that had been regrouped after the fall of Stalingrad. By the end of September, the front formed a 1,000 (!) kilometer long curve from Kolozsvár to Nagyvárad (Oradea/Grosswardein) and from there to Arad and Temeschburg. Friessner also had at his disposal the Hungarian 3. Army which provided two corps for the front. Connecting with Wöhler's 8. Army the Hungarian 2. Army surrounded Kolozsvár.

It was clear from the beginning that this line could never be retained. It was just a matter of waiting for a new Red Army offensive to be mounted, an event which Friessner feared would come very soon. There was a rumour going around that Stalin had decided that the fall of Budapest should coincide with the annually celebrated anniversary of the October- revolution!

On 6th October, fighting broke out for the Hungarian puszta. Though theoretically the Red Army was far superior they found it incredibly difficult to beat the German forces. As always, breaking through the lines posed little problem for the Red Army. The Hungarian section proved to be fragile and they gave up easily. Deeper into the enemy lines where what counted was well ordered structures and tactics the Soviets were weaker. Though the Russians were stronger in numbers the

Germans managed to surround more Soviet corps with their tank units, while they in fact had very little material at their disposal. It was notably the three armoured divisions of Fretter-Pico's 6. Army, the 1., 13. and 23. PzD. that made life difficult for the Soviets. The battle at Debrecen went on for days but inevitably the Red Army won. With the breaking through of the front at Arad and Szalonta, just to the south of Nagyvárad, the German 6. army was forced to beat its final retreat to the west (to preserve contacts Wöhler's 8. army was forced to retreat as well). The Red Army had lost an estimated 11,000 soldiers, nearly 6,000 men were made prisoners of war and no less than 1,000 tanks had been destroyed. The losses were heavy but not insurmountable. The Soviet tank production line was incredibly efficient. On the Soviet side losses of men and material were generally replaced for 90% while on the German side the recovery level was just over 60%.

The German armoured divisions had been badly hit. The entire 6. army only had fourteen Pz.V's, twelve Pz.III's and 41 assault cannons, the equivalent to the strength of one average tank division. The 23. Pz.D. alone, commanded by Von Radowitz, had sacrificed no less than 37 tanks and armoured vehicles.

After this heavy struggle and this meagre success, it was obvious that the celebration of the October Revolution in Moscow could not be linked to the conquering of Budapest though they were in sight of the city. By the end of October, the only thing separating the Red Army from the gates of Budapest and the Danube was the river Tysa (Tisza/Theiss). By this time tension was high in the Hungarian camp. Just as in August when Bucharest had been taken, increasingly fewer Hungarians wanted to suffer defeat with Hitler's Germany.

Since the Klessheim fiasco, Horthy had been trying to find ways to get out of the war but he was plagued by the same problems that had beset Ion Antonescu. It was with increasing fear that Horthy and most Hungarians watched the Red Army advance on Budapest. Rumours about the loathsome way in which Russians had treated Hungarian civilians reinforced the defeatist climate in Budapest. Reluctance to reach a settlement with the Red Army kept the Hungarians in the German camp, though, it was perfectly clear that the 'brothers in arms' relationship was practically over. What was significant about the shift in onus was that German military power in Hungary had increased greatly since the time of operation 'Margarethe' as had German political influence. The Commanding SS and Police Führer, Otto Winkelmann, carefully reviewed the situation in Budapest from the policing angle. SD, SS and Gestapo factions were at his disposal day and night. Dr. Edmund Veesenmayer, the uninvited guest who had accompanied Horthy on his train journey back to Hungary in May, in his capacity as Hitler's special envoy, now followed all the political developments in the Horthy household with Argus-eyed vigilance. Under the rigorous command of Eichmann more and more Hungarian Jews were being rounded up and handed over to Nazi extermination camps. The economic pressure on Hungary had also tightened. What was also worrying was the fact that under German rule Hungarian fascists, Ferenc Szálasi's Nyilas (Arrow Cross Movement) were gaining power and influence.

Horthy decided that the only way in which he could extricate his country from these problems was by approaching the west. Hungary was then confronted with the same problems that had faced Antonescu and Romania. On 22nd September, several of Horthy's envoys were received by the British General of the 8. army, Maitland Wilson. The negotiations went slowly because the Allies first had to deliberate amongst themselves. Horthy's overtures failed for the same reasons that the talks in Bucharest had once failed: the western Allies did not want to make any agreements that would exclude the Soviet Union. By this time, it was already obvious that after the war the Balkans would be in the hands of the Russians. That was a political and military fact and the western Allies did not want to burn their fingers.

Hitler's favourite commando leader, Otto Skorzeny. In October 1944 he arrested Admiral Horthy in an efficiently organized commando operation because Horthy had been trying to join forces with the Allied Powers. It was because of this operation and the freeing of Mussolini from Gran Sasso earlier on in the war that Skorzeny became known as 'the most dangerous man in Europe'. This photo was taken shortly after he was arrested by the Allies. After the war he lived in Spain.

Ferenc Szálasi arriving at the castle in Buda in October of 1944. With the help of German troops the Arrow Cross Movement seized power and afterwards anti-Jewish pogroms broke out.

When, in that same month, Horthy's military advisor Vörös reported that the Hungarian units were on the point of collapsing at the front and that at any minute the Red Army might storm Budapest, Horthy realized that he would have to take action. With a small group of people he could trust Horthy discussed what would be the best way of getting Hungary out of the war. Most of the politicians were given little information about the plans for fear that some of them might betray him. It appeared that for Hungary the only possibility was to lay down its weapons and withdraw from the war without encouraging conflict with Germany. Bearing in mind what had happened in Bucharest it was not very realistic to believe that this might work. Straight after the coup against Antonescu, Hitler had gone on to bomb Bucharest and the Romanians and Germans had entered into battle. Horthy was cornered and there was no alternative so he concentrated on compiling the declaration that he was going to broadcast by radio. The authorities in Moscow, with whom he was secretly in contact, urged him to make the U-turn at the beginning of October.

After the disastrous sequence of events in Bucharest, the Germans were very guarded this time around. Horthy's palace was under surveillance day and night and it was no secret that Budapest was negotiating with the western Allies and with Moscow. On 10th September, Hitler had summoned his favourite man for difficult jobs, the lanky SS officer Otto Skorzeny, to Wolfsschanze in East Prussia and had given him instructions to join forces with Friessner and Winkelmann and restore order in Budapest, if this should become necessary. Skorzeny, who was born in Austria and whose face had been disfigured with honourable scars gained in a sabre duel during his student days, was the right man for the job. In September 1943, Skorzeny had successfully mounted a commando operation in Gran Sasso to save Benito Mussolini from the hands of Italian partisans. Tito, the Yugoslavian partisan leader, had once almost fallen into one of Skorzeny's traps. Because of his speed and efficiency Skorzeny's operations were usually successful and the losses incurred low. He was the kind of man Hitler liked and it was for good reason that he was chosen to go to Hungary which, to Hitler's mind, was strategically very important. Later in the war, Skorzeny was commissioned to do three other jobs: to bomb the bridge at Remagen, to create a distraction manoeuvre during the Ardennes offensive (Operation 'Greif' involving German special forces in American uniforms) and to defend the bridgehead Schwedt on the Oder. None of these operations was as successful as those in Gran Sasso and Budapest but they did provide plenty of interesting material for the memoirs which Skorzeny was to recount no less than four times over.

Skorzeny arrived in Budapest under the assumed name of Dr. Wolff and was joined by the SS General Erich von dem Bach Zelewski, who arrived on 13th October. His brutal fighting in Warsaw had impressed Hitler who maintained that with such anti-partisan experience this stocky SS officer would certainly also be effective in Budapest. As far as Skorzeny was concerned von dem Bach Zelewski was more of a hindrance than a help. The methods of the two SS officers were rather different. Von dem Bach Zelewski immediately wanted to reduce Horthy's historic castle residence to a pile of ruins by firing a big Bertha (a 65cm cannon) while Skorzeny's ideas were much subtler.

In the end, Skorzeny's politics prevailed. In September and October the power struggle began in Budapest. In and around Budapest, hundreds of thousands of Jews had been herded together in ghettos and camps and were awaiting deportation to Auschwitz and elsewhere where they were required to help in the German war industry. Jewish building brigades worked on fortifying the city in preparation for the anticipated battle of Budapest. The city offered protection for many refugees who had come from the east fleeing from the advancing 2. and 3. Ukrainian front armies. Arrow Cross men became more brazen by the day and started intimidating the Hungarian authorities and the Jewish inhabitants of the city. Horthy reacted by arresting a number of leading

Arrow Cross Men on 16th September. On 8th October the Gestapo retaliated by arresting General Szibard Bakay, one of Horthy's last military confidants. In the meantime Skorzeny's right-hand man, the SS-Hauptsturmführer Von Fölkersam, worked out the details of operation 'Panzerfaust', the plan to attack the Hungarian stronghold. Veesenmayer had been in close contact with the Arrow Cross movement when making arrangements for an interim government to take over in the event that Horthy should attempt to leave the German camp.

On 15th October 1944, the time was finally ripe for action. After close talks with those he could trust, mostly family, Horthy resolved to broadcast a declaration to the nation in which he would urge Hungarians to lay down their arms and become neutral. Horthy was an honourable man so he first wanted to inform the Crown Council, Prime Minister Lakatos and above all else, Edmund Veesenmayer of his intentions. In reality this was hardly necessary because the Nazis were completely up- to-date on what was going on and already had their plans drawn up. On the political front, Veesenmayer and a new special envoy of Hitler's, the German ambassador in Italy, Rudolf Rahn, would be enlisted to win Horthy back to the German camp with a diplomaticall tour de force. For this purpose Rahn was specially flown in to Budapest from Munich by Condor. If this should fail there was always the military plan to fall back on. Skorzeny was plotting against Horthy. There were also German army units dotted around the city - equipped with 40 heavy Königstiger tanks (sPz.Abt.503) - which could intervene militarily at any given moment. For security reasons Horthy had not told the Hungarian army what was going to happen, so no plans had been made for defending his residence.

The German campaign went according to plan. Horthy's son who had been very involved in all his father's secret discussions with the Allied Powers was supposedly invited by an emissary of Josef Tito to attend secret negotiations. At first, the Hungarians were wary of the proposal but finally, on the morning of 15th October, Horthy's son decided that, accompanied by a couple of guards, he would meet them. The rendezvous, code-named 'Mickey Mouse', was a trap set up by Otto Skorzeny. Horthy's son had hardly set foot in the building when a huge group of SD men descended on him. He was knocked unconscious, rolled in a carpet and rushed to the airport from where he was flown to Mauthausen concentration camp near Linz in Austria. In the operation the Germans had only lost one man, a person of high rank, the SD Chief in Budapest, SS-Hauptsturmführer Otto Klages who was shot in the stomach during an exchange of fire with Hungarian security men outside the building. Skorzeny, who himself had escaped by the skin of his teeth, had posed as a civilian standing next to a car that had supposedly broken down in front of the building where the 'rendezvous' had taken place. He had given the German authorities an excellent trump card.

Now that Horthy junior had been kidnapped Veesenmayer was in an even stronger position than before and 15th October became an even worse day than it already was for Horthy. Horthy first informed the Crown Council of his plans. Partly because up until then they had known nothing whatsoever of the regent's plans, the Council was not very quick to support him. A little later, at noon, Veesenmayer arrived. He was unsuccessful in his attempt to make the fatigued regent change his mind. Shortly afterwards, Rudolf Rahn, Hitler's special envoy, was equally unsuccessful in his bid to influence Horthy.

From the very start, Rahn had been rather pessimistic about his mission to the Balkans. He described the area as a 'place packed with lunatics'. Rahn also had a very low opinion of the German diplomatic service which consisted of more SA and SS people than persons who were versed in diplomacy. In this respect, what had happened in Bucharest had been very revealing. Rahn had blamed much of the failure on Von Ribbentrop, the minister of Foreign Affairs. This vain man (he had bought the aristocratic prefix 'Von') had really managed to rise high in the Nazi hierarchy on the basis of a mutual misunderstanding between Hitler and himself. Von Ribbentrop had originally believed that Hitler would be the man to restore the German Monarchy. For his part Hitler thought that the clever widely travelled wine merchant must be 'a man of the world' who would be good of selling his National Socialist programme abroad. Through this miscalculation on both sides Von Ribbentrop had, with the support of his overambitious wife, risen to the position of Minister of Foreign Affairs. His mother-in-law had once commented that it was her 'most stupid son-in-law who had gone furthest career-wise'. She was not alone in her low opinion of Von Ribbentrop. The intelligent propaganda minister Goebbels also realized that Von Ribbentrop was not all that bright. He sometimes sarcastically referred to him in public as 'the wine merchant'. Rahn had the strong impression that with this rush assignment, noted down on a single sheet of paper, he was really being asked to clear up the Ministry's mess for them.

Rahn, a professional diplomat who had previously been posted in places like Syria and Tunesia, succeeded in giving the unfriendly tone of Veesenmayer and Horthy's discussion a more civil turn. 'I wish I had met you before', Horthy complained. While they were engaged in discussion, Horthy's message was being broadcast to the nation. The revolt against Germany was now a reality. The Germans were shocked. Just before going in to talk with Horthy Veesenmayer had shown Rahn a telegram from Berlin which made it clear in no uncertain terms that if things were to go wrong as they had gone wrong in Bucharest both men would literally lose their heads. The atmosphere was only made worse by Von Ribbentrop who, frightened that they might see a repetition of the Bucharest tragedy of August 1944, kept telephoning and hysterically reporting that everything was about to go badly wrong. When Bucharest fell the Nazi's most important diplomatic mission in Eastern Europe had failed. Von Ribbentrop could not possibly afford to lose Budapest as well. Rahn tried to calm the Minister by exclaiming 'at least credit us with some sense' and hung up.

Veesenmayer, Friessner and Skorzeny decided that there was now no more time to lose. They would immediately have to recover their hold on Budapest. Tiger tanks carrying soldiers from the 'Maria Theresia' cavalry division, Waffen-SS parachutists (the Fallschirm 600 Fighter Battalion) and the 'Jagdverband Mitte' (previously jägerbataillon) surged towards the castle. Horthy realized that his guards did not stand a chance and so ordered them to refrain from shooting back. Despite this there was a quick exchange of fire. In the confusion not all of the Hungarian units had received the message that they were not to resist. For Skorzeny it went like the operation in Gran Sasso. The resistance was broken down with little effort.

Photographs that have been preserved of the 'Panzerfaust' siege show that the German army clearly felt supreme. Soldiers of the Waffen-SS cavalry division 'Maria Theresia' can be seen relaxing and smoking cigarettes at the palace in Boeda after the assault. Just as he had done with Mussolini, Skorzeny personally accompanied Horthy from the political arena. Horthy broke down completely and cried. He looked for support to Rudolf Rahn whose hands he grasped and whom he begged to spare the life of his only surviving son. The regent was flown out of Hungary to castle Hirschberg at Waldheim in Beieren where he lived in exile and from where he was eventually liberated by the Americans at the end of the war. He did not return to Hungary until after his death. His remains were exhumed and re-buried in 1993. Despite promises to the contrary Horthy's son remained imprisoned throughout the war. He was not released from Dachau, the camp to which he had been transferred, until the end of the war. Himmler was extremely satisfied about operation 'Panzerfaust'. 'May I compliment you on your excellent work' he wrote to Veesenmayer. Rahn took his leave and Veesenmayer was glad to see the back of the 'busybody'. The feeling was mutual. Rahn was relieved to be able to leave the

German soldiers of the 22.SS Kav.D., 'Maria Theresia', equipped with anti-tank shells laugh and relax after having stormed the castle in Buda. The Hungarians gave in virtually straight away. The confiscated weapons lie scattered on the ground.

Balkans and fly back to Italy. He was pleased to see that the 'Panzerfaust' operation had produced few fatalities but not confident that things would end well.

After Horthy had been removed from office, things became much grimmer in Budapest. A branch of the German intelligence service took over the Budapest radio station. The unit was led by a certain SS-Untersturmführer, known as Kernmayer. The events are described so graphically in the revisionist book 'Die Letzte Schlacht' written by Erich Kern that it is almost certain that Kernmayer and Kern must be one and the same person. Kern named the man who took over the radio station Ruhle. The Arrow Cross men were glad to be able to use the facilities offered by the radio station to widely broadcast their grand Hungarian and anti-Semitic views. In the night of 15th and 16th October, hundreds of Jews were killed by groups of teenage Arrow Cross members. A number of Jews doing construction work had, in a brief moment of euphoria, discarded their bands with yellow stars and dropped their spades and pickaxes. This gave the Arrow Cross movement an excuse to unleash their long bottled-up hatred. That night hundreds of Jews were thrown from the famous Ketting and Margarethe bridge into the Danube and shot. Pogroms took place at other places in the city, notably in the Népszinhastraat area and in Teleki square but this will be explained in more detail in the next chapter.

In political terms much changed as well. Ferenc Szálasi's Arrow Cross movement ('Nyilaskeresztes Part'), prepared by Veesenmayer to step into power, took over and ruled the country in a very violent way. For Szálasi it was the moment he had been waiting for all his life. Szálasi believed that he was predestined by providence to free Christian Hungary from the threats of communism, Slavic 'provinciality' and the 'Jewish problem'. Born on 6th January 1897, Szálasi was of Hungarian-Slovakian and Armenian stock. His authoritarian father had made a career in the army and Szálasi who, like his brothers, had followed in his father's footsteps possessed promising military talent. As a young man he had served in the general staff in the First World War. In 1925, he was admitted to the highest military ranks in Hungary. By 1932, he had become a popular lecturer in military history. The rest of Szálasi's career would have been wonderful had he not chosen to change the whole course of his life by embarking on a political career. It was not a rational decision. The man was convinced of the import of his historic mission. He truly believed that providence had predestined him to make Hungary the 'superpower of the Carpathian region and the Danube basin'. Szálasi's first political book appeared in Germany in 1933, the year that Hitler rose to power. It was entitled 'Plan for the reconstruction of the Hungarian State', on the face of it not a radical standpoint in view of the fact that demanding the revision of Trianon - the Hungarian version of the Treaty of Versailles - was equivalent to being sincerely patriotic, but Szálasi took things too far. His revisions were taken to sickly extremes and he did not shrink from propagating the use of violence. Szálasi fervently believed that in the interest of building up Hungarian hegemony other peoples of the Balkans should be suppressed. His aggressive politics was complemented by Nazi-like anti-Semitism, and based on cooperative notions for the transformation of the economy inspired by what he saw Mussolini had done in Italy. What was particularly striking was that Szálasi, like Hitler, saw it as his sole task to create such a 'huge Magyar State'. He claimed 'he who does not serve me absolutely must be eradicated'. If nobody was willing to bow to the sort of compliance that was required this was no problem for Szálasi: 'Even if I remain alone in this I shall still create the Hungarian State from the secret power that lies within me' he proclaimed.

In talking of 'secret power' Szálasi was alluding to the preferential role that would be given to Hungarian Christians played in Central Europe (against the Turks) and he would certainly be needing such 'secret power' in the coming months. The Red Army approached the towers of Budapest and many Hungarians believed that the Arrow Cross Movement which was now in power would only prolong the war. Szálasi had the virtually impossible task of mobilizing the Hungarians for this final battle with the Germans. At the same time, though, it was Szálasi's mission to convince the people that they would also be fighting for some kind of big Hungarian ideal, what he termed 'a great fatherland ideal', which could only be realized if they joined Nazi Germany. Szálasi also had plans to publish a further number of political standard works in which his ideas would be preserved.

With the Arrow Cross Movement it was clear from the start that they could never be anything other than an interim regime, not only because of developments on the front, but also because their power base was simply too small, even though Szalasi's numbers of followers had increased over the years (1935: 8,000, 1937: 19,000, 1940: 116,000 and in 1944: 500,000 party members) and he could depend on the support of a further 100,000 Hungarian rightist radicals. However this was still not enough for a broad consensus on such an important issue as fighting on the side of the Germans. The party's popularity quickly dwindled when the chances of winning the battle diminished.

Still, there was one last objective left for Szálasi to pursue. The Jews that he hated so much would not be allowed to escape from his power and from the destructive plans that the Arrow Cross Movement and Adolf Eichmann had in mind for them, even if it meant fighting to the death. In this respect, Szálasi and Hitler thought the same: both dreamed of a military revolution and a new beginning. Hungarian economic resources would pour westwards, new tanks and planes would be built, V missilies would be showered on Antwerp and London and new Me-262 fighter aircraft would patrol the German airspace acting like an umbrella over 'Festung Europa'. Both dictators believed that with sheer will-power and persuasion they could shape reality. The fist of National Socialism had been balled once again, only to fall and miss its target with enormous destructive force. In Hungary the bizarre and irrational politics of National Socialism were to colour the last bloody chapter. The story is one of collaboration, ghettos, bureaucratic murderers, teenage terrorism, the last gassings at Auschwitz, death marches and forced labour and of a series of remarkable large-scale and prestigious military offensives and economic plans.

The annihilation of the Hungarian Jews

On the night of 18th March 1944, a small convoy of vehicles from the SS moved into Hungary accompanied by tanks of the Pz.Lehr division. The action was part of operation 'Margarethe' and the vehicles constituted the advance guard of Adolf Eichmann's SS Commando Group which was about to set in motion the last massive deportation and execution of European Jews. Their target was Budapest, a city with a Jewish community that had, up until then, managed to remain intact. It was also a city with much Jewish commerce.
Eichmann was in excellent spirits. On the night of 18th March, he had shared a bottle of rum with his close colleagues Dieter Wisliceny and Hermann Krumey in celebration of his birthday and had wished them every success in their impending mission. When the black convoy of military vehicles had entered Hungary and had proceeded towards Budapest Eichmann had noticed that everywhere they went they were warmly welcomed by the Hungarians. Before entering the country, he had loaded his revolver in readiness but it was a precaution that had proved to be unnecessary. The Hungarians were prepared to renounce their independence without putting up a fight. This was clearly a sign of what was to come because Hungary, so wrote Eichmann after the war, would be the easiest victory of his whole career. In retrospect it is all rather puzzling if one thinks about exactly when in the war the extermination of the Hungarian Jews began. Only after March 1944 ('Margarethe') and October 1944 ('Panzerfaust') were the Germans more or less free to do as they wished in Hungary. By then it was clear that Germany was going to lose the Second World War and the Germans knew very well that after the war they would be required to answer for their atrocities. Nevertheless the Hungarian Holocaust turned out to be a remarkable success for the Germans which says something about the dogged determination of the Nazis to win 'their war against the Jews' if nothing else. It also says a lot about

the Hungarians on whose territory and with whose cooperation this was all allowed to happen. Finally it tells us something about the Jews who were the victims of such terror and about the outside world that looked on without attempting to intervene.

When Eichmann entered Hungary in March 1944, and shortly afterwards installed himself in 'The Majestic', a luxurious hotel on the Schwabenberg in Budapest, Hungary was still a last haven of peace for European Jews. Up until then it had been a little like an island, safe from what was happening in a continent that had further been 'cleansed' of Jews. From Russia to the Spanish border and from Norway to Greece, the Eichmann Commando had rigorously rounded up all Europe's Jews transporting them to the various death camps. It was ironic that the Jews were relatively safest in the countries that were most closely allied to Germany. Because Berlin viewed such countries as faithful allies they were more or less given political autonomy and were, therefore, able to determine policies themselves when it came to their own Jewish communities.

In Hungary, just as everywhere else, Eichmann was very systematic in his approach. On arriving in the country, his 'closest colleague', Wisliceny, was immediately sent out to establish contact with the Hungarian and German authorities in the city. Eichmann was particularly keen to meet 'experts', people who knew something about the 'Jewish question' in the Danube metropolis. It was not long before Eichmann was invited to dine with his first Hungarian host, Dr. Laszlo Endre, former judge, anti-Semite and writer who was said to be 'dying to meet Eichmann in person'. Wisliceny had introduced Eichmann to Endre because he had understood from SS and SD authorities in Budapest that Endre believed it was extrememly important to 'rid Hungary of the Jewish plague'. Wisliceny had indeed put Eichmann in touch with the right man. With Endre, Eichmann only needed to hint at the matter of deporting Jews and the Hungarian was immediately enthusiastic. 'We did not need to waste the rest of the evening on further discussion' Eichmann recalled in his memoirs, 'so that left us free to concentrate on the business of tasting all the beautiful Tuscan wines.' The fate of the Hungarian Jews had been determined that evening. A short while later, Endre was made Secretary of State for Political Affairs. The word 'Political' here being in effect a synonym for 'Jewish'.

The Hungarian Jews could only be exterminated if the Hungarian authorities sanctioned this so Eichmann was pleased to have struck up such an alliance. Up until 1944 Hungary might have been a paradise for the 750,000 Jews who lived there, but this was soon to change. In reality Hungary had been an anti-Semitic country. Its policies and legislation were very anti-Semitic, even by East European standards. To an extent these hostile feelings had their roots in religious differences. The Jews lived in a country that was predominantly Roman Catholic (circa 10 million Catholics). In addition, Hungary had 2.7 million Calvinists and 720,000 Lutherans.

In the country's economic sector too there was quite a lot of enmity towards Jews. Most Hungarian Jews were middle class citizens. They constituted 5.1% of the population, of this number 0.33% were in farming and 1.6% were civil servants or in the armed forces but in the professions and the business sector they were proportionally over-represented. So it was that 49.2% of the country's judges were Jewish and more than half of the general practitioners were Jews. A high percentage of people in banking were Jewish (59.4%), likewise many of those in industry (75.1%). Furthermore 25% of all musicians were Jewish and 14.7% of the country's artists. In publishing 30.4% of publishers were Jewish and among academics 31.7% were Jews. With so many Jews in influential social positions prejudice against them could only increase and nationalistic sentiment was inevitably reinforced. Their demographic concentration also encouraged anti-Semiticism: twenty percent lived in Budapest. The aristocratic élite, to which Horthy belonged, resented the fact that so much economic power rested in the hands of the Jewish middle class, hence the antipathy towards this section of the community and the country's decidedly anti-Semitic politics.

The Hungarians made a first step in the direction of the Holocaust. In his monumental standard work on the persecution of Jews in Europe Raul Hilberg explains how the extermination process worked and how it was constructed in phases. The process went as follows:

1 identify
2 expropriate
3 concentrate
4 deport
5 exterminate

What is striking is that the first two phases at least were accomplished with little German support. In his research into the Hungarian Holocaust Hilberg made an inventory of Hungarian prime ministers who were pro-German and those who collaborated under pressure. It is ironic that over the course of the years the pro and anti camps alternated so that the tragedy that was coming to the Jews was sometimes accelerated only to be slowed down and then accelerated again. In no other European country were the Jews so uncertain of there future as in Hungary. The road to destruction was painfully slow but once the wheels had been set in motion the fate that was coming to the Jews was terrifyingly inevitable.

The ever changing policies towards Hungarian Jews began with the problem of defining who was and who was not, strictly speaking, Jewish. This was initially important in conjunction with establishing a numerus clausus at Hungarian universities to limit the number of Jewish entrants. Between 1939 and 1943, the Hungarian parliament assembled no less than three times to discuss this very issue. The main problem was to decide to what extent Jews should be seen as a religious group and to what extent they should be seen as an ethnic minority. It was mainly the Catholic Church that was pedantic about the definition because a small group of Jews (some 62,000 people) had been converted to Catholicism. In the end, the

Adolf Eichmann whose last deportations of the war were carried out in Hungary. He called the Hungarian Holocaust 'the most successful operation' of his career. The Hungarian authorities cooperated with him willingly.

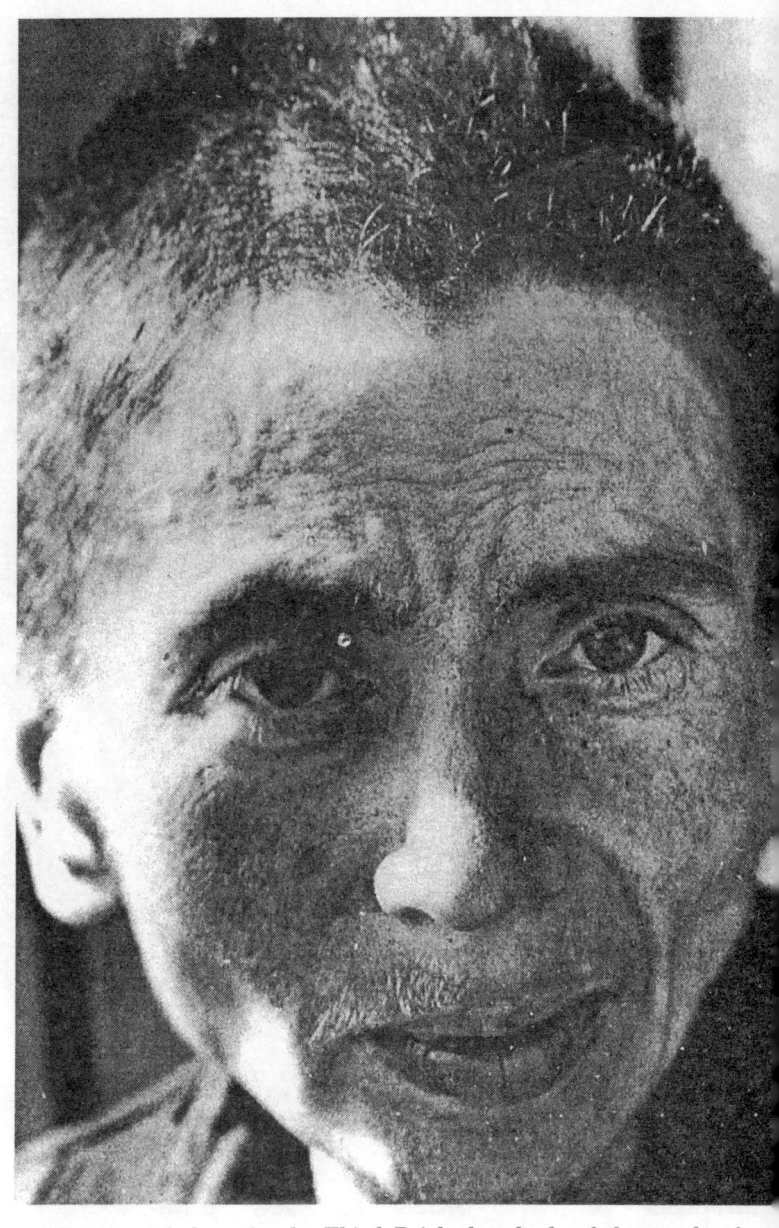

At the eleventh hour in the Third Reich, hundreds of thousands of Hungarian Jews were murdered by the Germans. The above photo shows a Hungarian victim who survived Auschwitz.

The deportations get under way. Hungarian Jews assembling for the journey with their belongings. Hungarian Arrow Cross men assisting the German authorities.

final piece of legislation on this matter was so precisely worded that even though 725,000 Hungarian inhabitants were officially registered as being Jewish lists were drawn up of 787,000 Jews. This had to do with the fact that the Hungarians had - voluntarily! - opted to adopt the law laid down in Nuremburg. In the Nuremburg laws on racial matters, drawn up in 1936, Hitler had given his own definition of what constituted 'Jewishness'.

It was important to establish exactly what made a person a 'Jew' because this later made it easier to take action against such people. The next step was to strip the Jews of everything they owned, in other words, to hand over their wealth to the Hungarian non-Jewish élite. This process did present Horthy with a major problem though. In October 1940, he wrote the following to Prime Minister Teleki: 'All my life I have been anti-Semitic, so I hate it when I see that banks and companies are run by Jews but we must be careful how we go about compulsorily purchasing Jewish property, because otherwise the country will go bankrupt'. This 'problem' was something that would affect the whole dispossession process and the entire Jewish economic infrastructure in Hungary. As the Jews traditionally constituted the middle class sector and as many of the country's remaining inhabitants were chiefly agriculturally oriented there were few people left to fill the economic vacuum. The Germans who had established their 'Jewish interests' early on also confirmed that this was a problem. 'The Hungarians are short of finances and expertise' wrote a representative of the investigation division of the OKW in January 1941.

The 'Arisierung' of Jewish economic interests was a laborious process but Horthy was realistic enough to appreciate the delicacy of the situation. Even the Nazis exercised some reserve. A number of the Jewish-Hungarian companies were important to German industry. Hence, the emergence of a remarkable kind of cooperation. During the war years the German steel sector poured heavy investments into Jewish companies (notably the aluminium branch) which were vital to the German aircraft building industry. In this connection,

Hilberg cites as an interesting example how close the ties which were existed between Dr. Westrick, manager of the German 'United Aluminium Works' company (VAW) and the Jewish director of the firm Aluerz, Dr. Hiller. After the invasion of Hungary in March 1944 Westrick quickly put in a request for Dr. Hiller's safety, the friend with whom he had enjoyed such a good business relationship. Westrick rightly feared that industry would become counter-productive once the spoils of 'Jewish plunderings' fell into the hands of the SS. Because of their overwhelmingly destructive urge they would make little efficient use of the potential that the Jewish economy had to offer. Throughout the war a perpetual internal economic battle was being waged between, on the one hand German industry and the Ministry of Warproduction headed by Albert Speer and, on the other hand the SS empire of Heinrich Himmler whose aim it was to secure economic and financial autarky for his 'SS State'.

While the 'Aryanization' of Jewish (predominantly industrial) business activity was a laborious process, the Hungarian political élite was more successful in its efforts to seize land owned by Jews. Up until 1939 some 5% of Hungary's land was in the hands of Jews but during the war years this situation rapidly changed as it was gradually confiscated. Their land was 'surrendered' to war veterans of the First World War as though the Jews themselves had not taken part in the fighting and were not themselves veterans.

Jewish people were economically exploited throughout the war in a different way as well. After war broke out with the Soviet Union in the summer of 1941, 130,000 Jewish labourers were quickly recruited for the Hungarian army. These men were split up into battalions and placed in existing Hungarian units. Once in the army they were given unpleasant jobs to do, like for instance clearing minefields. While Himmler was heavily involved in the process of exterminating Jews from other countries, Albert Speer was watching very interestedly to see how Hungarian Jews were employed in the construction gangs. In his endeavours to economically support the German war effort he was always on the lookout for new sources of labour. In 1943, for instance, there was an acute shortage of workers in the copper mining industry in the Yugoslavian town of Bor. Originally a French company ('Compagnie des Mines de Bor') the company had been left virtually unstaffed after the SS had sifted people out a little too rigorously. The local Jewish and Serbian population had been wiped out by the SS who had deported them and executed them. Speer then approached the Hungarian authorities and requested that they release 10,000 Jews for employment in the copper mines. After some hesitation, Budapest finally agreed to 'deliver' 3,000 Jews in exchange for 100 tons of copper per month: a business deal in which the Jewish people had become mere transaction objects. This was not the only 'slave deal' that was made during the war. Szálasi also preferred to do trade with Hungarian Jews rather than hand them over to the extermination camps. For the Hungarians, the Jews had become an export commodity.

The Hungarians were also guilty of deportation and murder. It was curious that the Hungarians found it easier to kill their 'conquered' Jews than their 'native' Jews. After the Hungarians had gained more territory following collaboration with the German camp, tens of thousands of Jews from outside the Hungarian buffer state fell into Hungarian hands. The sanctions exercised against these Jews were invariably stricter than those applied to Hungary's 'native' Jews. The so-called 'Ostjuden', for example, from the Carpathian-Ukraine region (captured from Czechoslovakia) were simply taken over the border and thus automatically placed under German jurisdiction. This was done without first consulting Berlin. At this stage, the German authorities were at a loss what to do about the Jews who were pouring in from other areas in Europe. In some places, they were, therefore, sent back over the borders again in their thousands only to be returned just as quickly by the Hungarian authorities from what was their recently gained land. Top SS man and Police Führer, Jeckeln, promised in September 1941 to do his best to 'exterminate the Jews as quickly as possible'.

A tragic mass murder of Jews took place on conquered Yugoslavian soil. On 20th January 1942, the Hungarian general Ferenc Feketehalmy-Czeydner ordered the people in the city of Novi Sad to roll down all their shutters. The city's Serbian and Jewish inhabitants were then led to the city's bathing area on the Danube. There they were forced to stand naked on a diving-board from where they were shot into the Danube that was frozen over. On impact the bodies made great holes in the ice. Thousands of Serbians and Jews were murdered on that day. A year later, the Hungarians brought to justice the general who had carried out the orders in Novi Sad, thus, demonstrating once again the indecisiveness of Hungarian policies. The general escaped to Germany and Hitler personally saw to it that he was not extradited to Budapest. After 1989 some historians claimed that the tragedy was planned by the Germans.

The Nazis wanted the extermination of Hungarian Jews to be organized in a more structured way, to take place according to the methods dictated for the whole of Europe. On the German side, serious endeavours were made to discuss and plan this issue. In April 1943, a meeting was arranged between Horthy, Hitler and Von Ribbentrop. Horthy defended the Hungarian standpoint on Jewish politics by arguing that Hungary was the first country to actually implement quotum controls for Jews. Hitler was not satisfied with this answer and he insisted on even firmer measures. He argued that the Jews should be stripped of their incomes and livelihoods. Horthy protested saying indignantly that he could hardly be expected to 'exterminate all the Jews'. Von Ribbentrop's stone cold answer to this was that extermination or confinement in concentration camps was the only solution. 'It's easier for you Germans' Horthy complained 'because you have fewer Jews.'

However, the worry of the whole Jewish question was soon to be removed from Horthy's mind altogether. It was partly resolved when German power in Hungary increased. After Horthy's return from Klessheim in March 1944, an extensive SS contingent had gone to Budapest. The new authorities there were top SS man and Police Führer Dr. Otto Winkelmann and the SS Commando Eichmann. They were assisted in their task by Seidl, Krumey, Dannecker, Wisliceny, Novak, Hunsche and Abromeit. The coordinator of all the German units stationed in Hungary was Dr. Veesemayer and his deputy Feine. The Nazi presence and influence was clearly reflected in the new Hungarian parliament installed on 22nd March 1944 of which Döme Zstojay was Prime Minister. In his cabinet, the Secretary of State for Political (Jewish) Affairs was Dr. Endre: Eichmann's man in parliament. By now, Endre and Eichmann had become close friends. Eichmann had given Endre his personal weapon as a sign of respect and in return Eichmann was frequent quest at Endre's family residence in Kiskunfölinhaza, south of Budapest.

Now that these political developments had taken place, Eichmann was able to commence his deportation operations in earnest. Already on 20th March, a preliminary meeting had been held with delegates from the Hungarian Jewish community. Eichmann kept them waiting for hours before calling them in to talk with a low ranking SS officer. During this first meeting, the Jews were given to understand that a Jewish council would have to be set up, that an inventory must be made of Jewish owned property and that no Jews were to be allowed to leave Budapest. Eichmann who could have, so some said, an almost hypnotic effect on people started to exercise his power even more in the days that followed. He would sometimes play on people's anxieties (he once called himself 'the bloodhound'), at other times though, he could be most amiable and accommodating. Eichmann guaranteed that if the Jews cooperated nothing would happen to them and he pointed out that the political and military situation was changing in Europe. The Jewish delegates were naturally delighted to hear that things would be different for their particular community. They were gullible and believed all the lies they were told. For their part the Nazis were delighted with the cooperation and gratitude they were receiving. The Jews showed their appreciation by rewarding Eichmann's commando with presents of lingerie, Eau de Cologne and paintings. SS-Hauptsturmführer Hunsche, who enjoyed playing the piano told the Jews that he would like to have a piano as soon as possible. Before the day was over, no less than eight instruments had been delivered. In the meantime, through its own Jewish newspaper, the Hungarian Jewish Council summoned its people to be obedient and to behave in a disciplined way.

During that same month, March 1944, laws against Hungarian Jews were tightened once again. The Germans fully exploited the existing situation. On 29th March, the 'prohibition on professions' was extended to include Jewish journalists, judges, academics and musicians which meant that all these people were instantly left without work. Very soon, it was only Jewish doctors who were allowed to keep on working but this was only because without their services the entire Hungarian health service would have more or less disintegrated. In economically destroying the Hungarian Jews heavy damage was done to the Hungarian economy as a whole. In Hungary, there were 110,000 registered companies, 40,000 of which were owned by Jews and most of these were closed down. Of the 30,000 companies which existed in Budapest 18,000 were shut down. On the same day that the 'prohibitions on professions' was enforced, the armband with the yellow Star of David was introduced. Only war invalids from the First World War who were 75% incapacitated and had been decorated with gold and silver medals after the war were exempt from wearing the yellow Star of David. From the beginning of April onwards, all Jews were prohibited from travelling and between 31st March and 28th April thousands were arrested to ensure that they could not organize a rebellion. Almost 8,142 supposedly 'dangerous' Jews were imprisoned.

The process of identifying and expropriating Jews was set in motion by the Hungarians. Once this had been accomplished, the Germans stepped in to take over the task of rounding up all the Jews and deporting them. To allow this ghetto-forming process to run smoothly and quickly the country was divided up into five zones, Budapest excluded, from which Jews were to be called up and deported in turn. Eichmann was again clever in his tactics. He first started rounding up Jews in zones I and II which were situated in the Carpathians and Transylvania thus hoping to pacify the Jewish Council by convincing Council members that the SS was only interested in deporting 'conquered Jews' who, in the past, had been dealt with severely by the Hungarians as well. He persuaded the Council that as far as their 'own Jews' were concerned they would never be hurt. Of course, not a word of this was true. In zone III (to the north of Budapest), zone IV (to the east of the Danube excluding Budapest) zone V (to the west of the Danube excluding Budapest) and finally in the capital as well people were deported en masse between June and the end of July.

The whole operation went amazingly smoothly and efficiently, especially if one bears in mind that the fate awaiting all deported Jews was common knowledge by this time and when one considers what the state of affairs was like on the front. Despite all this the extermination machine had been easily set going. The Jews were herded into ghettos in cities (such as Nagyvárad, Szeged and Sighut) or camps (Kolozsvár) or sometimes they were simply left out in the open (as in Marosvásárhely (Tirgu Mures). There was not nearly enough accommodation for all the people who had been herded together and all clues pointed in the direction of immediate deportation and extermination.

To ensure that this phase also went smoothly Eichmann had sent SS-Untersturmführer Novak and his deputy SS-Untersturmführer Martin to Vienna to partake in the railway conference due to take place in the Austrian capital. The conference, designed to plot how the transportation of Hungarian Jews to the German death camp of Auschwitz was to be effected, proved to be an example of incredible international cooperation in the middle of the Holocaust. Not only German civilian specialists were present at the conference but also Hungarian and Slovakian officials, including Hauptmann Lullay of the Hungarian gendarmerie. The main problem facing them was that the railway route via Lwow was out of bounds because of activities on the front. The Budapest-Vienna line could not be used, because that would arouse too much suspicion with the Jewish Council and the Jewish community in Budapest, so it was decided that transportation would have to go via Slovakia. It was agreed that four trains a day would be reserved, each with 45 wagons. The Hungarians would take care of the 'loading' of the trains.

Already by the end of April 1944 the first transportations to Auschwitz had got under way. Passengers were forced to send cheerful letters to their families in Hungary. The letters went to the Jewish Council in Budapest from where they were distributed. According to the deportees they had gone to Waldsee where they were having a grand time. At first it seemed as though the German's trick was working but when someone deciphered a badly erased Auschwitz stamp the Germans were found out. Panic in the Jewish ranks did little to improve their lot though. By the time the railway conference in Vienna was over, 200,000 Jews had been gathered in ghettos and this number was increasing by the day. The deportations then became quick and efficient. By 9th July, 437,402 Hungarian Jews had been sent to Auschwitz. Horthy and his loyal followers sorrowfully looked on but did nothing to try to influence matters until pressure from other countries, notably neutral countries like Switzerland and Sweden, increased. When the western Allies also started to talk of war crime compliance Horthy was galvanized into action. He had already seen to it that the Jews in Budapest were not placed in a big ghetto. Instead he had created 'Jewish houses'. Originally, the Jews, who comprised 200,000 of the one million inhabitants in Budapest, had lived in 52,300 different houses. By July, this had been reduced to 33,294 houses where Jews, living thirteen to a room on average, were accommodated. Horthy finally started to protest about the deportations, he forced trains to stop running and removed Endre from office. All of this culminated in a revolt on 15th October in which the Arrow Cross movement seized power.

By the time Szálasi came to power, the transporting to Auschwitz had been completed. The gassings in the Polish camp, the last of its kind that was still open, were coming to an end and the Germans by then needed the surviving Jews for other purposes. Since just about every German labourer had been sent to the front to fight there was a drastic shortage of manpower throughout Germany and the Jewish community was able to provide free labour. In particular the SS-'Wirtschafts-Verwaltungshauptamt' (SS-Gruppenführer Kammler) was interested in enlisting Hungarian Jews to help build the underground aircraft and V-2 factory he was planning to construct. He required tens of thousands of workers for this purpose and the German authorities in Budapest were more than pleased to supply the 'slave-labour' required for the job but there were a number problems. The German railway network was disrupted and overloaded which meant that the Jews could only reach their destination on foot.

Three days after Szálasi came to power, the German authorities decided to march 50,000 Hungarian Jews westwards. These marches were to go down in history as the death marches to Hegyeshalom. A the border town on the Austrian-Hungarian border Hegyeshalom was then in German hands. It was the place where the Germans also wanted to employ Jews to build the 'Südostwall/Reichsschutzstellung' (a kind of Siegfried defencework of the east). Poorly fed and thin from their time in the ghettos the Jews set off, stumbling westwards through the snow and ice. The route took them through Piliscsaba, Dorog, Süttö, Szöny, Gönyü, Dunaszeg and Moson-Magyaróvár and it came to be known as 'death's highway'. The distance the Jews were expected to walk was 200 to 220 kilometres. They were sent off in groups of two to four thousand people and it took them seven to eight days to get there. All along the route people died of exhaustion and only Red Cross helpers came to occasionally relieve a little of the pain. At the embassies of neutral countries, people were shocked to hear what was going on. The Swiss and Swedish embassies sent a delegation to Hegyeshalom. The Hungarian Holocaust was followed by the eyes of the world, it was public knowledge and even certain SS officers were shocked at the sight of the long sad convoys of people. SS-General Hans Jüttner lodged a complaint with the authorities in Budapest about the suffering that the Jews were having to endure.

By the time the marches to Hegyeshalom were taking place, the Jewish community had become so disintegrated and so depleted that Eichmann and Veesenmayer had trouble finding 50,000 Jews who were fit enough to work. In the end, some 35,000 were sent to join the death marches. Szálasi also protested about the deportation of Jews, but with economic motives at the back of his mind. It was probably the memory of the fate of all the Jews who had been 'exported' to work in the Yugoslavian copper mines that prompted him to make it clear to Veesenmayer that he was only 'lending' the Hungarian Jews to the Germans. In Berlin, his request was, of course ignored but in any case it was virtually impossible to return the 'labouring Jews' for the simple reason that they were 'used up' at a fast rate. Many died through ill-treatment and the ones who did survive were sent off to concentration camps in the west such as Mauthausen and Gunskirchen at what was the end of the war.

The Jews who were left stayed in Hungary, many of them remained in Boedapest which eventually had its own ghetto. The ghetto occupied a small area of the city, a mere 0.3 of a square kilometre (the total area of Budapest being 207 square kilometres) and it was situated between Domony street and Magyaratád-Szabo street. By November 1944, there were still 120,000 Jews living in the Hungarian capital. The area they lived in was cordoned off with wooden fencing built by the same company that had constructed the barriers for the

Warsaw ghetto, a company owned by a certain Mr. Josef Auguszt. When the Red Army neared Budapest Auguszt disappeared leaving the last part of the job to Novak, his second-in-command.

On 10th December, just before the city was surrounded by the Red Army, the number of inhabitants in the ghetto had dropped to 70,000. By now, the Jews could not feel safe anywhere. In his two volume long standard work on the lot of the Hungarian Jews Randolph L. Braham makes mention of daily pogroms taking place within the confines of the ghetto. Even hospitals were included in such actions and doctors and patients were tortured and murdered. Such attacks were carried out on 11th and 14th January 1945. In one single attack on a hospital in the Maros street no less than 92 people were killed. In the accompanying siege many lives were also lost. Approximately 10,000 Jews died in this particular siege, many of them dying violent deaths.

The vast majority of the Hungarian Jews deported to Auschwitz lost their lives. A study carried out by Martin Gilbert provides details of the actual extermination process. Since the transportations that Eichmann organized to Auschwitz were incredibly efficient the last days of Auschwitz were very busy and a record number of gassings took place. Between May and October 1944, hundreds of thousands of people were put to death in the extermination camp and a great many of these people were Hungarian Jews.

The first train from Hungary arrived in Auschwitz on 16th May. Each train transported around 4,000 people. From this first train only seven people went into the camp, the rest were sent directly to the gas chambers. The second train arrived on 17th May, again bringing some 4,000 people most of whom were instantly gassed to death. An entry in a sinister SS bookkeeper's records noted that on that day the amount of gold accumulated from the teeth of Hungarian Jews amounted to 40 kilograms. The third train from Hungary arrived on 18th May. On that day only twenty women from the 4,000 people transported were sent into the camp. On 20th May came the fourth train. This time 34 men and 58 women went through to the camp and the rest were killed. In the space of just over four days more than 16,000 Hungarian Jews had been executed. On 21st May, the horror at Auschwitz reached its height. No less than three trains arrived from Hungary, two from the Netherlands and one from Belgium, one of the Dutch trains being packed only with gypsies. In the days, weeks and months that followed, new train loads of people streamed in from Hungary, the Netherlands, France, Italy and Greece, in short, from all corners of Europe that had fallen into the hands of Nazi Germany.

By November, Himmler was able to conclude that most European Jews had been killed and that the last gassings would take place on 25th November. On that same day, organizational changes took place. Auschwitz I and II were merged into one concentration camp and Auschwitz three was renamed, it was called Monowitz. On 12th January 1945, the Red Army broke through the Baranow bridgehead on the Vistula and moved quickly towards Auschwitz. The final roll-call was on 17th January, by then the camp contained almost 70,000 prisoners. People were transported westwards by train and all who could still walk were forced to go by foot in the bitterly cold conditions. At the last moment, the SS performed several final mass executions and blew up all their crematoriums. A small group of SS men stayed behind to guard the prisoners who had not left on foot. Hence, the reason that crematorium IV was operational up until the very last moment, it was not blown up until 27th January. When the Russian units of the 100. and 107. division entered Auschwitz few buildings and barracks were still standing but those that were left told their own shocking tale. The depots contained 368,820 men's suits, 836,255 ladies' overcoats and seven tons of hair. A mere 7,000 people were freed from the camp and most of them were very sick.

Those who had managed to survive Auschwitz were then sent on to Buchenwald, Sachsenhausen, Gross Rosen and

Mauthausen or Dachau. The camps in the west were overfull. Ever more prisoners were being sent to the west from the east and, with the battle against the western Allied Forces on the looming large, the Germans began to fear reprisals after the war so in various industries they quickly started getting rid of all their Jewish employees. All kinds of diseases broke out in Auschwitz which only intensified the suffering there. At this stage many ex-Auschwitz SS guards were sent to other camps which did not improve matters for the Jews in those particular camps. The aggression towards Jews in the last weeks of the war was terrible. In Stutthof concentration camp on the Baltic Sea over 3,000 Jewish women were taken onto the hearby beach and killed by firing-squads or driven into the sea and left to drown. On 27th April 1945, several days before the war ended, two ships sailed into the harbour at Kiel packed with Jewish evacuees. German SS men and sailors idled away their time by shooting the Jews on board while German army officers watched the spectacle from their gardens along the canal and photographed it. In other cities the train consignments of Jews, invariably from Hungary, were stoned by German civilians. It seemed that the ingrained hatred started by Streicher and Goebbels was impossible to eradicate.

The success of the German annihilation of the Hungarian Jews might give the impression that there was no opposition to this final phase of the Holocaust, but such a view is not completely true. There was opposition, but it was not forceful enough and it came too late in the war.
There has been some controversy about the part played by the International Red Cross (the IRC) in Hungary. Up until July 1944, the IRC did not interfere with the Hungarian Holocaust in any way. It was only when all the transportation to Auschwitz was more or less completed that they started to intervene. The slownless of the reaction had largely to do with the fact that the IRC abided rigidly by the basic principles laid down in the Geneva Convention of 1929 which stated that the IRC's role was particularly to help prisoners of war in wartime

by offering legal aid and providing food parcels. The Jews, however, were not seen as prisoners of war. The problem was viewed more as one of conflict between a regime and a minority group for which the Convention provided no jurisdiction. The pleas made by Jewish organizations, such as the World Jewish Congress, to the IRC to acknowledge that the Jews of Hungary were 'civilian internees' were, therefore, all made in vain.

A report on the activities of the IRC during the war revealed that the organization had defended itself by stating that it really had no choice in the matter because there were interests other than those of the Jews to be considered. On other fronts though the IRC and its helpers did do a great deal of good work in Hungary. They helped out with the emigration policy that saved some Jews from the Holocaust - this will be discussed later - and they were instrumental in saving thousands of children in the ghetto in Budapest which, by the end of the war, was populated mostly by children and elderly people.

Apart from the Red Cross, the Vatican in Rome also protested about the mass murder of Hungarian Jews but, as with the IRC, Pope Pius XII's indignation was heard much too late. It was not until 25th June 1944, that Horthy received a letter from the Pope expressing concern about the predicament of the Hungarian Jews, but the Pope's protest had immediate effect. Horthy defended the ghetto in Budapest. It is significant to see that, when protests did come, they were effective. The root of the problem lay in the fact that objections to the Holocaust were more of a modest and diplomatic nature than of a public nature. Instead of naming the murderers and turning the indignation of the world upon them cautious discussion was entered into behind the scenes. Already in July 1942, Harold H. Tittmann, ambassador for the US had personally warned Pope Pius XII that he would be 'morally damaged' and would 'lose prestige' if he remained silent any longer.

Just like the Red Cross the Vatican was well aware, throughout the war, of the atrocities that were continuing and of the suffering that was being caused for the Jews. Both organizations had a huge information network at their disposal and were also continually kept up to date on matters by Jewish organizations, the neutral press (notably the Swiss and Swedish press) and the western Allies. The Hungarian clergy also put up a degree of resistance. It was notably Cardinal Seredi, his locum tenens the deacon John Drakos and the papal nuncio Angelo Rotta who made their disagreement known.

Even within this group the real protesting only started after the deportations had commenced. When, on 15th May, deportation had just begun in zone I, Rotta wrote in a letter to the Hungarian Minister of Foreign Affairs: '100,000 Jews are being deported. Everybody knows what that means in practice ... it is our duty to protest.' On 27th May and 17th June, further letters of protest were sent from Bishop Apor of Györ (Raab) to Cardinal Seredi in which demandeds were made for action and Seredi duly passed on the complaints.

It was apparent that the clergy was putting much more effort into trying to free the small group of Christian Jews that came under the broad definition of 'Jew' than into helping Jews in general. As Hilberg argued, it implicitly indicated that they went along with the extermination of all other Jews. In Hungary, the Catholics protested about the fact that their Jews were forced to wear the Star of David, since this symbolized a 'rejection of God' and therefore constituted an affront to the Church. All in all, this typified the attitude of the Catholic Church in Hungary to the Jewish community there. A total of 20,000 'protection passports' were issued by the papal nuncio. This did not guarantee the safety of these Jews in Hungary but it went some way towards halting the terror against them. Their houses were not daubed with a yellow star in the usualway but with a yellow crucifix.

Szálasi's Arrow Cross movement tried to play upon these ambiguous Semitic sentiments within the Church. In Veszprem, they tried to persuade the priests to include in their mass a prayer of thanksgiving conveying that the annihilation of the Hungarian Jews was the will of God.

The bishop of the city refused to do this arguing that Christian Jews were also being deported.

The hesitancy of the Vatican to resist has been discussed at length in post-war literature on the subject. Certain people like Guenther Lewy who did research into the role of the Vatican during the war discovered that many of the archives of that period had been closed. Apparently nobody wanted to be reminded of this shady past. The help given by the Vatican after the war to war criminals wanting to escape to South America and elsewhere by means of the so-called 'monastery route' also confirms how unedifying the attitude was towards the tragedy of the jews. During the thirties and forties, Communism had been seen as the big threat and many members of the East European clergy who had collaborated with the Nazis clung to their anti-Semitic and anti-communist views after the war which only served to reinforce the attitudes already established in the west.

It was for this reason that the Croatian professor of theology, Krunoslav Draganovic, who had been responsible for the deportation of tens of thousands of Jews and Serbians was able to find refuge within the walls of the Vatican. It was not just the Vatican that turned a blind eye to its murky dealings of the past but also the Allies in the west. After the war, the German researcher Ernst Klee discovered that Draganovic had not only worked for the Vatican but that he had also been an East European expert and 'reliable anti-communist' for the CIC (Army Counter-Intelligence Corps) of the American army. Draganovic was therefore a rather special case, because he was working for two sides at the same time but there were other big names who surfaced in Rome as well. Walter Rauff, famous for the mobile gas vehicles and Adolf Eichmann who went under the assumed name of Ricardo Klement both availed themselves of the facilities offered by the Vatican to escape from Europe. Like Draganovic, Klaus Barbie, the Gestapo officer stationed in Lyon ('butcher of Lyon') worked for the CIC after the war.

The western Allies who, through the American ambassador to the Vatican, had made their criticism of Pope Pius XII heard, were guilty of gross negligence themselves. It was only at a very late stage in the war that the Allies started to bomb Auschwitz and even then these bombings were not so much designed to preserve more Jews from being killed but rather to put an end to the production of synthetic fuel which they suspected was being fabricated in the camps. Ironically this time in connection with the Allies oil production and the fate of the Jews once again came together on the strategic agenda.

It was not until 16th January 1945, that the Red Army carried out its first attack on Auschwitz. The Red Army made little use of strategic long-distance bombers which explains why their air force was only activated when Auschwitz came within their front area after the Red Army had broken through the Baranow bridgehead.

The western Allies got there a little earlier but they also were much too late. It was not until 4th April 1944 that a photographic reconnaissance flight was carried out above Auschwitz which precipitated the bombardment of Monowitz on 20th August, 13th September, 18th December and 26th December 1944. Evidently, these meagre attacks mounted late in the day did little to hamper the large-scale massacre of Europe's last Jewish community that had been going on. Politically also far too little pressure had been put on the Germans. It was only in March 1944 that Roosevelt actually called the 'Endlösung' a crime against humanity.

Obviously, there was much protest about the Hungarian Holocaust from the Jewish side. The resistance was chiefly organized by the 'Vaadat Erza v' Hazalah', a support and life-saving group. The committee was composed of a number of militant Zionist Jews who, up until then, had been able to escape the Holocaust by fleeing to Hungary. Now that the Holocaust had reached Budapest it was time for them to come into action. The president of the committee was Dr. Otto Komoly. The man who was most in the public eye and in direct conflict with Adolf Eichmann was the committee's vice-president, the judge and journalist Dr. Rezsö (Rudolf) Kastner. This militant group of Jews wanted to attack the Germans on three fronts. First they wanted to put up armed resistance for which they sought help outside of the country. In the second place they wanted to disrupt the transport of Jews to Auschwitz and in the third and last place, they hoped, through direct negotiation with the Germans, to be able to save as many lives as possible.

The committee's first two goals were not achieved. Great Britain was not forthcoming with armed aid. In the end, three commandos were dropped with instructions from London to only fight for the Jewish cause as a very last resort. The whole exercise was a complete fiasco. Veesenmayer who was kept well informed by his intelligence service at all times managed to arrest the three commandos in Budapest in July 1944. It now seemed that bombing the railway lines would be a more feasible option. The committee had discovered that, especially between the places Kosice and Oderberg, the route was vulnerable to air bomb attacks. This information was passed on to the western Allies via Swiss radio but enlisted no response.

The only course of action left was, to try and achieve results by going into direct negotiation with the Nazis. Kastner and his right-hand man Joel Brand were put in touch with Eichmann through Wisliceny. Eichmann who posed as the 'Tsar of the Jews' was interested in doing business with Kastner. After the war he wrote in his memoirs: 'Kastner became the key to instrumenting the extermination of the Jews'. The meetings between Kastner and Eichmann led to some of the most bizarre dealings of the whole Holocaust. Kastner implored Eichmann to free a few thousand Jews so that they could travel to Palestine. Eichmann agreed in exchange for a high fee (four million German marks for 600 Jews) and on condition that Kastner would help to keep the Jewish Council in line. 'I was prepared to turn a blind eye', wrote

Eichmann after the war, 'in exchange for a problem free extradition of the rest of the Jewish community.'

The negotiations between Kastner and Eichmann went further than that though. Between the two men arose what Eichmann called a kind of 'mutual trust'. It was with a degree of sadistic pleasure that Eichmann watched Kastner and Brand's frantic efforts to find somewhere in the world where they could send the Jews whom they just might be able to set free. 'Nobody wanted them', Eichmann wrote in contempt, 'Brand had to travel half way around the world.' Eichmann then came up with an absurd trading exchange suggestion. He said that if the Jews supplied Nazi Germany with 10,000 trucks one million of them would be released to the west. The Jewish World Congress would receive the guarantee that the trucks would only be used for the eastern front.

Eichmann who claimed to have received permission for this plan from SS-Reichsführer Heinrich Himmler pointed out that trucks were needed for the motorization of Waffen-SS divisions. Since 1944, there were indeed two SS cavalry divisions in Hungary, the 8.SS Kav.D. 'Florian Geyer' and the 22.SS Kav.D. 'Maria Theresia' which were stationed on the outskirts of Budapest and had taken part in operations 'Margarethe', 'Panzerfaust' and the battles in eastern Hungary ('Gruppe Plehps'). The units were commanded by two friends of Eichmann, the SS Generals Rumohr and Zehender. Units from these divisions had already been protecting Jews (whose freedom had been bought by Kastner) from the murderous plunderings of the Arrow Cross gangs in Budapest.

It is not exactly clear how serious these bizarre dealings really were. Eichmann writes in his memoirs that he can no longer recall who gave the order for this deal to be carried out. What he did remember was that both Heinrich Müller (Administrative Chief of Reichs Security) and Ernst Kaltenbrunner (RSHA Chief) were knowledgeable of the dealings. The plan was not altogether realistic. In the first place, the Nazis hardly had a million Jews left and in the second place, apart from all kinds of possible political consequences, the operation would be impossible from practical logistic and financial points of view. It is conceivable that Eichmann's request was influenced by his personal contacts with Waffen-SS cavalry officers who were in the middle of the process of setting up their divisions and by the knowledge that new Waffen-SS cavalry units (the later 37. SS Cavalry division 'Lützow' which was under the command of the brother-in-law of Hitler's mistress Eva Braun, SS-Gruppenführer Hermann Fegelein) were about to be established. Eichmann was also kept up to date on this matter through his friendship with SS-Standartenführer Becher of the 'Florian Geyer' division whom Himmler had personally sent to Budapest to further equip the Waffen-SS cavalry divisions. At this time, Eichmann mockingly called his friend Becher 'the horse merchant'.

In his memoirs, Eichmann also used the truck deal incident as 'evidence' that no one wanted to help the Jews and to prove that his deportations, therefore, provided 'the only solution' to the Nazis self created 'Jewish problem'. Quite apart from the reality aspect of this idea the 10,000 truck deal incident did prove that with defeat in sight the Nazis were more willing to negotiate. The Jews became increasingly valuable as bartering objects for the SS. At the end of the war, Himmler even used them as hostages to buy his own safety. In his memoirs, Eichmann speculates that with the truck deal Himmler perhaps wanted to create a basis for his later dealings with Count Bernadotte.

At any rate, Kastner whom Eichmann saw as a man of 'blood and soil' because of his Zionist sympathies managed to arrange for thousands of Hungarian Jews to be set free. According to Hilberg the number amounted to 18,000 (Eichmann spoke of a possible 20,000 released Jews). Drawing up the list of 'lucky ones' was a drama in itself. There were original lists and reserve lists. The sheer uncertainty of the Jewish lot up until the very last moment was well illustrated by a transport incident in Győr. A train Jews originally destined for Vienna ended up going to Auschwitz simply because of a shunting mistake made by the Hungarian railway company when a train that should have gone to Auschwitz ended up going to the west. The Jews who did arrive in Vienna waited for the end of the war. Approximately 1,000 of them died from the hardship and maltreatment they were forced to endure.

Dr. Kastner used all the resources he had to pay for this transport. Apparently the amount of cash handed over was not great but at such a time of scarcity the SS men were happy enough to be paid in kind, for instance with fifteen tons of coffee. This brought to an end the stories about Kastner and his exchange deals. Kastner remained however a controversial figure because in compiling the lists of the 'fortunate 18,000' he was simultaneously accused of having functioned as saviour and judge even though dozens of other people had helped him to draw up the lists.

After the war, a fierce debate flared up in Israel and all sorts of libel accusations were brought against Kastner in conjunction with his role in the war just at a moment when he was on the point of standing as a candidate for the Knesset. Kastner defended himself tooth and nail. 'I did not collaborate with the Nazis, they collaborated with me!', he protested. He made it clear that at the time there had been no possible alternative course of action. 'The situation in Hungary differed from that in Poland and Russia in that almost everywhere the farming community was hostile towards the Jews impatiently awaiting the moment when they could take over their property. There was no Hungarian resistance movement which was why dealing with the Germans was the only possible way of achieving anything' Kastner explained. Others were more critical and called Kastner's cooperating with the Germans 'a pact with the devil' and Kastner a little 'Quisling'. Even Horthy who was then living in Portugal was asked to comment. For Kastner himself the case soon ended. On 4th March 1957, as he left a newspaper office in Tel Aviv a jeep drove past at top speed, several shots were fired and one of them hit Kastner in the chest. On 15th March, he died from the wounds he had received. In 1958, in the Israeli high court, he was posthumously acquitted of all blame in connection with the Holocaust. In the eighties a play was staged about Kastner and his part in the war, it created the same kind of controversy that Spielberg's Schindler's List created in 1994.

During the war, Raoul Wallenberg, who became third secretary at the Swedish embassy, proved through his amazing rescue operations what an incredible person he was. Wallenberg was only 32 years old when he arrived in Budapest on 9th July 1944. He came from a wealthy Stockholm family of bankers and politicians and had inherited a flair for diplomacy. Certainly, in the task that lie ahead Wallenberg would be needing all the diplomacy he could muster because his ordeal in Budapest was going to be a difficult one.

Wallenberg felt very involved in and concerned about the Hungarian Holocaust. After having studied architecture in the United States, he had gone on to spend five months in Haifa, in Palestine, where in 1936 he had met Jews who had recently fled from Germany. He had been shocked to hear their stories about growing anti-Semitic feeling in the Third Reich. In the ensuing years, he closely followed all the developments of the Holocaust and in 1942 and 1943 spent some time in Hungary on business where he discovered that discrimination against minority groups was increasing and even filtering into Hungarian legislation too. In 1944, two workers from Manfred Weiss, a big Hungarian steelworks, approached Wallenberg and asked if, in his capacity as a neutral Swede, he would be prepared to mediate between the Jews, Germans and anti-Semitic Hungarians. Wallenberg put this proposal to the Swedish diplomatic corps which proved glad to expand its staff in Budapest. Wallenberg joined the Swedish organization and so embarked on a brave and fatal mission in Budapest.

From a number of points of view Wallenberg's case is an interesting one. In the first place, the fact that he succeeded in saving the lives of thousands of Jews was significant. In the second place, despite an extremely heavy workload he still managed to find time to send abroad detailed reports of the Jewish predicament, thus, effectively putting war criminals under pressure. Wallenberg was, therefore, often able to threaten that after the war was over the murderers would definitely be brought to justice.

Working together with leaders of the Jewish Council such as Samu Stern and Rabbi Ehrenpreis and with employees from the Swedish and Swiss embassies, Wallenberg versed himself as quickly as possibly in the turbulent Hungarian situation. Obviously, he had been too late to prevent the deportations to Auschwitz. What he could at least do though was issue 'emergency passports' to a number of Jews in Budapest which meant that these people were then given Swedish diplomatic protection. At first, only 300 to 400 Jews who had relations in Sweden were eligible for protection.

Wallenberg energetically continued his mission, partly with backing from the Jewish Council and he quickly managed to increase the number of protected Jews to 4,500 and later to over the 7,000 mark. According to estimates made by Randolf L. Braham Wallenberg had about 355 men, chiefly of Jewish origin, working for him when activities were at their peak. Apart from issuing emergency passports 32 'Swedish' houses were purchased in Pozsonyi street where nearly 10,000 Jews could be comfortably accommodated.

Wallenberg's whole operation was extremely complex. Not only was it necessary to apply all kinds of diplomatic pressure to protect the Jews from the marauding Arrow Cross men and the unstable political climate, but people also had to be provided with food. There was already a shortage of food in the city and with the Red Army getting ever closer this situation could only worsen. Wallenberg's efforts reflected great personal bravery in much the same way that Kastner's had done. Through their tenacity both men had somehow achieved the impossible. They had managed to halt the machinery of the Holocaust for just one moment and thus save thousands of lives.

Like Kastner, Wallenberg did not survive for very long after the war. After the fall of the Hungarian capital

Wallenberg remained in Budapest. The new Russian administration had little time for interfering busybodies from neutral countries. As always Moscow wanted to make a clean sweep and it did not tolerate critical observers. On one particular day, Wallenberg was invited to visit the Russian military headquarters, but he never returned from that visit. In a 1981 CIA report another reason for Wallenberg's disappearance emerged. Not only had he worked for the Swedish embassy but he was also allegedly linked to a more or less clandestine organization in America known as 'The American Council for War Refugees'. Now that the siege of Budapest was over and the effects of the Cold War were starting to be felt the Soviets had clearly decided that they had even more reason to ensure that a critic like Wallenberg should disappear. Wallenberg died in the KGB prison in Loebjanka in 1947. The ex-Soviet Union has since offered an apology stating that it was all a 'tragic mistake'.

Wallenberg was not alone in his heroic deeds and in saving people from the gas chambers. Though he was by far the best known hero, there were a number of other people who were highly successful but who simply failed to feature in post-war literature on the subject. The Swiss humanist and diplomat Carl Lutz, from Appenzell, was probably Eichmann's most effective opponent. Through setting up protected houses within the ghetto and outside of it the Swiss embassy managed to save no less than 46,500 Hungarian Jews. The Italian, Giorgio Perlasca, a former fascist who had fought voluntarily in the Spanish Civil War, also played a special part. When the war started, he was a businessman in the Balkans but eventually, upset by the tragedy of the situation in Budapest, he started to work for the Spanish embassy (he had learnt Spanish while fighting in Spain on Franco's side). Alexander Grossman, Carl Lutz's biographer, estimated that around 2,000 Jews were saved via the Spanish embassy. On one occasion, Perlasca found himself in direct conflict with Eichmann. The Italian had snatched two children from a deportation line and loaded them into his car. The SS officer who happened to stop him was Adolf Eichmann. 'The children are on Spanish territory', Perlasca shouted and after a quick exchange of words Eichmann gave in. As the Red Army drew closer to Hungary the Spanish ambassador packed his bags and fled so Perlasca appointed himself 'temporary ambassador' and carried on his work without Madrid realizing what had happened.

Perlasca was an impressive figure. Always well groomed he used to carry with him a smart walking stick with a silver knob on the end. The notion that Jews in embassy protected houses should be saved arose by coincidence. Perlasca did not want anything to upset his girlfriend. He placed a board on the outside of her house with the following text: 'The spanish ambassador's girlfriend lives here'. Several hours later the house was packed with Jews. After the war, Perlasca moved to Padua.

When Eichmann escaped from Budapest just before the city was surrounded by the Red Army he gave the Arrow Cross movement the order to burn down the ghetto. This order was not carried out partly thanks to the endeavours of Wallenberg, Lutz and Perlasca. They managed to put pressure on a high up German officer to 'protect' the ghetto by threatening him with legal prosecution after the war if he did not do this.

From the various sources that exist it is not possible to establish exactly who this German officer was. In her Wallenberg biography, Marton wrote that it was the SS General (August) Schmidthuber and Braham contended that it was SS General Schmidthuber who was commandant of the 'SS-division Feldherrnhalle'. In his Wallenberg biography Derogy indicates that it was an officer by the name of Schmidthubert and Hilberg mentions no name whatsoever. In view of the 'FHH' division references it is most probable that the person in question was not an SS- General but an army (Wehrmacht) officer and that he did not belong to the 'FHH' division (which was not in fact an Waffen-SS division!) but rather to the 13.Pz.D. who was under the command of Generalmajor Gerhard Schmidthuber.

Schmidthuber who was born in Dresden in 1894 and was formerly commandant of the 7.Pz.D. Decorated with several high military awards he perished during attempts to escape from Budapest in February 1945. According to eye-witness reports Schmidthuber, a middle-aged man, made 'a tired impression' and he certainly did not plan to fight for Budapest 'as though it were Berlin'.

Despite the successful efforts of a small handful of devoted people to save the Jews from certain death, hundreds of thousands of Hungarian Jews were still murdered in the Second World War. Estimates of the numbers killed vary between 180,000 (according to Hilberg) and 600,000 (Levai).

Wacht an der Donau

Horthy's deposition on 15th October 1944 not only made the way free for the anti-Semitic Arrow Cross movement, it also strengthened Germany's military and economic stranglehold on Hungary. Cleansings were carried out so that the Hungarian army, now under the permanent supervision of the OKW, came to be completely under German control. On the German military side people had learnt their lesson well. Shortly after the Romanian debacle, the Germans had escaped by the skin of their teeth in Hungary.
On 17th October, no one less than the highest ranking Hungarian commanding officer of the land forces, General Miklos, went over to the Russian side and from there ordered the soldiers of the 1. Hungarian army to pick up their weapons and cross over to the Red Army's side. Even General Vörös whom Horthy had kept well informed in connection with the imminent military debacle, had gone over to the side of the Allies and had supported the step taken by Miklos.
Friessner reacted both angrily and fast. He spoke of a great 'offence to Germany' and when he heard from Wöhler that units of the 2. Hungarian Pz.D. had decided upon their course of action he ordered that the commanding officer of the 2. Hungarian army division be arrested immediately. Just as with Skorzeny in Budapest the German retaliation was successful. The same evening General Verres was brought before Friessner. Friessner was extremely disappointed about the attitude of the Hungarians. Only the evening before, Verres had promised him that 'everything would stay the same.' Just twenty-four hours later he was Friessner's prisoner. At this point Verres reminded Friessner of Horthy's words: 'No country is obliged to offer itself up for another country.'

The German's thought differently. Undivided loyalty was one of the fundamentals of National Socialism and the

Germans certainly planned to make the Hungarians honour this principle. Now that the internal Hungarian-German crisis had been temporarily allayed new problems arose. The Red Army, now on the banks of the Tysa, was preparing for its big attack of the Hungarian political nervecentre: Budapest, the metropolis on the Danube where the last few members of Europe's last Jewish community awaited their fate in the ghetto and where Ferenc Szálasi dreamed of a new big Hungarian state.

This dream was quickly shattered. In October, the Red Army prepared for its big offensive on Budapest. All the while the German armies on the Tysa front were anything but stable. In the extreme south, bordering on where the Army Group F was stationed (in Yugoslavia), the Red Army had already reached the Danube. Composed alternately of German, Hungarian and Russian bridgeheads the front extended northwards along Szolnok-Polgan and Tokaj and the banks of the Tysa. The central and most northerly section of the front was defended exclusively by German troops (Fretter-Pico/6. army and Wöhler/8. army) while the most southern extremities were defended by the 2. Hungarian army that was composed of German and Hungarian units.

The Red Army opened its offensive on 29th October at Kiskunfélegyháza. It was no coincidence that the attack commenced in the Hungarian legions of the front. The Soviet plan of attack was soon clear. The Red Army planned to penetrate Budapest by progressing in a direct line from the Tysa and by passing through the industrial city of Kecskemét. In the early stages, the Red Army quickly gained ground. The Hungarian soldiers who were poorly armed and politically disoriented quickly retreated. Kecskemét was about to fall and it seemed to be only a question of hours before the Soviets would break through to the Hungarian capital but on 30th October the German 24.Pz.D. supported by a number of smaller units, intercepted. A heavy battle with tanks flared up, similar to an earlier confrontation at Debrecen.

The Puszta once again came under fire and set aflame, but it was clear to Friessner that the Red Army had learnt from its previousl mistakes. This time the Russian 46. army did not wrecklessly send whole legions of tanks into the battle. The units of the II. and IV.Gem. corps instead sent off their tanks in small clusters and backed them up with infantry and artillery. This made it impossible for Friessner to allow the assault units to first burst through and then 'cut off the enemy' as had been done in the past. The initial panic had been assuaged but the sheer pressure of the units bearing down on Kecskemét could not possibly be beaten down by the Germans. Friessner hastily telephoned the German military representative in the city, General Von Greiffenberg, and directed him to immediately close off all roads on the south-east side of Budapest so as to stave off a possible Red Army invasion. The situation grew even more threatening when the Germans realized that though the Red Army's progress might have been briefly slowed down just before they reached Kecskemét, big Red Army units were now dispersing themselves on every side of the city and were filling up the weakest holes in the German defence system 'like water seeping into a well'. On 1st November, Red Army units penetrated as far as Kunszentmiklós and the next day they marched on to Bugyi. On 4th November, units of the Russian 7. Guard army had broken through the Hungarian 20. division's defences and had reached Cegléd. The Soviets were now closing in on Budapest from the north and the south. The chaos was complete when, on the very same day, November 4th, the Margarethe bridge in Budapest was blown up due to an accident with a gas main and a number of people were blown up with it. All kinds of rumours quickly spread. It was supposed that the Red Army was already in Budapest and that the Germans had blown up the historic bridge as a precaution. Everyone in the city frantically started hording and the Jews in the ghetto braced themselves. Perhaps help would come in time ...

Friessner now sent his best units to the front at Kecskemét, such as the 23. and 24.P.D., the Pz,Gren.D. 'Feldherrnhalle' ('FHH') and the 1.Pz.D. of the LVII.Pz. corps and the III.Pz. corps under the command of Hermann Breith ('Gruppe Breith') but all to no avail. By 7th November, Friessner's Army Group South had been pushed back to the Danube along the whole length of the front that protected the south side of Budapest. Only Budapest which now formed a huge bridgehead on the eastern bank was still in German hands. Fretter-Pico and Wöhler's units to the north of Budapest retreated to the north-west through the Matra range of mountains.

As far as the Red Army was concerned pushing the German troops back to the Danube and into the Matra mountains was merely the second phase of their offensive. On 27th November, the units of the 3. Ukrainian front to the south of Baja broke through the 2. Hungarian army which precipitated great concern in the German ranks. Not only did this constitute a threat to Budapest from the south but it also meant that the oil fields of Nagykanizsa to the south of lake Balaton might fall into the hands of the Red Army. It was not until 4th December that there was quiet on the front between the southern periphery of lake Balaton and the river Drava (Drau) at the point where the 2.Pz. army was stationed. It was the task of this unit, which fell under the command of General Maximilian de Angelis, to protect the oil fields. Working in coordination with the Ob Southeast (to the south of the Drava) Friessner managed for the next few months to keep the front stable in the so-called 'Margarethe-Stellung' which was a series of weakly built out defences running along the lakes Balaton and Velencei. This was partly made possible by the fact that fighting was chiefly being focused on Budapest, also by the fact that the Germans were about to develop military strategies that would bind large Russian units to them.

In the operations that took place between 27th November and 4th December 1944 the Red Army's chief interest was in the prestigious target of Budapest. At first, the German 6. army situated on the northern periphery of

lake Balaton was able to cope with the units of the 4. Russian Guards. This advantage was not to last for very long though. The Red Army soon sent reinforcements from the 4. Russian Guards army to the western bank of the Danube and pushed into the Gerecse and Pilis Heights to the north-west of lake Balaton. Units of the III.Pz. corps, the LVII. corps and the LXXII. corps tried, without success, to hold back five Soviet army corps. The 4.Kav.Brigade was quickly brought in from where the 2.Pz.army was stationed, where things were relatively quiet, but that was not enough to prevent the Red Army from penetrating, from Bicske and the industrial area around Tatabánya and Felsögalla through the Danube to the east of Komárom (Komorn, Komarno) by the end of December 1944. The headquarters of the Fretter-Pico army group was transferred to Tata.
During this whole period, Budapest itself was permanently under the pressure of the Russian IV.G.Mech. corps that managed to push back the 8.SS Kav.D. 'Florian Geyer' to the outskirts of the capital. Up until now the bridgehead on the eastern bank was still intact. In the meantime, the 6.G.Pz. army and the Army corps 'Plijew' of the Red Army situated to the north of Budapest moved through the Matra Mountains between the places Waitzen and Pásztó. The pushed the 8. army of Otto Wöhler to the far side of the river Gran (Hron). By Christmas Eve 1944, Budapest was effectively surrounded by Red Army troops.

At this crucial moment, political considerations again came into play. At Führer headquarters, the developments in Hungary had been followed with increasing anxiety. Heinz Guderian, the OKH leader, began to involve himself more in Hans Friessner's decision-making process. Guderian could not understand why Friessner had not been able to hold back the Soviets with his 'armada of tanks'. Guderian's criticism was unjustified because in all the battle areas the balance of power had been roughly 3 : 1 in the Soviets' favour. The Red Army was far better equipped and the Army Group

South was weak on infantry. Friessner, thus, had the same problems that the Soviets had had at Debrecen, namely, that it was impossible to win any battle only with tanks and without the back-up of infantry.

The breach with headquarters came quickly. Without further warning Friessner received the order at the end of December to immediately remove Fretter-Pico from office. 'They needed a scapegoat' wrote Friessner after the war, but Friessner was to be punished too. On the night of 22nd December, General Wenck, 'Chief of Staff of the OKH' telephoned the Army Group South with the message that Friessner was to be immediately replaced by Otto Wöhler, General of the Infantry and Commander of the 8. army. Friessner demanded an explanation and rang Wenck and Guderian, but nobody was able to give him a satisfactory answer. Finally, Wenck admitted that it had been 'a spontaneous decision on the part of the Führer' and the communiqué that was eventually released from Hitler's headquarters was: 'Der Führer dankt'. Friessner packed his bags and passed over his responsibility to Otto Wöhler on 24th December, the day that Budapest became fully surrounded by the Red Army.

Hitler's decisions concerning to the Hungarian front were directly related to his general strategic and political philosophies about how the war should be further conducted. In recent times, Hitler had become increasingly involved in Hungarian matters. He had personally seen to it that units of the Waffen-SS, the German Wehrmacht (IX.SS Geb.corps) and a number of Hungarian divisions in Budapest firmly stood their ground despite the fact that they were gradually being closed in. Budapest had been declared a 'Fortress' ('Festung') that must be defended from house for house and from street for street to the bitter end. This 'Festung' concept derived from Hitlers precise description in his Führer's dictate of 8th March 1944 of what was meant by 'Festen Platz'. He had explained: 'You must see to it that the enemy does not seize this operationally strategically important city. Allow yourselves to be closed in thus engaging as many as possible enemy troops and, creating space for successful counter-offensives.' Hitler had also written clear directives about the task of a commandant in a 'Festung' of this sort: 'the commandant must be suitable for the job; a hardened soldier in the rank of general. With such a duty in mind he must put his honour as a soldier to the test and seek to fulfil his task to the bitter end.'

One cannot help wondering what the 'operational importance' of Budapest was and how Hitler imagined that these 'successful counter-offensives' were going to be realized. To Hitler the Hungarian operations were all part of the Third Reich's final struggle, a miracle he believed in till the end. He hoped that, just as in the Seven Year War of his big hero Frederick the Great, there would be a sudden dramatic turn about on the battlefield. An offensive initiated in the west would signify the start of this struggle, but the real final battle would be fought in the east, on Hungarian soil!

The attack in the west was code-named 'Wacht am Rhein' and went down in history as the Battle of the Ardennes. The late autumn of 1944 saw many historic moments. After the Bomb Plot of 20th July 1944, Hitler seemed to be more convinced than ever that providence had elected him to pursue this mission to the bitter end. Holding on more stubbornly than ever before to his old theories, offensive operation plans and rigid attitude towards the Jews, was what enabled Hitler to keep to the same course until the end of the war.

By the autumn of 1944 Germany's prospects were bad. On 22nd June 1944, the Red Army had opened a big offensive against the Army Group Centre which had driven back the Nazis as far as Warsaw and had obliterated the Army Group Centre. No less than 25 German divisions perished in the fighting. In the north the Germans were forced back to East Prussia. In Courland, more than thirty divisions of the remaining units were cut off and only able to receive supplies by water. In the south, as we have already seen, Bulgaria and Romania had fallen to and only direct German intervention had been able to save Hungary. In his endeavour to hold back the Red Army Hitler had turned Budapest into a fortified city. Finland suspended its hostilities towards the Soviet Union on 4th September 1944.

The heavy defeats incurred on the front left their impression on the troops. Between 1st June 1944 and 1st November 1944, the German combined forces on the east front were reduced from 2,620,000 to 1,840,000 men. By November, there was a shortage of 40,000 officers. They were fighting against 5,290,000 Red Army soldiers. Because the Germans also had troops stationed in Courland (Latvia, 32 divisions) and in Hungary (17 divisions) very few divisions were available for the main front extending from East Prussia to the Carpathians. The Germans only had 82 big units for this front of which sixteen were panzer divisions or panzer grenadier divisions. By contrast, the Red Army had 225 infantry divisions, 22 Pz. corps, twenty smaller Pz. units and three Kav. corps. Apart from all its other problems Germany was also having trouble on the south front (Yugoslavia) and in Italy where a further 30 divisions were deployed. The situation on the western front was also worrying. The section from the mouth of the Schelde to Westwall passing through South Holland which extended as far as Switzerland, had been fairly stable since September 1944. The western Allies were by now on the point of invading Nazi Germany itself.

Now that Germany had missed its historic chance to turn D-Day into a Dieppe Hitler wanted to gain time by mounting a big military operation in the west. His plan was to repeat the success of May 1940 by organizing a major attack from the Ardennes thus creating heavy losses for the western Allies, cutting them off from the interior and providing 'a year's leeway'. The attack was to be mounted by top German army and Waffen-SS units under the command of Field Marshal Gert von Rundstedt. The Germans would cross the Meuse and go on to win back Antwerp, a seaport that was very important to them but which had been seized by the Allied Forces on 4th September 1944. Without this vital port the western Allies would be unable to penetrate the German Reich and their plans to invade Nazi Germany would be temporarily disrupted. Hitler hoped not only to gain time for his military activities, but also to undermine the enemy politically. By depriving the Allies of a quick victory and giving them the prospect of a long drawn out struggle Hitler hoped to create more room for negotiation. With the time gained in the west efforts could be concentrated on the east again and on ensuring that Germany remained supreme.

As far as Hitler was concerned the heart of the eastern offensive was in Hungary. By holding on to Budapest and mounting a few preliminary offensives Hitler hoped to conquer the western bank of the Danube. After the Ardennes offensive, western Hungary would then function as a springboard to Eastern Europe and Hitler had two underlying main aims. By mounting such offensives he hoped to protect and preserve the last natural oil reserves available to the Third Reich, the oil fields of Nagykanizsa in Hungary and, he also hoped to win back the Romanian oil at Ploesti. Hitler always used to say, 'my generals understand nothing about economics', but with this masterly plan he believed that things could still go in Germany's favour. If these actions should prove successful on what was, for the Russians, a front of lesser importance (Moscow had not equipped it as well as the main front on the Vistula) Hitler would then mount a follow-up operation in the north. The units stationed in Courland were, in relative terms, stronger than those of the Germans on the Vistula. Closing in from the north they could approach behind the Soviet forces and together with the Hungarian operations seriously jeopardize the Red Army.

Anyone examining such plans today, fifty years later, finds it hard to take them seriously. By this stage, the war had, as cited earlier 'already been lost in production-techincal terms', as Speer had said. As far as Hitler was concerned things were different, but then he did not think rationally. He continued to pursue a course set long before with unyielding tenacity. Exactly how obstinate he was about winning the war in the way he wanted to win it can be illustrated simply by the fact that both the Ardennes offensive (December 1944) and the big Hungarian offensive (March 1945) went ahead despite enormous pressure on other fronts and all the logistic problems that the operations brought with them. Straight after the failure of the Ardennes offensive the 6.SS Pz. army, the Waffen-SS' best army, was taken to Hungary by train. It was mad plan, but typical of the sort of foolishness that Hitler displayed until the bitter end. Hitler's Hungarian plans were executed at the cost of defending German soil which by then was looking very insecure behind the weak Vistula front and later the even weaker Oder front. Heinz Guderian had concluded, on the basis of reports received from Major General Gehlen that the eastern front was as shaky as 'a house of cards' but all his warnings were ignored.

Oil had always played an important part in Hitler's military-strategic thinking. Oil and raw materials in general had been one of the most important reasons for Hitler's 'much wanted' war: the war against the Soviet Union. Hitler had learned his lesson from events in the First World War. The food supply and economic blockades set up in 1917 had proven that in such circumstances Germany would, in the long run, always be forced to surrender. Just like its Japanese brother-in-arms Germany would have to become an autarky and that could only happen if 'Lebensraum' was gained.

This Lebensraum was based on two things. The newly secured land would be 'völkisch' (racially) repopulated and, it would have to furnish Nazi Germany with the raw materials required for its economy. In this context oil was vitally important. As Guderian rightly said in 1945, 'as far as Hitler is concerned oil is written in capital letters'. Throughout the entire campaign in the east, Nazi Germany's military operations and political dealings were largely dominated by the Third Reich's fuel supply situation. This was also the reason why, in 1941, Hitler had been hesitant to involve Romania and Hungary in the war against the Soviet Union: he was afraid that such involvement would mean having to share the Ukraine oil reserves with them. What was quite revealing was that on the eve of the campaign in the east all German military activity in Romania was completely devoted to protecting the Romanian oil fields, purely in Germany's interests. For similar reasons Hitler had sent Von Manstein to the Crimea where the 11. army was required to carry out a siege of similar magnitude in Sevastopol. On several occasions, he justified this move by pointing out that the Russians would otherwise be able to bomb the oil fields at Ploesti from the Crimea. The summer campaigns of 1942 and 1943 were completely dominated by oil. Hitler had hoped that at Stalingrad, on the Volga, he would be able to bring oil transportation across the river to a standstill and that by advancing in the Caucasus he would be able to capture the oil fields at Baku.

Hitler's concern about German raw material reserves not only stemmed from historic issues, but also from the fact that German strategic oil reserves were incredibly low. At the start of the Second World War in September 1939, German strategic reserves were only sufficient to support a five month long war! This situation had prompted the prediction from various sides, from the very outset, that Germany would inevitably lose the war because fuel shortages would bring everything to a standstill and there was certainly some truth in this belief. By the time Budapest was surrounded by Soviet troops the fuel situation in Germany had reached catastrophic levels. The Romanian oil fields had been lost and the German synthetic oil industry had been flattened by bombing. The only option left to Hitler was to gain the available Hungarian oil fields. But even then production levels were so low that the fuel reserve ratio between Germany and the Allied Forces would be 1 : 100. In no other military-strategic area was Hitler at such a great disadvantage.

From Hitler's point of view there was some logic to his argument. Without fuel German tanks would grind to a halt and without tanks Germany would lose the war. The possibility of loss was not an option for Hitler because as far as he was concerned the fighting had to go on till the bitter end. On 28th December, four days after Budapest had been surrounded, Hitler had made it perfectly clear to his highest army officers that Germany must keep on fighting because, he claimed, 'the future of the German State was at stake.' The whole German military organization, the economy and the population were geared to do battle.

This explains why the last phase of the war saw a remarkable degree of effort and determination on the side of the Germans. Once again any German civilian who could possibly be of any help in the war effort was dredged up. The Minister of Propaganda, Dr.Joseph Goebbels, tried to encourage the German people in his own familiar forceful way. More than 11 million women were involved in the war-industry. By combing industry, closing universities and schools, closing down newspapers and bringing the civil legal system to a complete standstill tens of thousands of men were made available for recruitment. On 18th October, the Volkssturm was established, meaning that all men between 16 and 60 years of age had to serve their country. It was predicted that this, together with the new 'wonder weapon', the V-1 flying bomb (Vergeltungswaffen, retaliation weapons) now being dropped on London and Antwerp, would mark a turning point for the Germans.

Other assets were the new Wehrmacht divisions, the Volksgrenadierdivisionen and the new Waffen-SS divisions that would lead Germany to victory. After the attack of 20th July, Himmler's SS forces became even more important. On 13th September, Hitler commanded that a first SS army be created, the 6.SS Pz.army, and that it be commanded by Joseph (Sepp) Dietrich who was known as 'the 'Blücher' of National Socialism'. The Waffen-SS grew until it comprised almost a million soldiers divided between nine SS army corps and some 38 divisions. They were the ones who, during the 'Wacht am Rhein' and later during 'Frühlingserwachen', the big Hungarian offensive, would have to take the lead.

It was also incredible to see how in 1944 the German war industry, under the galvanizing leadership of Albert Speer, had been able to force out more production. It would appear that Speer was the right man in the right place at the right time. With great vigour he started to revitalize the German weapon industry. He saw to it that repair jobs were carried out quickly and the distribution network was made more efficient all of which led to substantial increases in the level of weapon production. Manufacturing levels even surpassed those of the previous year. In view of the pressure Germany was under at the time from western Allied bombings this was quite a feat.

Speer's success came from the fact that he made merciless use of the availability of foreign workers. People who had been brought to Germany in their masses during the course of the war for the purposes of forced labour were now deployed in the war industry. In 1940, the second year of the war, there were 'merely' 1.2 million foreign workers in Germany. By 1944, there were 7.5 million foreigners in the country doing forced labour, many of whom were Jews and, with the end of the war in sight, the Germans preferred to employ them in the weapon production business rather than to let them die. 'I am ashamed to admit that I was only interested in these people's economic value' Speer confessed after the war. For instance, tens of thousands of Hungarian Jews were employed in the underground aircraft production project that was part of the so-called Dorsch plan, a megalomanic production plan aimed at creating enormous subterranean factories. Göring was enthusiastic about this whole idea and wanted to build as many of these factories as possible. Speer found the project too grand and expensive and succeeded in restricting the number of factories built.

In spite of sustained Allied air attacks the Germans had managed to construct a record number of new fighter planes by April 1944. This production project was given top priority because the European 'Fortress' had to be defended from the air. It was the job of Hermann Göring, Hitler's close confidant to rebuild the German airforce. A staggering 2,000 fighter-bombers came off the production line in April 1944 and the record was broken again in May when bomber production crept up to 2,212. Eventually, this culminated in an all-time record of 3,375 fighter planes in the month of September, 1944.

This achievement, partly made possible by the availability of Hungarian aluminium, was incredible when one considers that Speer not only had to contend with Allied air attacks but also had to fend off rival German organizations. As was the case everywhere within the Third Reich there was much competing for power and overlapping in the economic sector. Speer not only had to contend with Göring's four year plan and Robert Ley's labourer's front, but also with the ever-expanding imperium of the Reichsführer-SS, Heinrich Himmler. After the war, Speer wrote 'Der Sklavenstaat' in which he expressed his frustrations in this connection.

It was not only the Germans who were involved in production for the final conflict, the Hungarians too were expected to make their contribution. 'Germany has stolen 80% of our economic resources' Horthy complained to the Germans in 1944. Indeed he was right, the Hungarian economy had been swallowed up in the German war production programme. Immediately after the Klessheim conspiracy, Saur, Speer's right-hand man, had been to see Hitler and had received orders to put the Hungarian economy to best use in Germany. The Reich's Treasury (Statistisches Reichsamt) had then busied itself finding out what useful resources Germany's most recent ally could provide. Hungary proved to be a gold-mine for the Germans. What the Germans needed most was Hungarian steel which came from three different steelworks: Riema, Mavag and M. Weiss whose respective annual output at the time was 400,000 tons, 200,000 tons and 130,000 tons. Fortunately for the Germans the last company was owned by Jews so they were simply able to confiscate it. SS-Hauptsturmführer Kurt Becher (known as 'the horse dealer') negotiated with the Jewish owners who, in exchange for their businesses, were given free passage to neutral Portugal. The Hungarian aluminium production plants situated mainly in Budapest, Pecs, Kassa and Nagybajom were also vital to the German aircraft industry.

Obviously, all this work and effort was only of any use if fuel could be found for the newly manufactured tanks and planes. This was where Hitler needed the Hungarian oil fields and he was relying on the reserves of Nagykanizsa. By 1944 Hungary was producing more than 600,000 tons of oil on an annual basis. With German help the production level was being forced up. This was nothing compared to what the fields at Ploesti had been capable of producing but, in practice in March 1945, the Hungarian fields together with the small Austrian oil fields at Zisterdorf produced 80% of the remainder of Germany's oil production. As the oil supplies diminished so Hitler became more obsessive and his oil politics increasingly came to determine his strategic plans.

In reality not even the Hungarian fields, let alone the Austrian ones, were worth such elaborate military efforts. The total production of the Hungarian fields was barely enough to move the Army Group South. A further problem was that it was difficult to refine the oil in Hungary, where the refineries were so close to the front. In Hungary, there was a total of twelve refineries and capacity for 1,142,100 tons. A number of the refineries had been lost during the Red Army advances while others like the refineries in Budapest, Petfürdö, Almásfüzitö and Csepel (Shell) had been damaged during bombings. The biggest refinery, the Hovéd (Hungarian army) refinery of Szöny at Komárom (300,000 tons) only came into use towards the end of the war. Because of the problems Albert Speer went to Hungary in February 1945 to help supervise the laying of pipelines to Germany where the refineries were still operational. 'I saw the tanks of the SS assembling there for the final battle', he wrote in his memoirs, but he wasted no further words on the oil problem. By then, Speer no longer believed in Hitler's day-dreams and not long afterwards he started ignoring orders and was replaced by Saur.

In Budapest, these day-dreams were hard reality for the 70,000 soldiers of the IX.SS Geb. corps who were caught there. For them Christmas 1944 began with the surrounding of the Hungarian capital. At the very last moment, Adolf Eichmann had escaped from the city in his black Mercedes. He left behind him a ghetto of half starved children and old people terrorized by murderous Arrow Cross men and a depleted garrison. The soldiers were to hold the fort in war-torn Budapest where everyone was hoping to be rescued by the IV.SS Pz. corps that was making its way to Hungary from the weakened Vistula front. The authorities hoped that the freeing of the Hungarian capital and the whole western bank of the Danube would mark the start of the big German comeback in Hungary which was scheduled to commence after the Ardennes offensive was over. It was to be called operation 'Frühlingserwachen' and it was to be the Ardennes offensive of the east: a real 'Wacht an der Donau.'

Budapest is sacrificed

The whole world was shocked when on 16th December 1944, contrary to all expectations, the German army initiated a huge surprise counter-offensive in the Ardennes. After brief preliminary artillery attacks, the 6.SS Pz. army and the 5.Pz. army started marching towards the Meuse and Antwerp. Twenty German divisions broke through the 110 kilometre long front line and flattened the vanguard lines of four Allied divisions between Monschau and Echternach. The initial results looked spectacular in theory but the German attack quickly lost its momentum and it was not long before things ground to a halt. The terrain they were fighting on was rough and the German ammunition and fuel supplies far from adequate. Only by plundering enemy depots could they be certain of making any progress. Apart from anything else, the soldiers of the German units and the troops of the SS were worn out from the continual fighting they had been involved in on all fronts. The Allied Powers had absolute supremacy in the air and it was only bad weather conditions that kept their squadrons on the ground for a while.
Hitler was surprised to see that the Americans were prepared to put up a good fight and to defend their territory with great determination. The Allies won time which in turn put them in an even stronger position. This state of affairs gave Heinz Guderian reason enough to visit Hitler on 24th December at the Alderhorst, near Ziegenberg in Hessen in order to beg him to allow them to call off the Ardennes offensive. Guderian had been very critical of Hitler's plans in the west from the very beginning. As far as he was concerned German military effort should have been concentrated on the eastern front, in particular on the Vistula front, where a threatening calm before the storm was definitely constituting a direct threat to Germany.
Hitler grew irritated when Guderian reminded him that at Warsaw the Soviets had sustained 'a 15 : 1 military

advantage' over the Germans. He brushed off Guderian's remarks calling them 'lies' and insisted on continuing the painfully laborious Ardennes offensive. In an attempt to still speed up the action in the Ardennes a couple of new military initiatives were started up on 1st January, the very same day that operation 'Konrad' (to liberate Budapest) was initiated in Hungary. In the Alsace operation 'Nordwind', a supporting attack was commenced in which the 10.SS Pz.D. 'Frundsberg' constituted the core. Simultaneously, an amazing air attack was mounted: operation 'Bodenplatte'.

The 'Nordwind' operation progressed in much the same way as the offensive in the Ardennes. It got off to an impressive start, but it was not long before the Germans came up against the solid defences of the Allies. Operation 'Bodenplatte', under the command of General Peltz, turned out to be the most controversial German fighter-bomber attack of the Second World War. It was a typical all or nothing attack in which Hitler planned to flatten the western Allied air bases and the Allied air force by mounting a surprise attack with hundreds of fighter planes. The attack took place early in the morning of 1st January: the timing was good. Many of the servicemen were still asleep or were recovering from the celebrations of the night before. More than 400 Allied aircraft were destroyed on the ground. This was a heavy loss, but one that was easy to recoup for the Allies. The Germans lost 300 planes. Such a loss was much harder for the Germans to deal with. Because of the high level of secrecy surrounding the attack the FLAK, the German anti-aircraft batteries, were not aware that it was going on so they also shot at some of their own aircraft which was one reason why the German losses were so high. Operation 'Bodenplatte' thus finally finished off the already heavily crippled Luftwaffe.

By the beginning of January, it was clear that neither 'Nordwind' nor 'Bodenplatte' was going to be successful in refloating the Ardennes offensive so Hitler decided to pull out the 6. SS Pz. army and send it to the eastern front. In

SS Brigade führer Joachim Rumohr, commandant of the 8.SS Kav.D. 'Florian Geyer' with his soldiers in the trenches in Budapest. Budapest was defended by the IX.SS Geb. corps which also had at its disposal two cavalry divisions of the Waffen-SS.

A German Waffen-SS soldier standing on guard in a street in Budapest with an anti-tank shell.
The population of Budapest did its best to ignore the mounting threats within the city but could not escape from the violent siege.

A Russian T-34 tank which had penetrated through to the centre of the Budapest 'Fortress'. The city is reduced to a burning ruin. After heavy fighting Budapest capitulated on 13th February 1945.

practice this meant that the Ardennes offensive was over and had failed. Guderian could at least be thankful that the army was at last on its way to the eastern front, but when he heard that Hitler now planned to deploy his troops in Hungary Guderian was exasperated.

Even though the Ardennes offensive had not given Hitler the leeway he had hoped for he stuck firmly to his original Hungarian plans. In the military meetings of early January 1945 he reiterated how important it was to hold on to the Hungarian oil fields. With the task of having to protect these fields the German army did not 'have time to sit still.' 'First the oil and then the central front' said Hitler on 22nd January. He told Jodl that the Hungarian oil fields were of 'vital importance' which was a sentiment he was to repeat later when speaking with Admiral Dönitz, commander of the German navy.

Meanwhile, military action was getting fully underway in Hungary. On 1st January when operations 'Bodenplatte' and 'Nordwind' had begun operation 'Konrad' had also been initiated and the battle to free Budapest was already going on by then. All these operations put together were nothing more than a prelude to 'Frühlingserwachen' but that will be discussed more fully in later chapters.

The notion that Budapest should be defended was something that was perfectly obvious and beyond dispute for Hitler. Already in November 1944 Hitler had instructed that the Hungarian capital should be placed under OKH supervision. Hitler said at the time 'if Budapest falls then the success in the west will be halved!' He was referring of course to the Ardennes offensive. When it came to defending Budapest Friessner had serious doubts partly because he had little confidence in the Hungarian military which was supposed to provide half of the garrison. When a previous attempt had been made to recruit Hungarian armed soldiers only 29 men had turned up out of the 1,862 who had been called up to fight.

Originally SS General Winkelmann was appointed 'Festung'-Commandant in Budapest but only five days later the task was handed over to SS Obergruppenführer Pfeffer Wildenbruch. Friessner's position as Commander-in-Chief of the Army Group went to Otto Wöhler a quiet cigar smoking officer who, through having previously worked with the 8. army was familiar with the situation within Army Group South. Fretter-Pico was replaced by General Hermann Balck, a professional soldier who was known for his intractability and for the fact that he did not mince his words. After the war, Balck wrote that the Reichsführer-SS, whom he had only ever met once, was no friend of his, because he was 'too rude towards the SS divisions.' Balck also clashed with Von Rundstedt, an officer who epitomized the old Prussian diehard mentality. He found that the old chap was too preoccupied with his 'First World War experiences.' When he was appointed commandant of the 6. army ('Armeegruppe Balck'/Balck's Army Group) on 23rd December 1944 at the OKH in Zossen, this gave him the chance to start afresh with a clear slate. This slate did not remain 'clean' for very long though. Immediately after his arrival, and his first encounters with the front, through Heinz Gaedcke, General Chief of Staff, Balck rang up his good old friend Wenck and exclaimed: 'The situation is a mess!'

That was something that Karl von Pfeffer Wildenbruch and the garrison at Budapest already knew. What awaited them, though, was an important military task. As 'Mainstay' and 'Fortress' Pfeffer Wildenbruch had to make sure that the Red Army was forced to fight a fierce battle in every street of Budapest. In this way the Red Army had to concentrate on Budapest so fewer troops were available for the offensives on the oil wells. Again, valuable time could, thus, be gained, time that Hitler needed for the realization of his next grand military plans. If Budapest was well defended such defences would protect the city like a breakwater from Soviet upsurges on both banks of the Danube (on Slovakian as well as on Hungarian territory) or at least stall the Soviet advance.

On the river Gran the front was not very strong. Later, in January 1945 it soon gave way under Soviet pressure.

Preserving Budapest was obviously also a matter of political prestige. In historical terms it was the gateway to Vienna and it formed the political heart of Hungary. The city always was, and still is, incredibly beautiful with Buda lying on the hill overlooking Pest. The city was famous for its medicinal spas. Already in the Habsburg era Margarethe island was known as a good place to visit. People would go there to admire the magnificent parliament building in Pest, designed by Emerich Steindl that, second to Westminster in London, was the biggest parliamentary building complex in the world. Majestic old bridges, such as the Széchenyi-Kettenbrücke, linked together the west and east banks of the city. Preserving Budapest was also a sign of neutral power and an indication that Germany was still capable of providing opposition. Put together all these considerations made Hitler decide that Budapest should be declared a 'Fortress'.

Yet, as was to be seen from the 'Konrad' operations, the decision to preserve Budapest was above all else militarily inspired. From the start, Hitler was prepared to sacrifice every last man if this could possibly have meant providing more space for military manoeuvre within Hungary. When Hitler had withdrawn the 6. SS Pz. army from the Ardennes offensive, he had partly justified the action by arguing that 'there was at least one place where he could still develop his plans' thus indicating in no uncertain terms that he was still hopeful of achieving positive results in Hungary.

On Christmas Eve 1944, Budapest was surrounded by twenty divisions from seven different corps of the Russian 2. and 3. Ukrainian front.

At that time, there were approximately 70,000 German and Hungarian soldiers in the city and an estimated 800,000 civilians. As has been seen, Karl von Pfeffer Wildenbruch had the dubious honour of leading the Budapest garrison in the hopeless struggle. The commandant of the Budapest fortress was a man who had certainly been put to the test. Both his sons had died on the eastern front and the Waffen-SS division which he had been in command of for a short time, the 'Polizei' division, had suffered huge losses in the war. Balck who was very critical did not think much of Wildenbruch's military capabilities. After the war, he wrote that 'at best one could say that Budapest was being led by a politician'. What Balck was referring to was the fact that Wildenbruch was selected more for his SS loyalties than for his strategic capacities.

Wildenbruch's troops consisting of some 33,000 Germans and roughly 37,000 Hungarians (Soviet sources erroneously quote higher numbers) formed together the IX.SS Geb. (Gebirgs) corps, a misleading name in view of the fact that Wildenbruch did not have any mountain troops. Such name-giving typified German sentiment in conjunction with army units. Whereas the Russians were increasingly inclined to create new units and new names, the Germans held on to the old names for purely nostalgic reasons. Budapest was not the most appropriate of places for mountain troops. It is surprising to learn that Wildenbruch had at his disposal two Waffen-SS cavalry divisions, namely the 8.SS Kav.D. 'Florian Geyer' and the 22.SS Kav.D. 'Maria Theresia'. These two units, led by SS-Brigadeführer Rumohr and Zehender were sister units. Veterans in these troops had often served in both units. The very fact that these troops had arrived in Budapest at all, complete with all their horses, showed how desperate the military situation was getting on the German side. There were simply no other units available. It would, thus, be the destiny of the majority of Heinrich Himmler's cavalry soldiers to die in the streets of Budapest.

Alongside of the cavalry divisions Wildenbruch also had the remainder of the once so proud 13. Pz.D. of Generalmajor Schmidthuber under his command and what was left of Oberstleutnant Wolff's 'Feldherrnhalle' unit (named after the Feldherrnhalle in München where Hitler's revolt of 1923 was quashed). Apart from that the

IX.SS Geb. corps consisted of a number of very small battle groups and emergency battalions. There was for instance Kündiger's combat group composed of the remainder of the 271.V.G.D and SS-Pol.Rgt.6 ('Kampfgruppe Dörner') as well as several emergency battalions and an SD combat group. The vast majority of the Hungarian units, which were part of the I. Hungarian army corps (commanded by Major General Ivan von Kinshind Hindy), consisted of infantry from the 10. and 12.I.D. There were also motorized units of the Hungarian 1.Pz.D. and the 1.Kav.D. in the city supervised by Captain Vertessy. Finally, the garrison had a series of smaller units such as Sturmart.Gruppe Billnitzer (Generalmajor Ernö Billnitzer), Oberst Janza's Flak-Rgt.12 Budapest, Sergeant Sipeki-Balazs' university assault battalion, the life-guard battalion from the castle in Buda and the Arrow Cross and Gendarmerie units of General Kalandy.

Not one of these units was complete at the moment when the city was surrounded at the end of 1944. The number of heavy weapons available in the city was limited. Few documents remain from Army Group South, the army under which IX.SS Geb.corps fell, so it is difficult to ascertain exactly how big Wildenbruch's troops were. It is probable that the corps at least had a number of 'Hetzers' (probably from the cavalry divisions of the SS, notably 'Florian Geyer') and motorized artillery ('Hummels'). Photographs found in Russian archives of the situation after the city was liberated show the remains of several Panther tanks and eight-wheeled armoured vehicles which came from the 13.Pz.D. and the 'FHH' division. One can undoubtedly add to this a number of Hungarian armoured vehicles and conclude that the total number of armoured vehicles possessed by the IX.SS Geb. corps would have amounted to around 70. All these units were, of course, hampered in their operations by shortages of ammunition and fuel. In street fighting situations armoured vehicles also constituted vulnerable targets.

What was at least as important was the artillery that Wildenbruch had at his disposal, but this was more or less restricted to (Flak) anti-aircraft devices. In particular, the 3.7 cm Flak and the 2 cm Flak situated near to the castle in Buda were successfully used against Russian dive-bombers and were also useful in ground combat situations. The heavy Flaks, the dreaded 8.8 cm German cannons, were concentrated in the 'Portugall' battle group and dispersed on and around the Adlerberg (Sas-hegy), as well as in Buda.

From the very beginning the fighting in the battle for Budapest was fierce. The Red Army resented that at such a late stage in the war they were being drawn into such a devastating conflict, which probably explains why the Soviets tried to avert fighting by first attempting to negotiate with the Germans. The attempts were fruitless. The two men sent to negotiate on 29th December 1944, a man by the name of Steinmetz and I.A. Osztapenko both lost their lives during their mission. Tass verified that they had been murdered by the Germans. According to German Wehrmacht sources though both negotiators had been German prisoners of war forced to carry out this mission and, once they crossed into German territory, they had immediately gone over to the German side.

After the war, the historian Peter Gosztony revealed that on his way to Budapest Steinmetz had driven over a land-mine and had been killed. On returning from his failed talks with Rumohr, the commandant of the 8.SS.D, Osztapenko had been shot down, supposedly accidently, by a Hungarian battery and had died. One Hungarian source put the blame on an artillery battery (Hummels) of the 'FHH' division but this was promptly denied by the Germans. A certain Walter Rothe (2./s.Sf.Pz.Art.Rgt. 'Feldherrnhalle') declared under oath in 1986 that the negotiators had lost their lives in a Soviet mortar attack. This version of the story was verified by Hauptmann a.D., Erich Klein, also a former soldier of the 'FHH' division. 'I already told two NKVD officers of this in 1948 when I was in Soviet detention' he commented. He added 'their reaction was one of fury, but we were never again accused of having killed the two parliamentarians.' What was, at least, certain was, that after the talks had failed the siege of the city had gathered momentum. What was about to happen in Budapest was terrible.

Right from the very start of the battle of Budapest, the German defenders had absolutely no chance. Wildenbruch was aware of this problem as well but he put all his faith in the promise that Hitler had made on 24th December 1944 straight after the city had been encircled. At that time Hitler had ensured Wildenbruch that he could depend on the support of rescue forces. The units that Hitler had in mind were those of the IV.SS.Pz. corps which would be diverted from the front at Warsaw to Hungary for that express purpose. For the IX.SS Geb. corps this therefore meant that until these reinforcement troops came to their rescue they would have to manage to survive in Budapest.

The first crisis came barely three days later when the Red Army drew in very rapidly on the eastern side (Pest) and simultaneously on the western side of the city (Buda). The Soviets who were well equipped with tanks, panzer vehicles, artillery and air support deployed their strongest units. Once the outer defence lines had been broken through on both sides the Russians were able to close in fast on the Danube, the river that bisected the beautiful city. It seemed as if the fate of the German garrison in Budapest had really been determined in the first days of January 1945 when pressure on Buda suddenly eased off. This had not only to do with the fact that the Germans had placed many of the 'Florian Geyer' division on the slopes of the steep approach to the castle. The slowing down of the Soviet attack was also directly related to the tempestuous start of the 'Konrad' operations in the Gerecse and Pilis Heights to the west of Budapest. On 1st January, the units of the IV.SS Pz. corps, a division of the German 6. army (Hermann Balck), embarked on their mission to free Budapest. They gave no preliminary

The beautiful city of Budapest was left in ruins when, after fifty days of fighting, the cannons were finally subdued. Its ancient bridges had been blown up by the Germans.

The surrender of the IX.SS Geb. corps in Budapest. The commandant of the German garrison, Karl von Pfeffer Wildenbruch, is seen here leaving his headquarters for the last time. Russian soldiers lead him to imprisonment. Much of the 70,000 strong garrison of soldiers was wiped out. Barely 700 soldiers managed to get through the German defence lines on the western side of the city. Wildenbruch survived his term in prison and returned to Germany after the war.

artillery bombardment so that the attack came as a complete surprise for the Red Army. The 4. Russian army was immediately forced to surrender land to the superior troops of the Waffen-SS tank divisions and to the supporting German Wehrmacht divisions. In order to ensure that the Russian army did not yield and retreat into the mountains the Red Army called back a number of its divisions that were involved in the siege of Buda and diverted them to where the 4.G. army was. On 1st January 1945, the Germans that were busy defending Buda had nine Russian divisions against them but by January 5th this number had dropped to four. Wildenbruch's troops were once again given a little breathing space.

In the low-lying area of Pest, though, the battle continued as before. Heinz Guderian warned that the eastern bridgehead was rapidly going to collapse. He pleaded for a more rigorous combing out of the garrison so that every man who was capable of carrying a weapon could be sent to the front. For Wildenbruch it was getting more and more difficult to block the gaps that were appearing in the front. The street fights that were taking place were extremely bloody. By 6th January, the IX.SS Geb. corps losses had risen to 5,621 men.

Ammunition supplies also shrank rapidly, because the ammunition was being used up so quickly. This became a matter of great concern for Hitler and his generals. If Budapest were to fall too quickly, this would seriously jeopardize all Hitler's plans for a spring offensive. Budapest was an important binding element holding down a great many Russian troops. Hitler, therefore, hoped that by initiating the 'Konrad' operations he would be able to keep Budapest safely in German hands.

By now, it was clearer than ever before that Budapest really was serving as a 'breakwater' for the front. Red Army units had crossed the Gran river and passed into the Slovakian hinterland. In this way, the Red Army constituted a threat to the flank of the SS panzer corps in the Gerecse and Pilis Heights and was even threatening the oil refineries at Komárom. By quickly bringing in new troops the Germans managed to prevent the Gran front from collapsing. Nevertheless, at the same time it was more important than ever before for the IX.SS Geb. corps in Budapest not to lose ground.

Hitler started to look for ways to reinforce the IX.SS Geb. corps. The units executing 'Konrad' could rely on light reinforcement and support from the southern units around Zámoly. Hitler, on the other hand, wanted to do something for the troops in the city. Every effort was made to airlift supplies so that the IX.SS Geb. corps could at least be kept going. For the Luftwaffe, especially the transport division with its Junker 52 aircrafts (and the odd He-111), this was again a difficult time. Just as at Stalingrad it required great courage to navigate between heavy anti-aircraft devices which was what the pilots had to do if they were to get into Budapest.

At first, planes were able to land on the horse-racing course in Pest but when even that had been occupied by the Red Army, supplies had to be dropped in the ever shrinking area of the city centre into which the Germans were compressed. At first, up to 100 flights a day were laid on to supply the Kessel but this number soon diminished. By now, only light aircraft could service the city and they had to land in the wider city streets or on a small remaining grass strip in Buda. From records found later in Führer headquarters explicitly describing various situations we know that Hitler involved himself personally in this problem. He knew that it was vital to bring in supplies and mail from the home-front in connection with the morale of soldiers in the IX.SS Geb. corps, Pfeffer and Wildenbruch realized that too. Every pilot that survived the journey was immediately taken to headquarters in Budapest from where he was ushered to bunkers where the wounded were kept. In this way the injured soldiers of the garrison were reminded that the outside world had not forgotten them.

Hitler contemplated using seaplanes and gliders and even helicopters (then still in an experimental phase in Germany) to take provisions to the troops in Budapest.

We know for certain that pilots in gliders and light 'Fieseler Storch' aircraft braved the journey to the Hungarian 'Fortress'. These crafts belonged to the Luftflotte 4 (K.G.4 and the 'Staffel z.b.V Reich') commanded by General Conrad. They landed on a strip of land near to the Vár-hegy (Vermözö pasture land) that Hitler himself had found for them. It was not long before the Russian artillery there saw what was going on and quickly ploughed up the land. The Germans soon called the area the 'Blutwiese' (blood land), because the remains of shot down German planes were scattered all over the area. In all, 73 gliders of the DFS 230 type flew into Budapest but only 43 of them ever reached their destination. Eleven of them were shot down by Russian Flak fire and twenty-one aircraft had to make emergency landings or turn back. According to a report brought out in March 1945 by the OKL 49 pilots had been reported missing in Budapest's airspace.

Finally, endeavours were even made to ship supplies to Budapest. A ship loaded with 4,000 tons of ammunition was sent off to Hungary but ran into difficulties. The north bank of the Danube was in Soviet hands and the final section was occupied by the Red Army. Only a small portion of the supplies actually got through to the city in small consignments.

These consignments were only sufficient to prolong the battle for a little while in Budapest. All hope now rested on the soldiers and on the results of operation 'Konrad' to the west of the city. The troops in the Kessel were in constant radio contact with the troops that were on their way. The German forces in Budapest desperately hoped that they would now be quickly released because, as one high up official of the IX.SS Geb. corps reported, the local population was 'starting to become hostile towards the German forces.' On top of this, the huge number of wounded soldiers, 4,000 men by 7th January, was putting pressure on the 'Fortress'.

Relief was not in sight, though, because the 'Konrad' attack had come to a standstill at the intersection between Bicske and Zsámbék. Afterwards, after having captured the city of Esztergom (Gran) further north on the Danube, the German supreme command decided to direct the emphasis of attack northwards. 'Wiking' penetrated as far as Pilisszentkereszt. By now, it was 11th January and Hitler was beginning to lose patience with the situation in Budapest and the new 'Konrad' operation ('Konrad' II) seemed to be petering out. A suggestion made by General Janza of Flak-Rgt.12 to mount a combined attack involving 'Konrad' II and a massive drop of parachutists at Budaörs with the aim of liberating Budapest was rejected as being too complicated. In the Army Group South diary mention was made of the fact that Hitler 'did not want to fly in any more forces now that the situation with regard to Budapest had become so uncertain.'

Hitler had more faith in the success of a military operation to be mounted more to the south, between lakes Velencei and Balaton and was afraid that the operations in the Gerecse and Pilis Heights would turn out to be 'a neverending battle.'

In reality this meant that things were over for the IX.SS Geb. corps. The first debacle after that occurred in Pest, the flatter region of the city which was harder to defend than Buda. In conjunction with the 'Konrad' operations the Red Army had more units stationed there than on the western side of the city. On 13th January, what remained of the eastern part of the garrison was driven back as far as the Danube and from 15th January onwards the soldiers were driven into Buda. On the same day, the Horthy bridge was blown up. On 17th January the Franz Joseph bridge was blown up and the next day, on 18th January, the Ketting bridge and the Elisabeth bridge were destroyed as well. The last men to save themselves on the Buda bank of the Danube were those still alive in the 'Schmidthuber' Group (13.Pz.D.).

Wildenbruch's garrison had been reduced to a mere 34,000 soldiers who, together with the remaining 300,000 inhabitants of the city, were crushed into the remaining four kilometres of the Kessel. In the bunkers under the Var-hegy 11,000 wounded were just about surviving in pitiful circumstances.

Because food and ammunition supplies were depleted and the military-strategic outlook was so depressing, the men's morale was low. On top of all the other pressures of war the half-starved soldiers were suffering from the cold. January is the coldest month of the year in Hungary and at the end of January 1945 the temperature fell to minus 20° C for a short while. Soldiers were so demoralized that some started going over to the Russian side. Otto Wöhler, commandant of the Army Group South did what he could to boost the men's morale, but to no avail. 'We have not forgotten you' he said. On 27th January when Hitler's orders of the day came, he was full of praise for the men of the garrison and for their bravery and resilience. At that time, a number of high military awards were dropped by parachute for the German officers. Wildenbruch was decorated with the much respected 'Ritterkreuz' and a number of medals went to other officers in Budapest, such as: SS-Hauptsturmführer Gustav Wendrinsky (SS-1./Pz.Jg.Abt.8), SS-Obersturmführer Franz Liebisch (Squadron leader of 8.SS 'Florian Geyer'), Usdau Lindenau (Chief of Staff of the IX.SS Geb. corps), Major Hans von Schack (Commandant SS-Kav.Rgt.16 'Florian Geyer'), SS-Hauptsturmführer Joachim Boosfeld (4. Squadron SS-Kav.Rgt.16) and SS-Untersturmführer Hermann Maringgele (2. Squadron SS-Kav.Rgt.15). The Hungarians followed the German example by promoting Hindy, Commandant of the I Hungarian Army Corps, to Generaloberst.

It was no coincidence that Hitler's news bulletin reached the garrison on 27th January. On the very same day, the planned third attempt to relieve the troops in Budapest, operation 'Konrad' III, had been abandoned. After the original Blitzkrieg-like results in the low-lying area to the south of the Gerecse and Pilis Heights, the IV.SS Pz. crops had got into difficulties on the Váli river where they had come up against heavy Russian tank attacks near the little town of Pettend. After the war Manfried Schönfelder, Chief of Staff of the IV.SS Pz. corps, wrote that this was when the Red Army had 'taken over the initiative' and apparently Hitler had come to the same conclusion too because he decided to definitely call off 'Konrad' III and ordered the IV.SS Pz. corps to switch over to the defensive. With the situation as it was in Kessel conditions in Budapest were now rapidly deteriorating. Ammunition was running out and food supplies were scarce. The wounded had to survive on the mere 15 grams of pulses and the half slice of bread they received each day. On 5th February, Adler hill fell into the hands of the Red Army, the 8.8 cm Flak of SS-Obersturmführer Kurt Portugall, the 3.7 cm and the 2 cm Flak of SS-Hauptsturmführer Hans Heinrich Klaus and SS-Hauptsturmführer Friedel Gregner had to be withdrawn to the grounds of the university and the castle.

On 11th February, General Janza was given orders to prepare the men of the garrison for fleeing from Budapest. Wildenbruch called together all the remaining officers. He informed them that they were soon to escape from the city and shortly afterwards Führer headquarters was informed of the plans being made in Budapest. By radio Wildenbruch intimated that holding out in the city could only lead to two possible outcomes: unconditional capitulation or certain massacre, both hopeless alternatives.

Janza had been put in a predicament. He had already been forced to abandon his parachute plan of 11th January, because if his garrison had broken out in a westerly direction, through the narrow valleys, the result would have been ulterly disastrous. Finally, they had settled on breaking away in two directions. The bigger group would go in a north-westerly direction while the smaller group would pass out through a house near the Blutwiese where they would escape by entering into the underground drainage canal system. When the signal to escape was given, according to estimates made by Kurt Portugall, circa 18,000 soldiers had assembled, some 6,000 of whom were injured but could still walk. This was all that remained of the IX.SS Geb. corps. The escape got off to a bad start. The Red Army immediately opened up artillery fire on the convoy of emaciated soldiers. Just as at every other stage of the siege of Budapest, the Russian soldiers knew exactly what the Germans were planning. Throughout the entire campaign in the east the Russians had always been one step ahead of the Germans when it came to intelligence. This 'tradition' had continued during the struggle for Budapest. The attempt to escape from Budapest had very much resembled the beginning of the decisive summer battle at Koersk in 1943. Then also the Red Army had been completely up-to-date on the German's plans and had been able to disrupt the operation from the start by firing well aimed artillery shots even before the German's had got underway.

The Germans who made their escape above ground-level were simply slaughtered. Only one group of 600 to 700 soldiers, led by Oberleutnant Schöning, commandant of the Pz.Gren.Rgt. 66 and Oberleutnant Wolff, commandant of the 'FHH' division had managed to pass through Red Army lines at Budakeszi. After passing dangerously through the enemy lines the unit finally reached the German defence line, but not before Schöning had been heavily wounded. Many soldiers were transferred to field hospitals suffering from serious frost-bite, like for example Harry Phönix, commandant of the II./Art.Rgt. 8 'Florian Geyer'. Others, such as SS-Hauptsturmführer Albert Klett, Chief of the 6. Squadron SS-Kav.Rgt.16 'Florian Geyer', died within sight of German lines. Ernst Schweitzer, a soldier of the 13.Pz.D., was so frozen that he literally crossed over the German front lines on his hands and knees. He was then transported further by truck but got caught in the cross-fire of his own side when Hungarians mistook the truck for a Soviet vehicle. Others who had successfully escaped from Budapest were in such pain from the freezing conditions that they committed suicide when they were no longer able to walk. This was for instance what happened to Oberstleutnant Kucklick (Pz.Rgt.13).

The escape that had started underground also turned into a fiasco. When the troops finally resurfaced they were quickly tracked down. At 11.30 a.m. on 12th February this garrison unit, chiefly composed of 'FHH' soldiers and soldiers from the Nachrichten-Abt.8 'Florian Geyer' (SS-Sturmbannführer Rietger) was completely wiped out. A total of about 785 men made it as far as German territory, approximately 1% of the entire garrison.

The scene in Budapest on 12th February 1945 was terrible. The Vár-hegy and the Gellért-hegy were covered with the bodies of thousands of dead German and Hungarian soldiers. Near to the Mathias Church thousands of prisoners of war were still under arrest and awaiting their fate. The streets were covered with discarded pieces of uniform from soldiers trying to find cover and disguise themselves as civilians.

One of the prisoners of war was Karl von Pfeffer Wildenbruch. A photograph exists which records his arrest and the fact that he looked utterly devastated. The Russians kept him imprisoned and it was not until 1955 that he was released from Woikowo and returned to Germany. Others who remained under arrest for a long period were Ernö Billnitzer and Hindy's right-hand man, Oberst i.G. Sándor Horváth.

In comparison to other army officers they were the lucky ones. Many others had not even survived the battle. Both commandants of the Waffen-SS cavalry divisions, Rumohr and Zehender were found dead. It is possible that they had committed suicide. Schmidthuber of the 13.Pz.D. was killed as was Helmut Dörner who fell during the fight at the Bolnay academy. The Ia of the 13.Pz.D., Oberstleutnant Von Ekkesparre had been killed in the Wienerstrasse, Major Pabst (Pz.A.A. 13) was also killed in action. Hindy, the commandant of the I. Hungarian Army

Corps was arrested and tried in Budapest on 29th August 1945.

Others, like the commandant of the SS A.A.8 'Florian Geyer' SS-Sturmbannführer Walter Drexler, went missing and were never found.

As the old Arabian saying goes: 'On the day of victory no one is tired'. On 13th February 1945, the date officially agreed to as marking the fall of Budapest, a Russian whirlwind raced through the city. German bodies were pulverized under the tracks of Russian tanks and the remains of dead soldiers were left on the streets for days on end by way of protest, to show how enraged the Russians were that the battle had been such a long exhausting affair. Hungarian and German prisoners were forced to bury the Russian soldiers who had died. Raids were carried out in the city and plundering and rape continued. Arrow Cross men were arrested and executed and in order to 'cleanse' the city everyone with a German surname was arrested. The Russians just made use of telephone books to find people. This action led to the deportation of 30,000 people.

Some of the wounded were simply killed off. A number of the bunkers beneath the castle containing injured soldiers who could no longer walk were filled with petrol and set alight. The cries of the dying were smothered beneath the resounding sound of artillery shots announcing a new Red Army victory. Others were more fortunate though. Otto Dülberg of the 8.SS 'Florian Geyer' recalled how, on the morning of 13th February, Soviet soldiers descended on a military hospital containing many wounded where about ten people died every day and where there was one male nurse, who himself was wounded in the head, to look after them all. Here the Russians behaved decently but they left the patients without provisions and to fend for themselves. After ten days of starvation, the patients in the emergency hospital were moved to a hospital near to the railway station on the south side of the city. The building had been badly damaged, all the windows and doors had gone and the conditions were indescribable.

Huge columns of smoke rose from the citadel, Horthy's old residence, the place where Veesenmayer and Rahn had feverishly tried to influence the Hungarian regent. How long ago that all seemed now and how pointless everything had been. Looking out over Pest from the castle one could see the scars of war everywhere. Bridges lay in ruins in the Danube, the very same water that had been stained red by the blood of Jews in the pogrom and water that flowed from the west, from Vienna, the next target on the map of the Russian commanders.

The 'Konrad' Prelude

Budapest was only one of the trump cards that was to help the Germans carry off their military plans. Their other plan was to set up a German offensive and fight for the western bank of the Danube, to make sure that Budapest remained in German hands. It was for this purpose that the IV.SS Pz. corps was transferred from the Polish front to Hungary.

The men of the IV.SS Pz. corps themselves were surprised by the sudden order to regroup elsewhere. On 24th December 1944, a certain telephone call was received at the divisional headquarters of 'Wiking', the 5.SS Pz.D. At that point in time 'Wiking' was fighting together with 'Totenkopf', the 3.SS Pz.D., in the defensive lines of the 'nassen Dreieck' (wet Triangle) to the east of Modlin. The 01., SS-Hauptsturmführer Günter Jahnke, was given to understand that the IV.SS Pz. corps must go directly to Hungary by train. The IV.SS Pz. corps which fell under the command of SS-Obergruppenführer Herbert Otto Gille was astonished to receive such an order. The Allies and the majority of German soldiers and generals felt that the central front (Army Group A and Army Group Centre), which was closest to German soil, should be given highest priority, but no one of course disputed orders received from higher up. Hitler simply initiated his Hungarian offensive and his soldiers were expected to support him whether there was logical to the reasoning or not.

The next day, the battle group Dorr (SS Panzer Grenadier Regiment 9 'Germania' commanded by SS-Obersturmbannführer Hans Dorr), the reconnaissance section and the 'Norge' battalion of the 'Wiking' division were put on a train to Hungary while other troops continued to assemble. Gille immediately realized that the task ahead was an important one. The IV.SS Pz corps had to take with them all the provisions they would be needing, scant ammunition and food supplies included. The soldiers were relieved to be moving. 'We were glad to

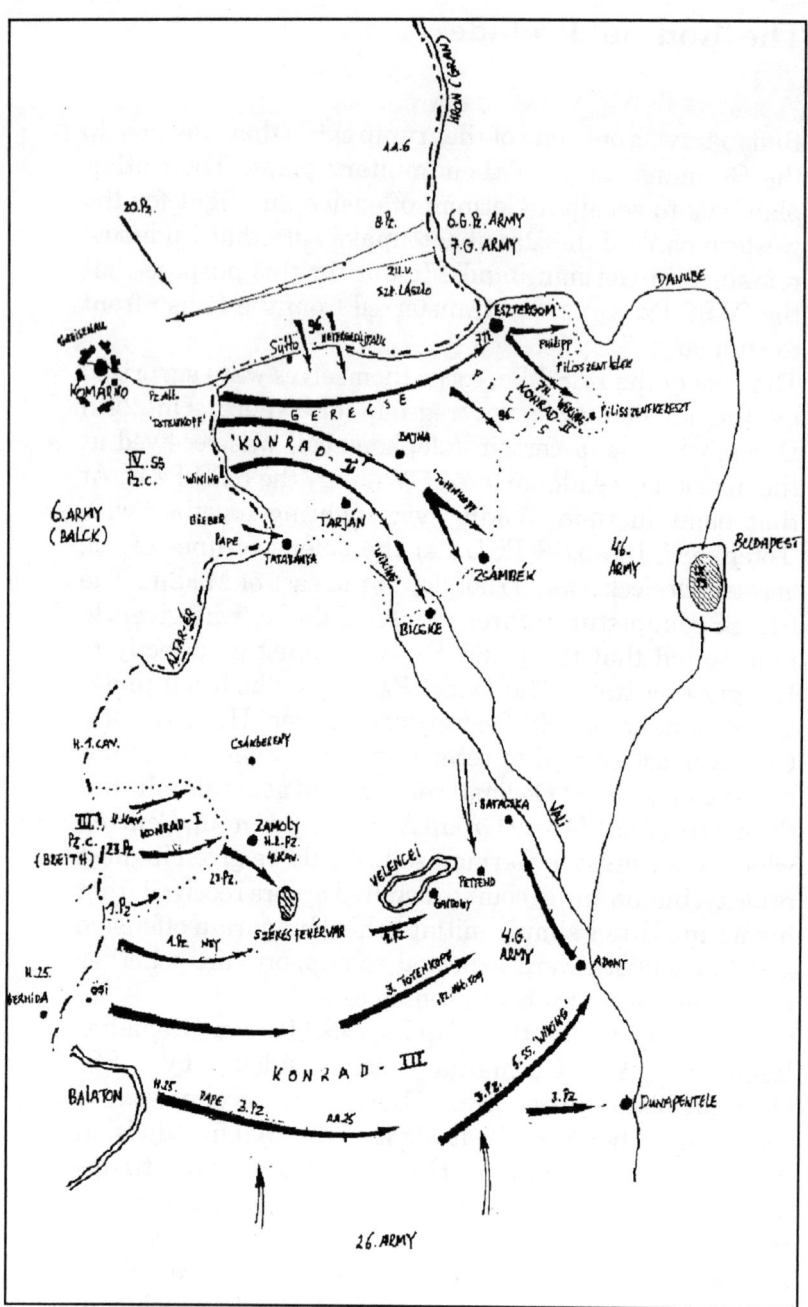

The operations 'KONRAD'

be leaving the 'Modlin Fortress", remarked Jahnke after the war, 'everyone there feared being surrounded because it was unlikely that we would have ever escaped.' As the trains carrying German soldiers pulled out of Modlin station they were shelled by Soviet artillery fire.

In moving from Modlin to Budapest the IV.SS Pz. corps in effect switched from one 'Fortress' to another. They hoped, though, that this time they would not be the besieged but rather the liberators. The IV.SS Pz corps consisted of two of the best Waffen-SS divisions. After the war, the Soviet Field Marshal, Zhukov, had complained: 'everywhere I went I came across the 'Totenkopf' division'. This 3. SS Pz.D that took its orders from SS-Brigadeführer Helmuth Becker, had fought in the main front line areas both in the west and in the east and had for a long time been led by the chief commandant of KZ Dachau, Theodor Eicke. 'Wiking', which fell under the command of SS-Oberführer Karl Ullrich and constituted an élite division, was the 'pampered child' of the well-known SS General, Felix Steiner. The unit was composed not only of German soldiers but also of volunteers drawn from Norway, Denmark, the Netherlands and Belgium. The Germans had managed to involve them by calling this a crusade against Bolshevism. Both divisions were completely flattened on the eastern front more than once but each time the legions were replenished with new recruits. In the period between 22nd June 1941 and 31st December 1944, (the eve of 'Konrad') the 'Totenkopf' division lost an astronomical number of men, a total of 53,794. No other division within the Army Group South sustained such a disastrously high level of losses. 'Wiking', which was a professional and experienced division, suffered 11,098 losses.

When, early in the morning of 1st January 1945 commanders of the 'Wiking' division arrived in Hungary, nobody realized that the corps would be going into battle the same evening. The first day of the new year was supposed to mark the beginning of a military turnabout for

Germany. On the western front Hitler had commanded that on the same day 'Nordwind', (the attack in the Alsace) and 'Bodenplatte', the accompanying air attack, were to begin. In Hungary the prelude to 'Frühlingserwachen', code-named 'Konrad', was about to begin. From the very start this military initiative was plagued by two major problems: shortage of time and ambivalence. The time problem derived from the fact that the Red Army dictated the pace of the fighting. In Budapest the Germans had been forced into the defensive and the Red Army had driven back the remaining troops of Army Group South to the Margarethe lines situated between lakes Balaton and Velencei and to the Gerecse and Pilis Heights where the peaks rise to 700 to 800 metres above sea-level. The garrison in Budapest was under such great pressure that the Germans had to react fast if they were going to keep the city in German hands. Therefore, the 'Konrad' offensive turned into a hastily organized military operation.

The ambivalence derived from the fact that originally there had been two main plans in circulation; two ideas of ways to achieve the same goal. The 'Konrad' operations, seen as the prelude to 'Frühlingserwachen', were not only aimed at retaining Budapest, but also at ridding the western bank of the Danube of Red Army troops. This was an ambitious plan, especially in view of the time factor and Budapest's position in all this. The area that lent itself best to such a large-scale manoeuvre was that of the Hungarian plains between the country's two biggest lakes and the manoeuvre was known colloquially as plan 'Paula'. The quickest route to Budapest was through the Gerecse and Pilis Heights: the 'Konrad' plan. After his usual indecision, Hitler settled for the 'Konrad' plan. It was true that this mountainous area was not particularly suitable for a mobile military attack but then neither had the Ardennes been in 1940. The German tanks had at that time made an amazing breakthrough at Sedan and Hitler hoped that he would be able to pull off a similar trick in Hungary.

Otto Wöhler, commandant of Army Group South. Wöhler replaced Friessner and had the unenviable task of having to execute Hitler's ambitious Hungarian plans. On top of this he had to contend with the bad relationships between certain of his highest officers, some of whom came from the army and some of whom originated from the SS.

General Balck who, according to some, was one of the best generals of the Second World War. Balck who was commander of the 6. army had a dispute with one of his leading corps commandants, Otto Gille.

Herbert Otto Gille, commandant of the IV.SS Pz. corps. A vain and particularly brave officer who had under his command two excellent Waffen-SS divisions: the 3.SS Pz.D. 'Totenkopf' and the 5.SS Pz.D. 'Wiking'.

Hans Gaedcke, Herman Balck's right-hand man. Balck and Gaedcke had a 'father and son relationship'. Gaedcke supported Balck through thick and thin whenever there was any unrest with the Waffen-SS.

There were three German officers who had key parts to play in the whole 'Konrad' operation. First and foremost, there was of course, Otto Wöhler, commandant of Army Group South and former commandant of the 8. army.
Wöhler had the unenviable task of having to realize Hitler's ambitious plans. Understandably he was, therefore, pretty tense about things. Several historic descriptions of events highlight the way in which Wöhler gave his Army Group divisional commandants a 'cold' reception on the eve of the onslaught. Wöhler had good reason to be concerned and dissatisfied. He had to start up a quickly improvised operation in mountainous terrain. For the attack that was to be concentrated on Budapest Wöhler's most important unit was Hermann Balck's 6. army, notably the IV.SS Pz. corps of SS-Obergruppenführer Herbert Otto Gille.
It was an unfortunate combination. Balck and Gille did not get on at all well. Balck came from a traditional military background and Gille was a Third Reich officer from a nouveau-riche family, a man who had made his career within Heinrich Himmler's SS imperium. Both men were brave, self-willed and vain. Balck saw himself as a military genius - a view supported by certain German military experts - and he doubted whether Gille was equipped with the necessary skills. Perhaps Gille did not have the required social background but he was held in high esteem by his subordinates. After the war, one of the Bundeswehr officers referred to Gille as having been 'one of Germany's best generals.'
With heavy pressure being put on military progress in Hungary and with the increasing personal intervention of Hitler (OKW) and Guderian (OKH), tension was rapidly mounting within the Army Group ranks. Well aware of what had happened to Friessner, his predecessor, Wöhler saw to it that he remained compliant towards his superiors and firm with his soldiers. In practice this put pressure on Balck who had to make Gille account for his actions and this in turn led to conflict.
Balck was known for the uneasy footing on which he stood with SS officers, something which was only

intensified by the stance of his Chief of Staff, Heinz Gaedcke. 'When Gaedcke heard that Gille was on his way to Hungary he turned pale' wrote Balck in his memoirs when recalling his first days with the 6. army. Gaedcke knew Gille from the time in Kessel in January 1944, when Tscherkassy on the Dniepr had been surrounded. He had come to know him as a 'difficult and headstrong' man. However, Balck revealed nothing more about the background to this conflict. In a letter written in 1989 Gaedcke threw a little more light on the situation. He explained how at Cherkassy Gille had refused to release a 1,000 or so drivers from the 'Wiking' division who were needed at the front and to help soldiers to escape from Kessel. In view of the fact that the 'Wiking' vehicles could not be saved and, therefore, had to be destroyed such help was vital. Gille had ignored this order for so long that he had almost been courtmarshalled. Through the 01., Günter Jahnke ('Wiking') of the SS, a very different story had been told after the war. At the time of breaking out, Gaedcke had apparently taken over the rearguard. Later he had appeared at the river on horseback and without his troops. This had precipitated an argument between Waffen-SS officers and Gaedcke.

Nobody can now verify the story. What is important, though, is to know that this relationship made cooperation more complicated. Balck took Gaedcke's warning directed at Gille seriously. There was a high degree of solidarity between Balck and Gaedcke. Both had served in the 1.Kav.D. and Gaedcke characterized their relationship as a 'father and son' relationship. 'When I met Gille my worries were confirmed' wrote Balck after the war adding,' Gille was undoubtedly very brave but he was also self-centred and lacking in strategic insight.' In reality the problem probably arose more from the fact that Balck and Gille were too similar rather than from the fact that they were too different. They were both rather stubborn by nature and that led to conflict. The German Wehrmacht was rightly irritated by the fact that in the case of the SS they not only took their orders from the Army Group but also from higher up (Himmler)

through their own SS channels which only complicated matters. On top of this there was the usual rivalry between units just as in any army as there is, for instance, between the land forces and the navy in the American army.
Somehow Wöhler had to try to bring together these extremities and be productive. It was an advantage that both officers were warmongering types. With an operation like 'Konrad' which relied so heavily on improvization this was a positive asset. After the war Gaedcke wrote: 'The situation was not completely hopeless. In the past, we had always been weaker in numbers but every time the strength of our leadership had been our saving factor. In addition, we had excellent units, like for instance, the 96. I.D.,' commented Gaedcke in one of a number of letters written after the war. Not surprisingly Gaedcke said nothing about the Waffen-SS Pz. corps which had been the spearhead of the offensive.

The operation got off to a hasty start. Troops had been instructed to congregate around the áltar-ér canal at the foot of the Gerecse and Pilis Heights and the offensive commenced on 1st January at 18.00 hours with no preliminary artillery fire. While a number of 'Gneisenau' (watch) battalions and the Heeres-Pz.Abt.208 (equipped also with Pz.Jg.IV 'Zwischenlösung') defended the Komárom oil area, armoured tanks (including several 'Tiger' type tanks from 'Totenkopf') rolled past in their winter camouflage on their way to Budapest.
The Red Army was taken by surprise and thrown into confusion. The German attacker had at its disposal two Waffen-SS panzer divisions ('Wiking' and 'Totenkopf'), the Gruppe Pape (i.e. several army tank regiments commanded by Günther Pape, ex-officer of the 'FHH' division) and a few combat groups (Kgr.Bieber'-271 V.G.D. and two battalions of the Hungarian Waffen-SS). The Germans were only opposed by one weakened Russian army corps: the 31. corps. This unit of the Red Army only had three weakend infantry divisions at its disposal and one tank brigade equipped with 27 T-34 tanks. The Russians had a

Hermann Harrendorf, commandant of the 96.I.D. During the 'Konrad' I operations this unit crossed the Danube and took the Red Army by surprise on the northern flank.

Gille with his famous carved walking stick is greeted by Karl Ullrich, divisional commandant of the 5.SS Pz.D. 'Wiking'.
To the right and in the background is the O1., Günter Jahnke, whose diary on the Hungarian operations is a valuable historic source.

Gustav Harteneck, commandant of the I.Kav. corps.

Manfried Schönfelder, Gille's right-hand man. After the war he wrote an extensive report on the Hungarian operations which also conveyed all his frustrations in this connection.

Herman Breith, commandant of the III.Pz. corps in Hungary. The III.Pz. corps had chiefly a supportive function.

48 kilometre long front to defend so they did not stand a chance against the Germans in this sudden attack launched by the 6. army. The experienced 96 I.D. led by Oberst Hermann Harrendorf approached from Slovakia, crossed over the Danube and hit the Red Army in its flank taking it by surprise. The units of the 4.G.D. of the Red Army were startled by these nightly incursions across the Danube that was packed with drifting ice. Between Süttö and Nyergesúfalu the front was disbanded and the soldiers held out against attacks from 'Jupp Stalin' tanks and Soviet Pak until the first tanks of the Pz.Rgt. 'Totenkopf', commanded by SS-Sturmbannführer Berlin, reached them. Only then could the plentiful wine cellars of the Hungarian Danube towns be plundered. The wine produced there was high in alcohol and known for its pungent character. From the wine hills surrounding the villages the drunken revelry of Soviet soldiers could soon be heard. In fact, the whole start of the military operation was characterized by alcohol abuse. The attack had begun the day after New Year's Eve which meant that many of the soldiers went into battle with hangovers. To the south of 'Totenkopf', 'Wiking', SS-Obersturmbannführer Fritz Darges' Pz.Rgt. 5, broke through the Russian lines. The tanks were immediately followed by 'Germania', SS-Pz.Gren.Rgt.9 under the command of SS-Obersturmbannführer Hans Dorr.

In the industrial areas of Felsögalla and Alsógalla 'Wiking' was backed up on the southern flank by the 'Gruppe Pape'. The outcome was the same here as in the area where the 96.I.D. and the 'Totenkopf' division was operating. The Red Army was unable to hold back the attack even though parts of the IV.SS.Pz. corps were still dribbling in by train which meant that the German attacker was not at its full strength. But Wöhler had no time to lose and goaded his men on.

In the ensuing days, the offensive slowly lost its élan for several different reasons. The area where the fighting was taking place was mountainous with strata of brown coal. It was, therefore, difficult for motorized vehicles to gain access. More than once tanks had to be towed through the hills by artillery tractors. Many of the roads were mined which meant that the German units were forced to keep away from the main routes. The narrow mountain roads were easy for the Russians to barricade. The Pak (anti-tank) lines in particular, made life difficult for the IV.SS Pz. corps. By now, the Red Army was aware that the German troops had mounted an offensive on Budapest. More and more Russian units were gradually being released to fight in the Gerecse and Pilis Heights. As has already been mentioned, the forces that were brought in were from units that had been deployed to fight against the garrison in Buda and troops that had been stationed further south on the front near the places Zámoly and Mór. The Russian 18. panzer corps, moving in towards the Gerecse and Pilis Heights from the south, played an important part too.

Therefore, the pace of the attack began to slacken not long after 'Konrad' had begun. Wöhler and Balck were most unhappy about this state of affairs. They angrily lodged a protest at 'Wiking' divisional headquarters, where Herbert Gille and Karl Ullrich were stationed. 'I have the impression that the officers do not possess the qualities they had at the beginning of the war' recorded Wöhler in the Army Group South's diary. By the time the two men reached headquarters, they had become a little more subdued. 'The officers were angry until they saw the state of the terrain where 'Wiking' was having to operate and then they changed their tune', recorded 'Wiking's' 01., Günter Jahnke, in his diary.

Tension mounted in the German camp when the attack came to a halt on the 5th January at the road junctions of Zsámbék and Bickse. To the annoyance of the Germans the front on the river Gran was also growing increasingly restless, thus making it virtually impossible, as Wöhler had wanted to do, to recruit extra soldiers from this area for the 'Konrad' operation. The 8.Pz.D, the 211 V.G.D. and the Hungarian Szt. László division were needed (at the very minimum) to protect the front on the north side of the

Danube. Only the 3.Pz.D. was released and Wöhler knew that he was taking risks.

This panzer division was incorporated into the corps installed to the south of the IV.SS. Pz. corps. Wöhler, who by now felt Hitler breathing down his neck, wanted to get the Waffen-SS offensive moving quickly again by encouraging the 'Gruppe Pape' near to the Felsögla industrial area to speed up its faltering attack. The III.Pz. corps (Breith) and the I.Kav. corps (Von Harteneck) based around Zámoly were busy carrying out this support attack.

On 6th January, it seemed that the tide was turning for the Germans. They were successful in two ways, one of which came as rather an unexpected surprise. The 711.I.D that had arrived from the Netherlands was a 'bodenständige' garrison division illequipped for such offensive operations. Amazingly, they managed to effect a breakthrough at the last weak spot in the Russian front. In view of the fact that no one had expected any achievements from this unit this came as quite a surprise. Shortly before the soldiers had been completely defeated in France. From there they had gone on to the Netherlands to get reinforcements and then this same rather shabby bunch of soldiers had suddenly popped up again on the eastern front where Hitler's prestigious Hungarian campaign was in full swing. The division was a motley collection of soldiers dressed in different uniforms. New soldiers who had come straight from the navy had not even had time to change their blue uniforms for Wehrmacht uniforms. Many of the soldiers were suffering from diarrhoea, because they had eaten their emergency rations, a couple of kilos of spiced Dutch biscuit, all at once while travelling to Hungary by train. Many of them had thought that it might be the last meal they would ever eat. Peering into the dark night they had seen the light flashes of the V missiles and had concluded that they were on their way to join the Ardennes campaign. The 'Wacht am Rhein' (watch on the Rhine), however, had been switched to the 'Wacht an der Donau' and knowing that they were destined for the eastern front had been, for many soldiers, justification enough to consume their entire schnapps and food rations. After the war, one Hungarian recalled how 'the unit was led by a strictlooking officer with a monocle'. This had undoubtedly been General Josef Reichert, who with his messily thrown together unit, had landed himself in the middle of Hitler's grand Hungarian project. Several units of the 711.I.D. had Dutch bicycles with them on which, slipping and sliding over the snow and ice covered roads, they were able to proceed faster than the troops moving on foot. Thus, it was that Esztergom (Gran), the city on the Danube with 20,000 inhabitants, fell into German hands almost without putting up any resistance.

This was an important conquest, because it stimulated the German high command to start putting more emphasis on the activities taking place on the extreme northern flank of 'Konrad'. Almost simultaneously a very turbulent attack was mounted by 'Wiking', notably Darges' Pz.Rgt.5 and Fritz Vogt's 'Norge' battalion (composed of Norwegian volunteers) which amounted to a second success. Darges relentlessly goaded his tanks eastwards attacking and almost completely obliterating a Russian convoy until, far ahead of the remaining 'Wiking' troops, they reached Hegykastély, an old castle built between 1833 and 1840. Necessary supplies were flown in to fuel the attack.

In theory, this might have looked triumphant but in practice it was no victory for 'Wiking'. The success achieved at Hegykastély soon turned against the Germans. In typical SS style the whole attack was badly thought out which particularly irritated Balck. Brave but reckless the SS soldiers had now laid themselves bare to repeated concentric Russian attack in which, by the hour, more tanks came to swell the ranks. Within a short time, the old castle was reduced to a ruin by the Red Army. Drunk and desperate the SS commandants looked to outsiders for help. The soldiers, including some fifty Norwegian volunteers, began to attack the Russian tanks with anti-tank weapons. Later in the war, the battle at the Hungarian castle was described in detail in the SS

Karl Ullrich, commandant of the 5.SS Pz.D. 'Wiking'. After the war he admitted to being convinced that Budapest could have been liberated. The photo shows Ullrich when he was regimental commandant of the 'Totenkopf' division.

Günther Pape, commandant of the 'Gruppe Pape' which supported the 'Konrad' I operations by attacking the industrial area near to Alsógalla. After the war he made a career for himself in the German army.

The Russian opponents of the German attacking forces: Field Marshal Malinovski and Field Marshal Tolbukhin. They called these battles the toughest since those of Stalingrad.

paper 'Schwarze Korps'. A new heroic myth had been born but the reality was different. After a terrible period of being under siege the SS had been forced to break out and escape westwards. Some contemporaries believed that the reason why Darges, a former official at Führer headquarters, had initiated such a reckless attack was connected with the fact that Hitler had sent him to the eastern front in order to punish him. One day Hitler had come across an insect at his headquarters and, plagued as he was by a morbid fear of bacteria, microbes and insects he had, in a fit of rage, issued the order that Darges was to be sent to the eastern front. For his part, Darges seemed determined to either die or receive the 'Ritterkreuz'. To him it had seemed that bringing about a tempestuous attack at Bicske would be the quickest way of achieving his ends. Bicske remained in Russian hands but Darges got his Ritterkreuz. By obliterating the Russian convoy of twelve trucks, six pieces of artillery and a number of horse-drawn vehicles Darges had earned recognition. In those days, the value of the Ritterkreuz had been greatly inflated.

The operation mounted at Hegykastély had been carried out in true Fritz Vogt style. Napoleon once said: 'The worse the man the better the soldier'. It was a description that seemed to fit Vogt, a man who was feared for his sheer recklessness. He had been known to wrench anti-tank shells out of the hands of soldiers and surge into battle. After the war, Hegykastély was demolished for fear that it would otherwise become a 'Mecca' for Nazi 'pilgrims'.

After the small victory at Esztergom and the Pyrrus victory at Hegykastély the Army Group South had to deal with two big disappointments on 6th January both of which constituted a direct threat to German oil interests. Because the activities in the Gerecse and Pilis Heights and the supporting actions of the III.Pz. corps and I.Kav. corps had demanded all Wöhler's attention he had not given much thought to how things were going with the 2.Pz. army. This unit, commanded by the Artillery

General Maximillian De Angelis, was responsible for the most southerly front area in Hungary which ran roughly from lake Balaton to the river Drava. This meant that it was the responsibility of De Angelis to protect the oil fields of Nagykanizsa. He was concerned about the Russian front reinforcements at Mestagnyoe-Marczali which was why he asked Wöhler for back-up troops in order to repress this front in a short, sharp offensive. Wöhler who had more than enough work on his hands coping with the offensive that was designed to protect the oil fields could not possibly pay attention to this matter as well. He pointed out what was happening to Herman Balck's 6. army and the Russians provided him with a second argument. On the very same day the Russian 6.G.Pz army (of General Kravschenko) and the 7.G. army (of General Schumilov) started up its long awaited offensive on the Gran.

Wöhler was made to pay for the fact that he had weakened the LVII.Pz. corps of General Kirchner (an old friend of Balck's) by having to move with the 3.Pz.D. to an area to the south of the Danube. The Russian troops broke through the lines of the Szt. László division that was made up of Hungarian parachutists, the 211.V.G.D. and the 8.Pz.D. In spite of their heavy losses, 23 tanks, they advanced at an amazing speed in the direction of Komárom. Panic then broke out at Führer headquarters and in the Army Group South. Komárom was an important road and rail intersection and the place where the only permanent bridge connection with Slovakia existed. Above all else, Komárom had big oil refineries which, in view of Hitler's oil obsession, made it a place of great strategic importance.

The Army Group gathered together all the units it could find to reinforce the bridgehead at Komárom. There it erected a provisional defence system with the help of the Pz.Jg.Abt.13, a section of the 13.Pz.D. that was not enclosed in Budapest and with the support of the army machine-gun battalion 'Sachsen', the army Flak-Abt.286 and the army Pz.Abt.208 (with twelve tanks). Units of the

8.Pz.D. (notably the Pz.Gren.Rgt.98 of Oberstleutnant Von Knoop), the 211.V.G.D. (Generalleutnant Johann Heinrich Eckhardt) and 'Szt. László' mounted localized counter-attacks. At this point the German troops discovered something strange. After closer inspection of demobilized Soviet tanks (many of which were American Sherman type tanks) the Germans discovered that they were packed with the spoils of war. Dead Russian soldiers often had three or more watches on each wrist and the posts that had been taken over by the Red Army were furnished with proper beds, presumably stolen from local inhabitants.

Thanks to the speedy arrival of the 20.Pz.D, led by General Von Oppeln-Bronikowski, that came from the area where Army Group A was stationed it was possible to divert the attack just outside Komárom. The front stablize along the Köbölkut - Libád - Kam - Darmotky - Kemend line. Komárom had, as its new city commander, General z.b.V. Herhudt von Roden. The defences were reinforced with emergeny battalions. 'That was a weight off my shoulders' wrote Balck in his post-war memoirs when referring to the successful deployment of 20.Pz.D. Balck's relief was understandable, especially since the Army Group had at one point even considered re-directing Breith's III.Pz. corps to the threatened Gran front as soon as possible. Had this happened the whole 'Konrad' operation would have been seriously undermined. The Russian attack was brought to a standstill. Though the greatest immediate danger had by now subsided, the Russian bridgehead was something that could not be ignored. 'Konrad' was under threat on the northern flank and the situation became urgent. There was general dissatisfaction about the speed with which the 8.Pz.D. had reacted to the attack. 'The commandant has failed', concluded Gaedcke and Fröhlich. The Generalmajor from Dresden who had been decorated with the Ritterkreuz, was replaced by Von Roden.

On 7th January, it became evident that in its present form 'Konrad' was no longer viable. Back-up attacks carried out by the III.Pz. corps and the I.Kav. corps had simply erupted and the Russian 4.G. army battled on relentlessly. 'It is the heaviest fighting since Stalingrad', commented the Russian Stavka. Despite everything the Russians managed to hold their own. From the south and from Budapest new reinforcements continued to pour in. The Red Army had mustered up omnibusses in Budapest to make the transportation of units to the front speedier.

The fighting had its repercussions in the mountains around Zsámbék and Bicske where heavy infantry and tank attacks flared up. There, the Russians amassed vast amounts of artillery. Within the IV.SS Pz. corps losses had risen to 525. Some 2,605 men had been injured and almost 400 were missing. The only positive development was on the extreme northern flank where the 711.I.D. was in action. This unit had followed the route from Esztergom - Pilisszentlélek- Pillisszentkereszt - Pomáz - Budapest and had gained a fair amount of ground. The 96.I.D. that had reached a stalemate in fights around Dorog and Sáriszáp was ordered by Wöhler to move to where the 711.I.D. was fighting and carry out back-up attacks. It was clearly evident that this amount of manpower would not be sufficient, because even the 711.I.D. was experiencing increasing resistance. Stronger units were required: panzer troops. Wöhler then ordered the 'Wiking' division to immediately move out to the northern periphery. 'Konrad' II, the northern variant of 'Konrad' I had been born.

From the beginning, 'Konrad' II was beset by the same kind of problems as 'Konrad' I: lack of time and ambivalence. The troops of the IX.SS Geb. corps yearned for the arrival of reinforcements from the IV.SS Pz. corps and from a southern direction the Russians gradually set about strengthening the extreme northern flank. At the same time, the alternative solution for the south, known as plan 'Paula', was coming more and more to the fore, because of all the set-backs.

The 711.I.D. continued marching on alone to Pillissentlélek. Then, they had to wait for the 'Wiking' division, the SS-Pz.Gren.Rgt.9 'Westland'. The soldier

Horst Lange (who had landed up in the infantry after following a short course to become a pilot) recalled that contact was first made with the soldiers of 'Wiking' when soldiers of the 711.I.D. were withdrawing from Pilisszentlélek whilst still fighting. While the 'Westland' troops were assembling they came under mortar fire. This unit was commanded by SS-Obersturmbannführer Franz Hack and they quickly headed for Budapest setting off along the same route as the one followed by the 711.I.D. To the north of this unit, following the road along the river (Esztergom - Nagymaros - Dömös - Pócsmegyer - Budapest) another small combat group known as 'Gruppe Philipp' joined the ranks. It consisted of five tanks, six SPW, II./'FHH' and the I.Art.Rgt.3 and was commanded by Oberstleutnant Ernst Philipp. This unit formed the most northerly flank of Konrad II. After the war, Philipp was surprised to hear that his mad attack with this insignificant unit had even been mentioned in the Army Group diary. Their objective, Budapest, was so far away that Philipp was hardly able to take the whole thing seriously which was understandable when one bears in mind how long the detour was. Georg Maier, the 1. General Staff Officer of the 6.Pz. army who, when the war was over, wrote a huge book about the military operations in Hungary, characterized Philipp's action as an 'Himmelfahrtskommando'.

Budapest was a more realistic goal for the 'Wiking' soldiers who were eager to join their SS comrades in Budapest. Passing through Pilisszentlelek the SS panzer grenadiers forged ahead to the east. The roads were cold and icy, but the Russians did not provide much opposition. At the same time, though, Hitler began to lose patience. On 10th January, he criticized the operation in the mountains calling it 'utterly pointless'. To his mind only a 'miracle' could turn operation 'Konrad' into a success. Indeed, the successful cleansing of the western bank of the Danube was further away than ever before. Even the ideal of holding on to Budapest could no longer be realized. The only thing that was still possible was, to liberate the garrison. For the 'Wiking' soldiers, who were unaware of

Hitler's overall strategic plans, that was their only goal. They were able to remember the terrible days in Cherkassy the battle of Kowel.

Balck and his right-hand man, Heinz Gaedcke, tried to come up with a sort of compromise solution. They asked at Führer headquarters whether it would be possible for the IX.SS Geb corps to attempt to break out to the west so that the IV.SS Pz. corps (Rgt. 'Westland' commanded by Hack) and the IX.SS Geb. corps might meet each other half way. A vanguard group from Von Wildenbruch's troops would then push forward in the direction of Pomáz. Guderian was the one who received the message and he was sceptical about the plans. He knew how difficult it was to make Hitler change course once his mind had been made up. A little while later, the reply came. The IX.SS Geb. corps was to stay where it was and Balck was given until 11th January to force a breakthrough.

The pressure on Gille to produce results increased. The Reichsführer-SS ordered the SS general by telephone to 'force a breakthrough!' The approach taken was important to Himmler because two of his cavalry divisions were stationed in Budapest. By 20.10 Hitler was exasperated and the order was received to stop the attack and start on the operation planned for the south (i.e. 'Paula' which was renamed 'Konrad' III). 'The Führer is afraid, that the fighting is proving fruitless' was what was written in the diary of Army Group South.

Several hours later, at 23.40, Gille reported that Pillisszentkereszt had been seized. The soldiers of 'Wiking' were excited. They were once again in radio contact with the soldiers of 'Florian Geyer' and 'Maria Theresia'. Soup was prepared and the military hospitals made space to receive the wounded that might come in from the Kessel. The announcement that Hitler had ordered the whole operation to be stopped came as a huge shock to all the men. Why stop attacking just before reaching the objective and after all the losses? Schönfelder and later Gille contacted their superiors. At Gille's request Wöhler got in touch with Führer headquarters. Afraid of offending

Hitler Wöhler was very careful how he worded things. 'I do not want to ignore orders, I just wish to pass on the latest news', was what was written in the diary. At 00.30 hours, Oberstleutnant i.G. Hermani reported that Hitler was not going to change his mind. At 00.35 hours, Gille made one final desperate attempt to change things. He contacted the Reichsführer-SS but, as usual, he had gone to bed early. SS-Obersturmbannführer Werner Grothmann who was only 29 years old did not dare to disturb Himmler. This was how 'Konrad' II ended.

'They all shook their heads', wrote 01. Jahnke in his diary. The 'Wiking' SS Grenadiers turned back when they were 21 kilometres away from Budapest. Once german troops were only 48 kilometres away from Stalingrad and this was less than half the distance. On the radio they could hear the desperate cries for help coming from Budapest! The 'Wiking' soldiers went to the health resort of Dobogókö from where they could see the church spires of Budapest. The soldiers were not given much time to think about what had happened. Very soon new orders arrived and they were required to regroup. Some days later, there was a minor incident in this same resort. The soldier Horst Lange recalled how, tired out, the soldiers of the 711.I.D. had returned to the resort to recover from the chaotic fighting in the woods when word arrived that the Red Army had broken through. Everyone dashed outside, but one soldier who had taken off his boots was unable to get them on again. Without boots on he would certainly have died in the snow and so the soldiers had no choice, but to leave him behind.

As soon as Hitler realized that the Germans could no longer hold on to Budapest he sacrificed the garrison. The soldiers in the city who preferred to fight to the death rather than be handed over to the Red Army still fulfilled a military function. Their being in Budapest made it necessary for Russian troops to remain stationed there which in turn meant that 'Konrad' II, according to the

'Paula' theory, would be freer to manoeuvre.

Even with the 'Konrad' III plans the ambitious idea of cleansing the entire western bank of the Danube - and, thus, of also holding on to Budapest - had not been abandoned. The main objective of 'Konrad' III was to get the IV.SS Pz. corps to advance towards Budapest from north of lake Balaton. After this mission had been successfully completed - i.e. after Hungary had been cleansed from the region to the north of lake Balaton to the Danube - operation 'Süd' would then be initiated (in effect a variation on 'Frühlingserwachen'). Together with the 2.Pz. army (operation 'Eisbrecher') and Ob.Southeast from Yugoslavia they would then proceed to disperse the Soviet units in the south.

However, the Germans had not yet got that far by a long way. Though the terrain conditions might have been in their favour, the Red Army was now much more alert than it had been during the 'Konrad' I operations. Besides, as far as the Germans were concerned, failing to gain air supremacy during the battle for the low-lying south might well have precipitated their downfall and finally, the IV.SS corps had lost much of its manpower. The number of tanks available in each division varied between twenty and forty but these numbers soon rapidly diminished. Even though many Russian tanks were also destroyed, estimates ran into the hundreds, the Red Army had big reserves to draw on.

For this new operation Gille had at his disposal his two SS panzer divisions, the 3.Pz.Div. and a group of smaller units like the sPz.Abt.509, the army Sturmart. Brigade 303, V.A.K. 403, Volkswerfer Brigade 17, Sturmgeschütz-Abt. 1335 and Sturmpz.Abt. 219. The 1.Pz.D. was deployed on the northern flank. To the north Gilles' troops were supported by the I.Kav. corps which was deployed in the Gerecse and Pilis Heights. To the south Gilles' corps would be protected by the III.Pz. corps. Breith's front line linked up with the 2.Pz.army.

At first, 'Konrad' III looked as though it was going to be a resounding success for the Germans. 'It was like 1940 all over again', wrote a soldier of the 3.Pz.D. after the war. On the northern flank 'Totenkopf' came into action; from the Berhida region the unit forged ahead along the banks of lake Velencei and, after four days, reached Gárdony and the river Váli. Also 'Wiking', which set off from the Csajag region, managed to make good progress. Working partly with thirty or so 'Königstigers' of the sPz.Abt.509 that was commanded by Major Burmeister and the 303 Army Artillery Brigade, commanded by Major Kokott, they too reached the Danube and the Váli within a matter of days. The death of the commandant of Rgt. 'Germania', SS-Obersturmbannführer Hans Dorr, came as a big loss to the division. A Russian grenade chanced to hit the regimental headquarters of Rgt.'Germania' in Sárosd. Dorr, an extremely experienced officer who had already been wounded fifteen times during the war, was wounded again but this time the wounds proved to be fatal. He died in a hospital in Vienna.

Because he had so often been fortunate in dangerous situations Dorr had built up the reputation of being 'indestructible'. Dorr himself had always been very casual about this, once brushing it off by saying: 'I'm just too tired to run for cover.' On the day of the Von Stauffenberg attack Dorr's photo had even reached the front page of the Völkische Beobachter. How he had fought at Tscherkassy was reported in detail and emphasis was given to the recognition he had received from the Führer. 'Dorr was wounded nine times', reported the article erroneously. The sixteenth wound was fatal.

On 21st January, the 3. Pz.D. of Generalleutnant Philipps conquered the city of Adony on the Danube. Terrified Russian soldiers fled by boat to the opposite bank while tanks of the German panzer division situated there fired relentlessly at the Russians.

After the initial days of the operation the euphoric mood ended for the Germans. The Váli became what Bicske and Zsámbék had been for 'Konrad' I. The Soviet armed forces

'Konrad' I and 'Konrad' II operations took place in the Gerecse and
Heights. The mountainous and wooded area was no easy terrain
he panzer divisions of the Waffen-SS. The few existing roads there
effectively made impassable by the Red Army which placed mines
anti-tank devices along the roads.

Optimism in the German ranks. Soldiers making music as they ma
For the first time in a long while the armies moved eastwards. Des,
the remarkable amount of ground gained the fighting was bloody and
the last moment the garrison at Budapest could no longer be saved.

brought in their reinforcements and did everything in their power to defend themselves. The southern flank of the 3.Pz.D. which had speedily been backed up by the 'Gruppe Pape' and a Hungarian infantry division also came under increasing threat from the superior Russian adversary. Despite all this it still remained a touch and go situation. The Russian Field Marshal, Tolbukhin, had even asked Stalin for permission to abandon the western bank of the Danube. Stalin had remained unbending with the result that the Russian 18.Pz. corps was virtually wiped out which, just as at Zsámbék and Bicske, had been positioned directly in the German line of attack. The Soviet losses were staggering. Between 18th and 21st January the Red Army had lost 193 tanks, 229 pieces of artillery, 257 Pak and 1,175 prisoners of war, but the front remained intact and the attack eased off.

At German headquarters, the first signs of panic could be detected. In the north-easterly direction progress had been blockaded, but it was not possible to stand still either pressure on the southern flank being as it was. 'We must find somewhere to break through', Gille intimated to Balck. When the supporting III.Pz. corps opened up its offensive at the Székesfehérvár (Stuhlweissenburg) road intersection this brought some relief. The operation turned into a joint effort between various units. It was decided that together with the Hungarian Waffen-SS battle group 'Ney' most of the panzer grenadiers of the 1.Pz.D would, under the strict observation of General Thunert, mount a frontal attack while the armoured section, 'Gruppe Philipp', would move along the south of the city towards Dinnyes on lake Balaton. The 1.Pz.D. attack was backed up by troops from the IV.SS Pz. corps, the 'Norge' battalion and a number of Pz.VI's (Tiger) together with the 23.Pz.D. on the north flank, a cavalry combat group (Gruppe Holste) and sections of the 24.Pz.D. (I./Pz.Rgt.24 of Rittmeister Weidemann) This last unit, in particular, provided good support for Thunert's attacking force. The I./Pz.Rgt.24 had about 24 Panther type tanks. Throughout the Hungarian campaign the I./24 unit served with a range of different units such as: the 1.Pz.D and 'Totenkopf' (in January), 23.Pz.D. (in February), 3.Pz.D. and 6.Pz.D. (in March) and the IV.SS Pz. corps (in April).

On 22nd January, the Székesfehérvár attack began. Székesfehérvár was a city with over 45,000 inhabitants and, since days of old, a place where main roads converged. The city, which was more than a thousand years old, was the site where big battles had been fought in the days of the Huns. The military operations of the Huns had been complicated by the vast amounts of mud in the area and this was something that again, later on, was also going to hamper 'Frühlingserwachen' operations. The attack was a success. The troops quickly managed to penetrate the Russian ranks on the western side of the city and a short while later the whole city fell into the hands of the Germans. This was where the 1,500th tank was destroyed by the 1.Pz.D. and where the Germans managed to capture forty Red Army tanks. They were also glad to have captured many Opelblitz, Hanomags and Russian trucks ('Studebaker') which meant that the 1.Pz.D.'s truck reserves were almost complete again. On the debit side a vast number of tanks were put out of action, albeit temporarily, by the fighting. By the time 'Gruppe Philipp' and the I./24 reached Dinnyes, only six tanks were still operational.

The battle group 'Ney' losses were so heavy that the unit urgently required reinforcements. The unit formed the so-called 'Sondertruppe der Reichsführer-SS'. Originally, the troop had formed a kind of life-guard brigade for Szálasi but ultimately the soldiers preferred to work for the SS rather than to serve under the Arrow Cross leader. Wöhler found this troop a little problematic and wanted to integrate it as quickly as possible into the SS to 'prevent political problems from arising.' The commandant of the unit in question was SS-Obersturmbannführer Dr. Jur. Karl Ney von Pilis, former Chief of the 'Hungarian East Front Fighters'. The Ia. was SS-Hauptsturmführer J. Graf von Karoly. As of March 1945 the unit consisted of three battalions and an FEB.

Around Baracska fighting started to intensify. At Szabolcs-Nagyteteny the SS had formed a small bridgehead over the Váli. A massive counter-attack of Soviet tanks at the village of Pettend finally put paid to any illusions that mounting an attack on Budapest might be fruitful. An estimated 200 tanks of the Russian 23.Pz. corps rolled over the plains towards the German lines. The attack was fended off by a number of combined units, four Königstigers (sPz.Abt.509), a couple of Sturmgeschützen (Sturmart.Brigade 303), units of the 1.Pz.D. and the 'Norge' battalion. The Königstigers were particularly successful. At Pettend they managed to demobilize between 40 and 50 Soviet tanks (T-34s and Shermans). 'We've managed to hold off the attack', reported Fritz Vogt, commandant of the 'Norge' battalion to 'Wiking'. In reply Karl Ullrich signalled back: 'Bravo Vogt!, Bravo Vogt! We are coming in with tanks to help you!' That should be enough for the 'Eichenlaub' remarked Vogt who was prone to exaggeration. After the war, several of the above-mentioned units including a 'Totenkopf' Flak unit claimed to have been responsible for repelling the Russians at Pettend.

The fierceness of the fighting plus the fact that the Russians had, as soldiers of the 1.Pz.D., noticed 'no fear whatsoever of tanks' meant that the German high command had to think up an alternative solution to the problem. Gaedcke spoke of going on as being a question of conscience and a new and somewhat curious solution came up. It might be possible to divert Gille's main thrust north-westwards so that, in cooperation with the I.Kav. corps, the Soviet troops between Zsámbék and Tatabánya could be wiped out. In this way, a little Russian 'Kessel' would be created in the old front area to the west of Budapest. The plan did not work, though, because, in the region to the north of lake Velencei, the Russians had dug themselves in very expertly. 'We must drag them out one by one' was the complaint recorded in the Army Group South's diary.

Indeed, this was easier said than done. The IV.SS Pz. corps, fatigued from the opening 'Konrad' III operations, lost almost 300 men a day. The Army Group understood that changing course and heading for the heavily defended north-west was therefore perhaps not the most sensible plan. For a brief while operation 'Süd' was even contemplated: just turn everything around and march south, possibly in coordination with 'Eisbrecher' of the 2.Pz. army. 'The directions of attack change with the day' complained Manfried Schönfelder at one point and one can sympathize with this view. Once again, as in every situation of crisis, tension built up between Balck and the Waffen-SS. However, the Red Army put a speedy end to all discussion. Renewed heavy attacks mounted by Achmanov's 23 Pz. corps left the Germans with no alternative other than to go quickly over to the defensive. The Germans left the ruins of Pettend, just as they did at Hegykastély.

'Wiking' was left with fourteen tanks, 'Totenkopf' with nine! The losses (dead, wounded and missing) for the Waffen-SS panzer division 'Totenkopf' had risen to 4,350 and 3,079 for 'Wiking'. The Waffen-SS divisions had lost 51 officers in the 'Konrad' battlefields and 157 officers had been wounded. In addition, there were the losses that had been suffered by other units in the fighting at Gerecse and Pilis Heights. The 96.I.D. had lost 2,107 men, the 711.I.D. 1,174 soldiers and the 6.Pz.D 785 men. The back-up corps fighting under Breith and Harteneck had also been hard hit. Both Kav. brigades had lost over a thousand men. The units that had fought on the Gran front had also suffered considerable losses. The 211.V.G.D. lost over 1,500 soldiers. By January 1945, the entire Army Group South had lost a total of 35,000 men, who had been killed, wounded and had gone missing.

The troops were exhausted by battle and there was a rumour going around that someone in the army had betrayed the soldiers of the Waffen-SS and that 'the Ic from the 6. army had gone over to the Red Army'. After the war, 'Wiking' officers confirmed this rumour. The betrayal had to do with the fact that nobody had warned them of the sudden Soviet Pz. corps attack. As the 01 of

'Wiking', Günter Jahnke, said in 1990: 'It was all rather incredible that such a big unit had been able to remain undetected and take us by surprise'. In the end, it turned out to have been nothing more than a rumour. Ic Lieutenant Wüstenberg was shot down during a reconnaissance flight above the front. He had been especially sent out on this mission by Heinz Gaedcke who wrote after the war: 'I have lived to regret having made that order'. Wüstenberg was simply the umpteenth person to die in the Hungarian drama. Jahnke epitomized German over-confidence when he proclaimed that the movements of the Soviet 23.Pz. corps could not remain hidden from the Germans. Post-war research into the German intelligence network have shown that intelligence was certainly not the army's strongest point. In Hungary, too, big blunders were made on a regular basis. During the 'Frühlingserwachen' operations German military intelligence even failed to detect a complete tank army. It was not therefore surprising that they also failed to see Achmanov's Pz. corps which was much smaller than any Pz. army.

Between 27th January and 3rd February the German troops gradually fell back to the outer lines. 'The radio messages from Budapest became increasingly pessimistic', wrote Günter Jahnke: 'We cannot be held responsible!' he added.

The prelude to Hitler's Hungarian military campaign went badly and after that the atmosphere within the German camp was so tense it could be cut with a knife. Because the 'Konrad' operations had failed so abominably one could say that the garrison of 70,000 German and Hungarian soldiers had in effect been led to the slaughter. By the time the three 'Konrad' offensives had ended, the German military situation had become worse rather than better than it was on New Year's Day 1945.

The tragedies in the Ardennes and in Hungary were not the only disasters. Despite repeated warnings from Guderian the Vistula front had been neglected by Führer headquarters for a long time. On 12th January 1945,

Army Group A and Army Group Centre had paid the price for this neglect, because on that particular day the Red Army began a massive offensive which would ultimately take them to the Oder and to within 100 kilometres of Berlin.

Already on 26th November 1944, the commanding officers of Army Group A and Army Group Centre had warned in their: 'Directions for the preparation of counter-offensives between Beskiden and Warsaw' of the imminent concentric attacks that the Red Army was preparing to launch from the Vistula bridgeheads. In order to successfully avert this huge planned offensive (the Soviets had more than 120 infantry divisions and 5,650 tanks), they emphasized the importance of having mobile German reserves on hand. Like this, two to three days after the start of the Red Army offensive, the Germans would bring in these troops to effectively stop the Soviet forces. That would be the only way to save the Vistula front.

Removing the experienced IV.SS Pz. corps was, therefore, going to prove seriously detrimental to the already weakened central front. On top of this, Hitler had also forbidden the Germans to back themselves up with reserves so that at the moment when the offensive began they were left with far too little space for manoeuvre. Even though the German intelligence knew with certainty one day before the offensive that the Soviets were about to attack the whole front just disintegrated. The Red Army managed to flatten Oberschlesien and East Prussia.

When Guderian met Hitler again on 16th January in the bombed out Reichskanzlei (Chancellery) in Berlin, he hoped that news of the disaster on the Vistula would finally have convinced Hitler that Army Group A and Army Group Centre were badly in need of reinforcements. But things went differently. 'As soon as I arrived' recalled Guderian in his memoirs, 'I asked Jodl about the latest developments and about how the front on the Oder was to be defended.' Jodl had disappointing news for Guderian.

Hitler had ordered that the Ardennes offensive should be abandoned and he had instructed the 6.SS Pz. army to go straight on to Hungary. 'When I heard this I lost my self-control', Guderian admitted. 'I conveyed my opinions to Jodl in no uncertain terms, but all he could do was shrug his shoulders.' At the military conference Guderian, one of the few officers who dared to tell Hitler the truth, raised the subject again. 'It turned into a debate lasting several days', recalled Guderian, but Hitler could not be dissuaded from his 'evil plan'. 'Frühlingserwachen' must go ahead even though Guderian - backing himself up with statistics - reiterated and emphasized that the eastern front was like a 'house of cards'.

A 'Sturmgeschütz' fully packed with soldiers heads towards Budapest where fellow soldiers are held captive. The 'Konrad' operations took place in January, the coldest month of the year in Hungary. The 'Sturmgeschütz' is daubed in its winter camouflage and the soldiers too have adapted their uniforms to the winter conditions.

The German panzer units were followed by infantry units. There was great discrepancy in the standards of the German infantry units stationed in Hungary. The 96.I.D. was a very professional unit. The 711.I.D. by contrast was a disorganised unit composed of soldiers from the airforce and the marines who had all been sent out to the eastern front.

Only in the early days did the battle have the dynamic 'Blitz' character of a lightning raid attack. Waffen-SS units passing through a village that has just been recaptured. At first the Germans were rather euphoric. Heinz Gaedcke said at the time: 'In the past our forces were often weaker at the outset but we always managed to win.'

Waffen-SS soldiers fighting in the Pilis Heights. The 'Konrad' operations were led by the 'Totenkopf' and the 'Wiking' divisions. Even before the 'Konrad' operations commenced the 'Totenkopf' division had lost an astronomical number of soldiers. 53,794 were dead, wounded and missing. During the same period 'Wiking' had lost 11,098 men.

A 'Sturmgeschütz' from the 'Totenkopf' division passing through a burning Hungarian village in the middle of January. The 'Konrad' III operation finally ran aground at the river Váli. The two Waffen-SS divisions of the IV.SS Pz. corps lost more than 7,000 men in the month of January 1945.

'Konrad' III. The units of the IV.SS Pz corps were able to manoeuvre more easily when they reached the lower-lying land between lakes Balaton and Velencei. 'Wiking' units assembling for the attack.

'Everywhere I went I came across the 'Totenkopf' division', complained the Russian Field Marshal, Zhukov, after the war. In Hungary too the 'Totenkopf' division was one of the most important divisions on the German side. Panzer grenadiers hitch a lift on a tank.

Hellmut Becker, commandant of the 'Totenkopf' division in Hungary. After the war he was accused of sabotage while during work was going on in Stalingrad and he was subsequently executed.

Josef Reichert, commandant of the 711.I.D., a weak unit that had the luck of the war on its side. It was more or less by coincidence that the unit managed to conquer the city of Esztergom. Afterwards the unit was active in the Pilis Heights.

Frühlingserwachen: Hitler's Spring Offensive

'We must emulate Frederick the Great', wrote the Minister of Propaganda, Dr. Joseph Goebbels, on 28th February 1945 in his personal diary. At this time, Goebbels frequently looked to history for his inspiration and for the hope he desperately needed to find. He hoped that, as had indeed once happened with Frederick the Great, the situation on the battlefield would change at the last moment and that things would turn in favour of the losing side. Goebbels certainly needed all the strength he could get. The Red Army had overrun and pillaged the German Reich to the east of the Oder and on the Rhine the western Allied Powers were pushing forward and preparing to penetrate through to the heart of Germany. Hitler, too, seemed to be looking more and more to the past for his strength and inspiration. He had instructed Goebbels to publish many stories about Frederick the Great and about the Punic Wars between Rome and Carthage. He hoped that if matters were placed in a more historic perspective the Germans would be able to understand current events better. As far as Hitler was concerned what was now being decided on the European battlefields was, who would rule Europe for centuries to come. It had to be impressed upon every German civilian and soldier that the future of Germany was at stake. If the Germans wanted to survive, as a nation, they would have to fight to the bitter end.

During these days of turbulence, Goebbels was visited by Sepp Dietrich, commandant of the 6.SS Pz. army which had just been fighting in the Ardennes. Dietrich informed Goebbels of the new plans that Hitler had for Hungary and for the 6. SS Pz. army. The army had received instructions to go to Hungary: it was the last vestige of hope for the Third Reich. Goebbels was very excited about the project and from that day onwards wrote continually about Hungary in his diary. 'We are going to make a new start', he declared. With renewed energy the man pursued his plans. In the special front paper 'Front und Heimat' he wrote articles in flowing prose spurring soldiers on to achieve even greater things.

After the Ardennes offensive had failed, the units of Dietrich's SS Pz. army had withdrawn to the other side of the Rhine to be patched up in an improvised sort of way. Afterwards, in strictest secrecy and by misleading routes, the whole army was transported eastwards. It was an ambitious operation. The railway network was badly damaged which meant that only four train loads of soldiers a day, at the very most, could pass eastwards. On top of this, there was renewed pressure to deploy the very same units on the western front. The situation was simular to that of operation 'Margarethe'. When, in March 1944, the commandants of the South Ukrainian Army Group heard that units were being released to go and occupy Hungary they all wanted to get hold of a division for their own purposes and on the western front the attitude was much the same. In January, a number of the Waffen-SS divisions once again became involved in the aftermath of the Ardennes offensive. At various points it looked as if the Allied Forces were going to break through and Waffen-SS units had to be brought in to stabilize the situation on the front.

Hitler, however, held on fanatically to his original plan to stage one last decisive battle in Hungary and slowly and in accordance with his wishes the trains started rolling again. During that period, Dietrich made his presence known in Berlin in a demonstrative way so that everyone would gain the impression that the Waffen-SS was making its way to the central front, a move which, to Guderian's way of thinking, would have been the only sensible one. In reality, though, the trains went to Győr/Raab) via Vienna. When the 6. SS Pz. army suddenly popped up in the area where the Army Group South was stationed this was, therefore, a big surprise.

The commanders of the Army Group watched in astonishment as the trains and troops arrived. Heinz Gaedcke quickly got on the line to Generalleutnant Von

Grolmann and asked: 'what, in God's name, is the meaning of all these troops?' but he was instantly silenced. The moving in of the 6. SS Pz. army was something that was top secret and, in the end, the initial surprise gave way to a certain sort of optimism. What officer would not be delighted to have this army élite group under his command? Surely this opened up all kinds of opportunities. On the other hand though, they had just returned from the Ardennes offensive which had been a bloody and traumatic experience for all the soldiers involved and anything but a success. The question was, how fit were the Waffen-SS soldiers to fight?

Balck and Gaedcke were both somewhat taken aback by this sudden 'SS invasion' of Hungary. Hungary had not only become a final outpost for the SS-Einsatzkommandos but also for the vast majority of the Waffen-SS. As well as the IV.SS Pz. corps ('Totenkopf' and 'Wiking') and the (ex) IX.SS Geb. corps ('Florian Geyer' and 'Maria Theresia') the I.SS Pz. corps (1.SS Pz.D. 'Leibstandarte Adolf Hitler', 12.SS Pz.D. 'Hitlerjugend') and II.SS Pz. corps (2.SS Pz.D. 'Das Reich', 9.SS Pz.D 'Hohenstaufen') had all arrived in Hungary. The I.SS Pz. corps fell under the command of SS-Gruppenführer Herman Priess; the II.SS Pz. corps was led by SS-Obergruppenführer Wilhelm Bittrich. In addition, there was also, where the 2.Pz. army was stationed, the 13. Waffen Gebirgsdivision der SS 'Handschar' (Croat.nr.1) and the 16. SS Panzer Grenadier Division 'Reichsführer SS'. Finally, there were several smaller Waffen-SS units that went to fight with others on the Hungarian front or helped to back up the Army Group, such as the Hungarian Waffen-SS (the battle group 'Ney') and the Osttürkischen Waffen-SS unit 'Harun al Raschid' (SS-Standartenführer W. Hintersatz).

The units of the 6.SS Pz. army were élite troops that had won their spurs fighting battles on various fronts. The same could not exactly be said of all the Waffen-SS which had served on the Hungarian front. Other qualitatively inferior units (which were not affiliated to the 6.SS Pz. army) were notably those of Islamic origin. 'Handschar' (SS-Brigadeführer Hampel) from Bosnia-Herzegovina had

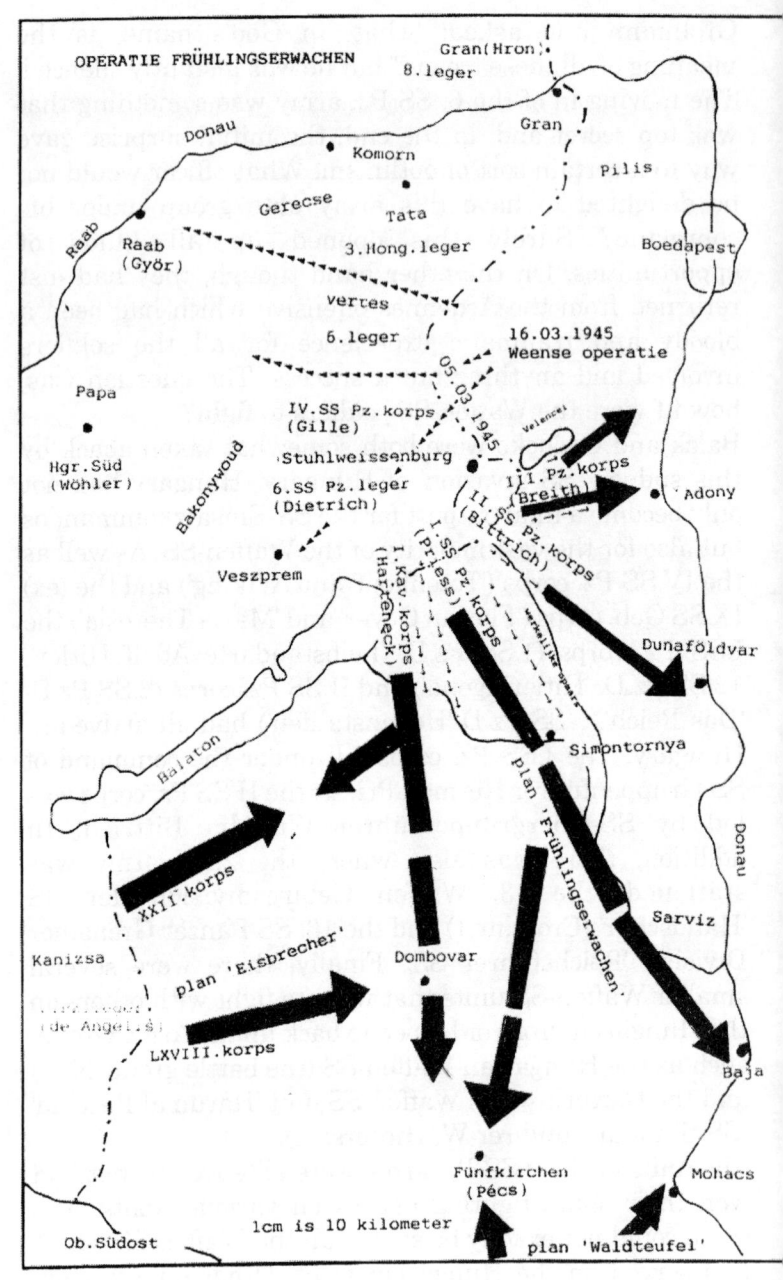

originally fought in the partisan battles staged in Yugoslavia. Despite the great endeavours made by Himmler - he had brought the Palestinian Grossmufti Mohammed Emin el Husseini to Europe and had announced that all Moslims and Nazis had a common enemy (he was referring of course to the Jews) - the unit was not a success. The Moslim soldiers were chiefly interested in directing their efforts towards burning down Croatian Christian villages so Himmler felt forced to divert them to the Hungarian front. 'The unit is completely unreliable', wrote De Angelis in a letter to Wöhler towards the end of January 1945. 'There are too few Germans: only two to every five Bosnians.' Wöhler was well aware of the problem. During a period of reprieve in France the entire division had risen up in protest when one battalion had made a deal with the French Resistance. The days when the Habsburg 'Bosniaken' regiment paraded through the streets of Vienna dressed in their splendid traditional headgear were gone for ever.

The 'Harun el Raschid' unit, formerly the 480 East Turkish battalion consisted of an amalgamation of different ethnic groups. In order to fully identify with his soldiers the unit's German commandant, Hintersatz, had become a Moslim and had changed his name to Harun el Raschid. For a time, the unit had served together with the controversial 'Dirlewanger' brigade, a 'Bewährungseinheit' that had carried out brutal murders in Warsaw. The unit was not suitable for going into battle against regular troops.

All in all the Hungarian front was a curious one, composed of volunteers drawn from a diversity of countries. 'Wiking' was made up of soldiers from The Netherlands, Belgium, Denmark and Norway. In the Army Group there were ethnic Russians and Ukrainians. Bosnians and six Italians (!), 434 Slovakians and Croats and 192 Spaniards (!) served in the 357.I.D.

Balck and Gaedcke had little confidence in the commanding capacities of the SS army. As far as Dietrich

was concerned he was, in Gaedcke's eyes a 'butcher' with 'little military knowledge.'
Indeed, it was true that Joseph ('Sepp') Dietrich, commandant of the SS army, was a typical product of National Socialism. Pride and obeisance were his salient characteristics. He was one of Hitler's confidants and his soldiers idolized him. After the war, the Waffen-SS officer Walter Krüger, of the 12.SS 'Hitlerjugend' division, described Dietrich as a 'people's general'. There were others though who doubted his military capacities and with good reason. Whenever an attack was mounted Sepp always let 'der Rudi' (his right-hand man, Rudolf Lehmann, and later on Generalmajor Krämer, Chief of Staff of the 6.Pz. army) speak for him. Jestingly, Dietrich would then say of his spokesman: 'He's been trained for this'. It was true, though, that in certain sections of the SS, where there was a shortage of General Staff officers, the SS relied heavily on army expertise. Apart from the 6.SS Pz. army there were others who, during the course of time, made use of the army's know-how, such as: the I.SS Pz. corps (Albert Stückler), the II.SS Pz. corps (Pipkorn), the 8.SS 'Florian Geyer' (Von Mitzlaff), the 22.SS 'Maria Theresia' (Erhard Mainka) and the 5.SS 'Wiking' (Kleine). It was in any case so that Dietrich had realized that certain things were best left to the experts. Towards the end of the war Dietrich gradually became more critical of Hitler who, in his eyes, was 'too involved in the details of battle.' On the whole, cooperation within SS units between the army and Waffen-SS officers was good. Stückler described Dietrich as an 'orderly man' with whom he got on well. Jahnke, 'Wiking's' O1., said of Major Kleine who was lost to the division when he had a car accident that he had been 'a good colleague.'

Once again Hitler's generals pored over their maps to think up new plans of action. The situation to the north of the Danube remained worrisome. During the 'Konrad' I operations a Russian bridgehead had been constructed there which was a constant threat to Komárom. Even though at a later stage, during the 'Konrad' III operations, this bridgehead had been substantially reduced in size (thanks to the combined efforts of the 8. and 20.Pz.D.) it still remained a threat. It was very tempting to use the troops of Dietrich's SS army (the I.SS Pz. army had arrived first) that were then trickling in to finally put an end to the problem. Such a plan was not without its dangers though. Wöhler estimated that some 1,000 lives, per SS division, would be lost if the Gran bridgehead were to be destroyed. This would then mean that, as far as the 'Frühlingserwachen' offensive was concerned, the SS units would be severely weakened from the very outset.

Ultimately, the temptation proved too great and Wöhler opted to demolish the Gran bridgehead. The SS corps selected to carry out the task was that of SS-Gruppenführer Herman Priess. The attack of the Russian bridgehead at Gran went down in history as operation 'Südwind'. The operation bore a certain similarity to another secondary operation, that of 'Nordwind' which had been organized in the Alsace during the Ardennes offensive. What both operations had in common was that they were both relatively small-scale. The Red Army's lines had been charted out. The front ran along the following places: Bart - Németszögyén - Bátorkeszi and to Karva and on the Danube. Wöhler aimed to eradicate the projecting defences by organizing a concentric attack. Apart from the Waffen-SS units the Army Group involved a number of other units: the 46.I.D. (Generalmajor Reuter), the 44. Reichs Grenadier D. 'Hoch und Deutschmeister' (Generalleutnant Von Rost), the sPz.Abt. 'FHH' (25 Königstigers commanded by Leutnant Piepgras), the Pz.Abt.208, sections of the 711.I.D. and the 96.I.D. (Rgt.Gruppe Hube) once again, crossed over the Danube, this time in a northern direction.

Operation 'Südwind' commenced on 17th February, four days after the fall of Budapest. It proved to be an operation that went exactly as planned which made it one of the most successful German victories of the last stages of the war. The Germans were even rather surprised at their achievements. 'We were glad to have the opportunity to fight there', said Hans Siegel, commandant of the II./SS Pz.Rgt.12 after the war. 'At last we were no longer threatened by Allied air attacks as we had been in the west. The Russians deployed few of their tanks and even the number of Paks was lower than we had expected. The advance went well.' On 22nd February 1945, the Army Group South conquered the places Bart and Beny which signified the end of the Russian bridgehead.

As far as the Gran bridgehead operation had been concerned Jochen Peiper, commandant of the SS Pz.Rgt.1 managed to achieve what had failed in the Ardennes: a strategic breakthrough. Together with the Königstigers, who effectively destroyed the Soviet Pak and the SS-battle group Hansen (SS Pz.Gren.Rgt.1 under the command of SS-Obersturmbannführer Max Hansen) the Soviet lines were successfully broken through and the German units were able to pan out in all directions. Both battle groups were German units that had built up reputations during the course of the Ardennes offensive as being more or less the best units. Peiper's battle group earned itself a bad reputation when after the war a law suit proved that Peiper and his men had been guilty of murdering many American prisoners of war at Malmedy. The 'Hansen' Group became well-known because after the war most of the few existing photos of the Ardennes offensive featured Hansen's unit in action. After the court, Peiper settled in Traves, in France, where he hoped to be able to enjoy a peaceful old age. Unfortunately, for Peiper though his past caught up with him. One day in the seventies his house was set alight and he died in the fire.

Reports received from the German Army boasted of triumphant victory. In a communiqué issued on 27th February it was stated that the Red Army had lost an estimated 20,000 men. The Soviets had allegedly lost 334 pieces of artillery and Pak. Despite the success of the operation German losses were also substantial. According to statistics in a 'Leibstandarte' biography both Waffen-SS divisions had lost around 1,200 soldiers. SS-Brigadeführer Otto Kumm, an experienced officer who, as early as in 1934, had served with the 'SS-Verfügungstruppe' and had for a time been commandant of the 7.SS Geb.D. 'Prinz Eugen' complained that the 'Leibstandarte' was 'in a sorry state'. Kumm had gone into the battle with thirty Pz.IV, thirty-five Pz.V and twelve Jg.Pz.IV in the SS Pz.Rgt.1. After the battle, the numbers had been substantially reduced and the division was left with twelve Pz.IV, eleven Pz.V and four Jg.Pz.IV.

The 'Hitlerjugend' division had also taken a beating. This unit had been deployed on the right-hand side of the 'Leibstandarte' and during the fight for the Gran bridgehead had lost one of its leading officers, SS-Obersturmbannführer Bernhard Krause who had been decorated with the 'Ritterkreuz', was commandant of the SS Pz.Gren.Rgt.26 and was killed at Muszla. He it was who had once uttered the famous words: 'If we ever win this war I shall write a book about how we should really have lost it.' SS-Sturmbannführer Kostenbader (I./26) then took over command of the regiment.

Priess, commandant of the I.SS Pz. corps, then asked the Army Group if his unit, which had been fighting at the Gran bridgehead, could immediately be relieved so that the troops would have time to prepare for the 'Frühlingserwachen' offensive. On 25th February, the first units were removed from the front.

In the Army Group South's weekly evaluation it was stated that the 211.V.G.D. and the 46.I.D. had both been badly weakened since the time of the battle at the Gran bridgehead.

Relief at the success booked at Gran reverberated around Führer headquarters where, up until then, only bad news had been coming in for months on end. 'Is it really so?' Hitler would keep on asking Hubertus Freiherr Von Humboldt-Dachroeden to which the latter would reply in affirmation: 'Yes it has really been resolved, everything is in order. Both SS divisions have already withdrawn.' 'Magnificent!' Hitler would exclaim. So with this victory behind him Hitler's final military brain-child, operation 'Frühlingserwachen' could see the light of day.

Encouraged by the 'warm recognition' received from Führer headquarters on 27th February Wöhler confidently set about preparing for the final ordeal. Once again the plans made were ambitious but the objective remained the same: to cleanse the western bank of the Danube, thus, opening up chances for further offensives in an easterly direction. 'I shall present Hitler with the oil fields at Ploesti in Romania on his 56th birthday', bragged Dietrich. Wöhler was, however, less optimistic and not least of all because of the low fuel reserves within the Army Group South. Despite all the boring for oil that had been initiated by Albert Speer in Hungary the troops were still threatened with chronic fuel shortages. This firstly had to do with the fact that Speer's production levels had been disappointing. Because of all the war activities the refineries at Almásfüsitö, Petfürdö and Szöny had all been put out of action. Wöhler questioned whether, even without any opposition from the Soviets, they would have fuel reserves enough to even reach Ploesti. On top of this, there were other problems facing the Army Group. The western part of Hungary was becoming increasingly overrun by large numbers of refugees who were fleeing from Stalin's troops. Some of these people were also drawing on the Army Group's medical facilities which were already overburdened. For instance, between 4th January and 17th March 1945 the 6.Pz.D. military hospital dealt with no less than 1,417 patients, evidence enough that the medical services were under great pressure. Every extra burden on the hospital was detrimental to the first aid emergency services. The Army Group was also desperately short of ammunition (just as with fuel they made use of secret supplies) and there was never time to reply to letters from the home front.
After a brief visit to Führer headquarters in the middle of February 1945, Wöhler felt a little more optimistic about

things. It seemed that Hitler had not lost the power to influence his subordinates and even Wöhler was somewhat 'hypnotized' by him. At first, it had seemed as though it would be a difficult meeting. Four alternative plans for ways of deploying the 6.SS Pz. army in Hungary had been put forward. Hitler and the Army Group did not agree, though. With the successful 'Südwind' operation still in the backs of their minds Wöhler and Balck were interested in keeping the operation small and manageable. The A and B plans which both involved mounting attacks chiefly in a northern direction (between the Danube and lake Balaton) were the two that matched their philosophy best. Hitler did not wish to hear of these plans and settled for plan C2 which involved a 6.SS Pz. army attack in a southerly direction supported by the 2.Pz. army ('Eisbrecher') and Ob.Southeast ('Waldteufel') which would attack in a northern direction. Hitler no longer had any trust in mounting an operation in the Gerecse and Pilis Heights. Just as during the 'Konrad' II operations when Wöhler also hardly dared to speak up, he once again became stunned into silence. He reported in the diary that Hitler was 'resolute' and 'confident' and that it would, therefore, indeed be best to adhere to his plans. Wöhler presumed that Hitler had more ideas up his sleeve such in the form of diplomatic plans or miraculous new weapons but in fact he did not. Even Balck was convinced. He knew that Wöhler was no National Socialist and that he could therefore take such statements made by him seriously.

When the units took up their starting positions, the situation looked impressive in theory at least. Of the 36 Army Group South divisions the Germans had combined eleven divisions in the main direction of attack. This main thrust consisted of four army corps that were to make a sweep in a southerly direction. A further four divisions linked up with the 2.Pz. army and another four went with the Ob.Southeast. This meant that the German attack base was nineteen divisions strong, exactly the same number as during the Ardennes offensive. The offensive

*'The 6.SS Pz. army is called the sixth because it only has six tanks left',
quipped Sepp Dietrich at the end of the war. To the left of the photo is a
German armoured vehicle that is missing a front wheel. The Waffen-SS
units could also no longer pass as élite units.*

Februar 1945. Soldiers of the German 8.8 (Flak) anti-aircraft division wait to see what is going to happen. As far as Hitler was concerned this operation in Hungary was to be the final and decisive battle of the Second World War. To make the opposition as strong as possible Hitler sent the last reserves of the Third Reich to the Hungarian front. Hundreds of tanks and almost 1,000 armoured vehicles assembled for what was to be the 'Ardennes offensive' of the east.

group consisted of somewhere between 220,000 and 240,000 soldiers. The four Waffen-SS divisions provided 271 tanks and motorized guns and 938 SPW with a number of extra tanks from other army units. Generalmajor Von Radowitz's 51 tanks from the 23 Pz.D. formed the reserve. On the northern flank, the 6. SS Pz. army was protected by Balck's 6. army. To the south of lake Balaton were the units of General De Angelis. His troops had been divided up into two corps (the XXII Geb. corps and the LXVIII. corps), which were commanded respectively by General der Gebirgstruppe Lanz and General der Gebirgstruppe Konrad. Just as with the Waffen-SS's units two divisions of these units formed the core of the so-called spearhead group. They were: the 13. Waffen Geb.D. of the SS 'Handschar' (under SS-Brigadeführer Hampel) and the 16.SS Pz.Gren.D. 'Reichsführer-SS' (of SS-Oberführer Baum). The Ob.Southeast provided the 291.I.D. and the 11.Lw.Feld D. for the front line.

Meanwhile, the Red Army that was having to face up to all these German troops had not been idle. Since the time of operation 'Südwind', the Soviets had been aware of the fact that there were new SS units on the front. Field Marshal S.K. Timoshenko had been brought in to draw up new plans for the Russian front and to reinforce the 2. and 3. Ukrainian front. Timoshenko planned to mount a Russian offensive as soon as possible, but not after first having let the Germans exhaust themselves in their offensive. The Red Army had always been very good at providing deep defence lines. On the western bank of the Danube four armies were laid on to combat the German attacking forces. The Russian troops were able to profit from the favourable lie of the waterways on their side (the Sárviz-Malom canal) behind which they could take cover. The 3. Ukrainian front had 400,000 soldiers and the 2. Ukrainian front had more than 500,000 soldiers. They had at their disposal more than 1,000 tanks. Finally, when the time was ripe for battle Timoshenko read the latest reports. He replaced some officers like, for instance,

General Zacharov of the 4.G. army who was taken over by General Zachvatejev and then sat back and waited for the Germans to open up their attack. Arrows pointing towards Pressburg (Bratislava), Brünn, Vienna and Nagykanizsa, the 2.Pz. army's oil area, had already been placed on the map. Timoshenko guessed that the battle would begin around 15th March. It almost seemed as if he could look into the future ...

'Frühlingserwachen' started on 6th March at 4 a.m. and from the very start just about everything that could go wrong did go wrong. The troops of Dietrich's attacking forces were up against heavy resistance from the Red Army. Since the thaw had set in, the roads had turned into mud-baths which inevitably delayed progress along roads that were already poor in the first place. The Red Army had dotted the whole of the route with minefields, bunkers and trenches. The soldiers were up against electronically activated flame-throwers. All in all, the situation was very reminiscent of 1914-1918 conditions. On the German side, something peculiar happened though when the battle began. At the front section detended by Bittrich's II.SS Pz. corps, there was no movement while a little to the south, where the I.SS Pz. corps was operating, the troops of the 'Leibstandarte' and the 'Hitlerjugend' had already started the offensive. It was not until 18.30 that the units of 'Das Reich' - in other words, not even the entire corps - stationed in the II.SS.Pz. corps' area, came into action.

The attacks mounted by 'Leibstandarte' and the 'Hitlerjugend' were certainly not spectacular. Under katsusja fire and hampered by the conditions and obstacles described above they plodded onwards. The 'Leibstandarte' proceeded along the Szabadbattyán - Tác - Csösz - Soponya - Káloz route with the 'Hitlerjugend' division fighting further to the south along the Kisláng Dég road. The Germans were quite intimidated by the Russian defence system. After their victory at Oedön Puszta, the commandant of the Nachrichten-Abt.12 'Hitlerjugend', Walter Krüger, walked through the city

215

and reported: 'The Russians had four 'Sperrigels', arranged one behind the other, all of which were well screened off and capable of firing in two directions. They had remained in their positions until the end because the corpses were still there.'

The units of Harteneck's I.Kav. corps, operating to the south of the I.SS Pz. corps, came up against similar problems. Only a few kilometres from where it had set off the whole 'Frühlingserwachen' operation ground to a halt. The atmosphere within the Army Group was very strained and tension between the army and the Waffen-SS only mounted. Heinz Guderian was enraged and he telephoned Sepp Dietrich who, on the night of 5th March, had assured Guderian that the 6.SS Pz. army was fully prepared for battle. How then was it possible that the II.SS Pz. corps had got off to such a late start? Dietrich did not know what to say and turned to Wilhelm Bittrich for help, the II.SS Pz. corps commandant. Bittrich could only complain at length about the huge amount of mud in which his troops had got bogged down. This, he explained, had been the cause of the delay and the reason why his men were so tired out. Another problem facing the troops at the front had been the fact that there had only been one access road, the road through Székesfehérvár which had led to such blockages that the panzer grenadiers had gone ahead on foot to the area they had to fight from. Guderian was not at all happy with this excuse. Bittrich had most probably simply made a mistake in estimating how much time would be needed to get to the 'Frühlingserwachen' starting positions and talking with Dietrich was getting Guderian nowhere.

After the war, the 'Chef des Stabes' of the I.SS Pz. corps, Albert Stückler, was not surpised: 'Bittrich was a very closed man, hard to fathom. Above all else, he was obstinate and not afraid of heavy criticism.' The Army Group South was indeed made up of a strange mixture of bizarre officers. The only person they all seemed to truly respect was the individual who goaded them on in these

Josef (Sepp) Dietrich, commandant of the 6.SS Pz. army. After the Ardennes offensive had failed the SS army had a 'second chance' to prove itself in Hungary. The whole operation was a huge disaster. 'Frühlingserwachen' began on 6th March 1945. Ten days later the Red Army opened up a devastating counter-offensive in the direction of Vienna. Dietrich, the highest Waffen-SS general feared arrest by the SS.

Maximillian de Angelis, commandant of the 2.Pz. army. It was his responsibility to protect the Hungarian oil fields. Because De Angelis had been given this one task Hitler had heavily restricted his operational scope.

utterly irrational military operations: Adolf Hitler. After the war, Heinz Gaedcke said: 'We were all caught up in the mad pursuit of that 'phantom': oil'. The way the operation was executed appeared to be as peculiar as the whole plan itself. The troops marched on without protest though perhaps privately they did have their misgivings.

In defence of Bittrich it should be said that the III.Pz. corps that was fighting on the north flank of the II.SS Pz. corps did not do much better. It is also conceivable that the state of the terrain where Bittrich and Breith were fighting was worse than in the area where Priess and Von Harteneck were waging war. The 3.Pz.D. which, during the 'Konrad' III operations had been very mobile, was hardly able to get started on 6th March. Bittrich finally moved into the offensive with a delay of fourteen and a half hours. Several times before getting going Bittrich had announced that the attack was about to start, but each time they only made small hesitant moves.

The shock of the developments of the first day was not eased by ensuing events. Though the Germans did admittedly gain some ground the whole battle was more reminiscent of a struggle between two phalanxes in ancient Greece than twentieth century mobile warfare. Already on 6th March, Wöhler knew that this was going to be no lightning raid attack. When in conversation with Dietrich, Wöhler had said, 'mud and new falls of snow have definitely ruined all the plans'. It was perfectly obvious that with so much mud on the ground any large-scale manoeuvres with tanks would be quite unthinkable. Like Wöhler, Dietrich was sombre about the prospects but not utterly without hope. When the fighting continued on 7th March in light snow Dietrich maintained that a breakthrough was not totally out of the question. He was concerned about the northern flank of the attack line, though, where Balck's 6. army stood. He was afraid that the German lines would be attacked at that point and Dietrich's intuitions were later proved right. Hermann Balck however, remained absurdly optimistic about their chances of stopping an attack on the northern flank of the 'Frühlingserwachen' operation.

On 8th March, Bittrich's units seemed to make a little more impact. Fierce fighting continued in the Sárosd - Aba - Káloz region. Aba was conquered on 12th March and units from the 'Das Reich' and 'Hoch und Deutschmeister' pushed forwards towards Káloz and Heinrich Major. At Káloz, the 44.I.D. managed to build a bridge over the canal there. The I.SS Pz. corps conquered Nagyhörcsökpuszta on 8th March and afterwards a group of mixed regiments, led by the SS officer Hans Siegel, conquered the town of Dég. The attack had been planned to start at sunrise and turned out to be an assault in which Siegel's 'Jagdpanther' was destroyed. Siegel did not allow himself to be daunted. Through the morning mist he rode into the city pillion on a motor bike and was able to see the Soviet assault units retreating. The I.SS Pz. corps' attack was halted at Simontornya.

To the north and to the south of where the Waffen-SS corps were fighting it was a similar story. At Breith on the northern flank, particularly heavy fighting developed between Dr. Köning's sPz.Abt.509 and the Soviet assault units. The predicaments of the 2.Pz. army and Ob.Southeast were not much better. At first, De Angelis had gained some ground but his attack came to a standstill near to Nagybajom-Jákó. At this stage feelings started to run high again between the army and the Waffen-SS. Hauptmann Steinbrenner of the II./211 got into an argument with a 16.SS Pz.Gren.D. 'Reichsführer SS' battalion. The latter battalion wanted to go into the attack before artillery reinforcements had arrived. Steinbrenner wanted to hear nothing of this reckless plan so the SS continued on their own and practically the whole battalion was wiped out. The Waffen-SS had experience of fighting in the Italian mountains, but here on the slopes of the Hungarian hillside vineyards they succumbed to defeat. De Angelis lost more than 500 of his men, a further 3,000 were injured and 150 went missing. The Red Army left behind

1,700 soldiers killed in action, 1,000 were imprisoned and 43 tanks were lost.

The Ob.Southeast did its best with troops which could hardly be said to qualify as army regulars. Most of the soldiers in the Ob.Southeast had up until then only fought against partisans. The only bit of good fortune for the Ob.Southeast was that when they came to the bridgehead over the river Drava the opposition, chiefly composed of Tito partisans and Bulgarian troops, was on the whole weak. At this stage, the troops were at least equally matched but the losses were heavy. On 7th March the Germans lost 700 men at the Drava due to death or injury.

After ten days of fighting, it was time to take stock of the depressing situation. The Army Group had lost 14,818 soldiers, 2,451 of whom had been killed. Forty-eight tanks had been destroyed and more than 1,000 men were missing. According to German records 5,100 Red Army soldiers had been killed, 1,300 had been taken prisoner and 210 tanks and 407 pieces of Pak and artillery had been lost.

By 16th March, patience had run out at Führer headquarters. Hitler demanded a breakthrough and urged the III.Pz. corps and both SS corps to get together and mount a combined attack. While Wöhler busily deliberated on the matter the Soviets drew their conclusions. Tismoshenko had a time schedule of his own to keep to. With deep satisfaction he had seen how the German attacker had been defeated by the solidity of the Russian defence system. Twenty-three Soviet divisions had successfully weathered the assault mounted by the eleven German spearhead units. Meanwhile, the 6.G.Pz. army which had moved in from the area to the north of the Danube had arrived on the scene. From war maps that have been preserved we can deduce that, at this stage, Wöhler was not fully aware of what was going on. The Soviets had noticed a weak link in the chain: a point on the northern flank of the German front that was being defended by Balck's 6. army.

By 14th March, 80% of the units called up by the Red Army had assembled and on 16th March the attack began with a devastating barrage of artillery fire. The sound of the thundering Soviet cannons drowned everything else. Where the 4. and 46. armies were stationed there were, in places, 160 to 170 cannons per kilometre of front. The 9.G army was brought forward from the reserves and, in short, the Red Army started to smell blood. The Army Group South waited in trepidation. The Germans firmly dug in their heels. They realized that now the initiative would be coming from the east. During the 'Konrad' III operations German soldiers had marched along the banks of the Danube but that felt like a long time ago. The Germans had barely moved forty kilometres from their starting positions. The water of the Danube flowed from the west, from Vienna! Now things had frozen over again and so once more the tanks could start moving.

The German military tragedy in Hungary was not the only disaster. On the western front, too the situation was deteriorating fast. At the end of February, Dresden had been bombed by the Allied Forces and on 5th March Cologne had fallen into the hands of the western Allies. On 7th March, one day after the start of 'Frühlingserwachen', the bridge at Remagen was seized, undamaged, by the 1. American army. The Rhine front was penetrated and Von Rundstedt had to clear the way for Albert Kesselring.
While Hitler and Goebbels discussed the historic importance of all their battles real history was no longer being decided on the battlefields. Between 4th and 12th February, the leaders of the Allied Powers had come together at Yalta for a political debate the main issue of which was the future of Europe. The time was ripe for bringing the Second World war to a military conclusion.

The Retreat to the Reichsschutzstellung

The Germans were taken completely unawares when, on 16th March 1945 (ten days after the start of 'Frühlingserwachen'), the Russian 'war machine' came into action in the Viennese operation. Just as during the fighting at Stalingrad, the risks taken with Balck's 6.army on the northern flank were great from the start. The Germans deployed Hungarian units and depleted German divisions. They were having to contend with a perpetual shortage of troops, but they hoped that operation 'Frühlingserwachen' would keep the Red Army occupied. The cannonade of 16th March adequately demonstrated that Timoshenko had more than enough troops to cover both stategic moves at once, in other words, to hold out against the new style 'Frühlingserwachen' while at the same time opening up an offensive on the Army Group's weaker northern flank.

Though the Germans were not sure about the magnitude of the Russian offensive, early entries in the Army Group's diary intimate that they were certainly taking the Russian attack very seriously. Soviet successes were recorded in the usual way: the hugeness of the Red Army was emphasized and this was used to explain away and indeed excuse any possible failure on the side of the Germans. 'Vast masses of infantry', 'huge groups', and 'massive assault attacks' were the kind of superlatives used to minimize the brilliance of Timoshenko's operation. The Viennese operation was simply a specimen of excellent military planning. The Red Army made good use of the defence means at its disposal. The Germans were allowed to bleed dry at a time when the ground was muddy. When things started to freeze over again, making the roads easier to go, the Red Army opened up its new offensive, one day later than planned.

Where the front lines were composed chiefly of Hungarian units, the Red Army found it easy to break through. Under the pressure of seven infantry divisions (and six reserve divisions) the Vertes front soon collapsed. Alongside these troops there was also the 6.G.Pz. army which the Red Army temporarily kept in reserve. The Russians would carefully seek out the weakest spots in the German-Hungarian defence lines and then attack at those very points with huge numbers of tanks. It soon became apparent that virtually the entire front in the Vertes mountain region was rapidly crumbling. Most hard hit by the Soviet attack was Colonel Schell's 1. Hungarian Kav.D., General Von Zsedenyi's 2. Hungarian Pz.D. and 'Totenkopf', the 3.SS Pz.D. of Helmuth Becker. Exhausted from fighting the 'Konrad' battles Becker's soldiers were easily split up. Before the battle began, both Hungarian divisions were so severely depleted that it had been concluded in assessment reports made at the time that they were really only fit for small defensive activities. It was no coincidence these units were the ones to receive the full blast of the Soviet attack.

Up until then relationships within the Army Group had been strained but now things quickly came to a head. Explicit orders had been received from Hitler to bring together various forces and let them push through the Russian defence lines. However, at the same time German officers were doing their level best to quickly find out what was happening on the northern flank. 'There is much drumfire but we cannot tell where the centre of gravity lies', noted 'Wiking's' 01. in his diary. Wöhler, too, was none the wiser but very soon he received word that the Hungarian units were fleeing en masse and at first it seemed that only two possible options were open to him. Either, he could opt to continue attacking in the vague hope of still making a breakthrough and forcing the Red Army into the defensive or, in the light of developments in the Vertes mountains, he could decide to call off the whole attack. Eventually, Wöhler went for a compromise. He decided to continue attacking while at the same time creating up a new defence line to the west of the Vertes mountains.

After consulting Heinz Guderian, Dietrich was given the thankless task of having to lead the immediate attack. In the Army Group diary mention is made of the 'relentless combat' that was envisaged and Guderian and Wöhler argued: 'We were capable of such breakthroughs in the past weren't we!' It seemed that now the postulations of German military leaders really were completely divorced from any sense of reality. Guderian, though, of all people, should have known better. The days of the French campaign and of leading his units forward a hundred kilometres a day only to astonish Führer headquarters with news of their amazing progress, 'we have reached the Swiss border!' were long gone. Only the 'Konrad' III and 'Südwind' operations bore a taste of the old-style manoeuvres.

At 21.30 hours on the evening of 16th March when Dietrich began to regroup his 6. (SS) Pz. army, General Balck's frontline was collapsing. Wöhler had hoped that he would be able to deal with this by assembling his troops on the western side of the Vertes mountains. In retrospect, though, his efforts were absurd. The Gren. Brigade 92 (mot.) (the battle group Lentz) was brought in the first section of which reached the area at 17.35 hours on 17th March and also the Pz.A.A.1 (of Major Dr. Koehler) and parts of the 96.I.D. and the 356.I.D. Where the latter two infantry divisions were concerned this involved troops of barely 500 soldiers. The battle group Lentz was a strange unit, since the French campaign it had been composed of German soldiers who had served in the French foreign legion. The unit formed a penitentiary battalion which operated in the Balkans as a 'fire brigade'. These troops were backed up by the 403 Volks Art. corps.

It goes without saying that these German units did not stand a chance against the powerful Soviet army. Nevertheless, Balck, within whose domain these battles were being fought, remained incredibly optimistic. He was convinced that his reserves were strong enough to stand up to the Soviet force but this was definitely not the case. These 'reserves' consisted of a number of battalions with a mere fighting force of some 50 men per unit! The Hungarian units at the front were utterly demoralized and the IV.SS Pz. corps that had fought during the 'Konrad' operations and had lost 7,000 men was very depleted. Wöhler and Balck began to argue about the situation. At the time, Wöhler wrote in the Army Group diary: 'Balck is showing his familiar optimism, even though there are no grounds for optimism'.

Early in the morning of 17th March, at 00.45 hours, Wöhler received a message from Heinz Gaedcke giving more clarity on the Red Army's offensive and movements. The Russians had already pushed passed Mór and captured Csákberény. During the course of the day two dangerous encirclements began in which the majority of the Army Group South soldiers could easily have been defeated. The Russian 4.G. army and 9.G. army moved southwards from Székesfehérvár threatening to corner the 6. SS Pz. army by forcing it towards lake Balaton. Meanwhile, the 46. army progressed northwards from a region to the north of Székesfehérvár thus threatening to surround huge sections of Balck's 6. army by pushing it towards the Danube. On 17th March, Wöhler had at first believed that Dietrich's offensive would continue but when he saw how the fighting was going he gradually realized that 'Frühlingserwachen' was over for good.

It was then that the Army Group received a little support. Hitler was by now as disappointed with 'Frühlingserwachen' as he had been with 'Konrad' so he agreed the very same day to allow the offensive to be stopped, but on one condition. Ever worried about the oil reserves Hitler commanded that 'Frühlingserwachen' could only be halted if the oil fields near to where the 2.Pz. army was fighting were not in any kind of danger. Wöhler put in a request for one division of the 2.Pz. army to be released in order to support the troops on the northern flank, he had in mind the 16.SS D. or the 1.V.Geb.D., but his request was flatly refused. Hitler hoped that once things had stabilized on the front it might be possible to resume the offensive and he commanded the 2 Pz. army to continue its attack. Wöhler promised to obey this order, because he would have done anything to escape from the

'Frühlingserwachen' operation. He recorded that they had agreed on a 'solution', but at the time of writing that he could not possibly have foreseen how bloody the fighting ahead would be.

Dietrich was ordered to stop the attack and regroup his soldiers. This time they were not going to march to the east but towards the north-west, roughly in the direction of Györ (Raab). The Waffen-SS commandant understood what this meant: a march back towards the Austrian border. All dreams of obtaining oil from Ploesti could now be definitely forgotten. The soldiers would simply have to be glad if they could escape in time from an area that was rapidly becoming encircled. The northern arc of the Red Army energetically unfurled itself on 18th March along the Veszprém - Pápa - Tét - Ménföcsanak line. The industrial area of Tatabánya came under threat and the 96.I.D. and 711.I.D. troops were driven ever closer to the Danube. Meanwhile 'Totenkopf' held its own in the Mór region, while 'Wiking' remained in Székesfehérvár, on the periphery of the offensive. There the Germans were able to hold off the Soviet attack, though the division's 'Westland' Regiment remained under heavy artillery fire.

The southern advance of the Red Army, in the direction of Várpalota, quickly gained ground and began to constitute the biggest threat to Dietrich's SS army. Priess' and Bittrich's SS panzer corps were forced to retreat in haste towards Györ, but this was easier said than done. The SS officers who had hardly had time to get used to the new style 'Frühlingserwachen' were once again required to regroup along the few roads which existed while at the same time coping with acute fuel shortages. Apart from anything else big sections of the SS troops, notably Bittrich's 'Das Reich' (the III./'Der Führer' at Heinrich Major) were prevented from moving by the presence of the Soviets and had no choice but to retreat while fighting. The 'Das Reich' division which had lost Ostendorf, its divisional commandant, was being led by Karl Kreutz.

The Germans were deeply disappointed about the most recent series of defeats. The Hungarians in particular were blamed for the whole military failure. In the Army

Group diary Wöhler recorded that: 'the Hungarians flee wildly from the Russians; their fighting capacity is nil'. The Germans assiduously sought new reinforcements to boost the Army Group. The brand new 232.Pz.D., commanded by Oberst Freiherr Von Ohlen, was immediately brought in. It was a division that had been created during the last year of the war and was composed of soldiers from the Pz.Feld.Ausb.D. 'Tatra' and had only a weak armoured section (Gem.Pz.Abt. 'Tatra') with antiquated Pz.Kw-III. and IV. tanks and four battalions of panzer grenadiers.

In the night of 19th March, the long awaited breakthrough from Dietrich's SS army finally came, literally at the very last minute because, after the success of the infantry breakthrough, the Red Army had now also wheeled its 6.G.Pz. army tanks into the battle. The unit was commanded by a young and energetic tank General by the name of Kravschenko and it seemed that the Soviets were determined to get rid of the SS-Waffen élite group once and for all. On 20th March, units of the I.SS Pz. corps, the 'Leibstandarte Adolf Hitler' and the 'Hitlerjugend' division became entangled in one of the columns of Russian tanks that had broken through the German lines. Though the German troops found themselves in an extremely perilous predicament they were able once again to prove that, even while beating a retreat, they were capable of putting up a good fight. In the chaotic struggle that followed some 31 Soviet tanks went up in flames.

The Red Army was able to recover its losses with remarkable ease. In no time, new tanks could be seen rolling onto the battlefield. Field Marshal Tolbukhin had deployed no less than 42 infantry divisions in the battle. The 'gate' to the north through which Dietrich had to fight and pass with his troops became narrower and narrower until finally it was only two and a half kilometres wide. Eventually, between 21st and 23rd March they effected a breakthrough. The entire operation was vaguely reminiscent of the German exodus from Budapest. Once

An inglorious finale. The last remnants of the 6.SS Pz. army being gathered up together by the Red Army. 'Panther' tanks abandoned on the roadside because they have run out of fuel. The tank at the front is possibly one from the Pz.Abt.208.

again, the units had been forced to run the gauntlet, though, now the Germans were more powerful than they had been in the Gerecse and Pilis Heights in February 1945.

Nevertheless, the casualties were shockingly high. Von Radowitz's 23.Pz.D. was partly trampled under foot. The Austrian 44.I.D, proud bearer of the 'Hoch und Deutsch Meister' order founded in 1526, was surrounded by the Red Army at Jenö. Panic broke out in the ranks and Generalleutnant Von Rost pleaded for help in one radio message after another. The 1.Pz.D. promised to do what they could to help but by this time the Austrian troops were under heavy fire and simply could not wait any longer.

Von Rost summoned together all his units and endeavoured, on his own strength, to take them battling through the passage that would lead to freedom. The entire exercise was a major disaster. The infantry division which had broken off slowly from the II.SS Pz. corps and had got off to a sluggish start had become a sitting target. The Red Army managed to wrap no less than five lines around the division. Von Rost then gathered the few armoured units he had, put them in the middle of his troops, placed the 131 and 132 grenadier regiments on the flanks and opened up a desperate offensive. They managed to break through three of the Soviet lines and then a grenade hit the SPW of the divisional commandant. Von Rost, Ia Major Vogel and the Ia Schreiber Vojacek were all killed in the confusion. The commandant of the 'Nachrichten-Abteilung', Major Mack and the 01 of the 132 Gren.Rgt., Leutnant Zimmerhackl were also killed in the same battle. The commandant of the Art.Rgt.196, Oberst Siehl was heavily wounded.

The 'Hoch und Deutschmeister' division was virtually obliterated altogether. In his memoirs written after the war Balck commented with regret, 'it was the only big unit under my command to be lost in the whole of the Second World War' and that was true enough. The few survivors were not left in peace. Oberst Hoffmann now took command and Rönnefarth was the new Ia. The Army

Group which was unable to miss any soldiers kept the unit in the field. By this stage, it was not a real battlefield situation any more. The Germans poured back towards Vienna and towards the Reichsschutzstellung, a series of weak fortifications on the Austrian-Hungarian border which, perhaps like the Margarethe Stellung of January 1945, might be able to provide some protection.

Now that most of the troops were retreating it was becoming impossible to hold on to the city of Székesfehérvár where 'Wiking' had entrenched itself. Gille and Karl Ullrich, divisional commandant of 'Wiking' attempt in a maintaining radio contact to follow the confused fighting going on around them. There was great unrest among the soldiers stranded in the city. Rumour had it that the Führer had issued orders to turn Székesfehérvár into a military stronghold. If this was true it would mean that the 'Wiking' soldiers would have to remain in the city and defend each and every house until the bitter end. Everybody knew what that would mean in practice. The division would be forced to go through what the Waffen-SS divisions 'Florian Geyer' and 'Maria Theresia' had been through in Budapest. On 21st March, a life-saving order arrived. Gille was instructed to break out of the city with all the equipment that was still mobile and head towards Urhida. Needless to say, the soldiers did not need to be told to leave. They left immediately and the very same evening 6.G.Pz army tanks entered the city. 'Everyone is on the move, where can we find a closed front?' wrote Günter Jahnke, 'Wiking's' O1 in his diary.

In contrast to the 'HuDm' and 23Pz.D., 'Wiking's' retreat went quite well. On 22nd March it was possible to withdraw Gille's and Karl Ullrich's units back as far as Papkeszi where Silvester Stadler, commandant of the 9.SS Pz.D. 'Hohenstaufen' and Hermann Breith, commandant of the III.Pz. corps congratulated them on their escape. Gille told of the rumours emanating from the orders made by the Führer that the city of Székesfehérvár was to become a 'Festung', but Breith merely shrugged his shoulders. It was one of the few occasions on the

Hungarian battlefield when the SS-Waffen and the army were actually in agreement with each other, though, Breith had refused to officially cover 'Wiking's' retreat.
Supported by the Flak Abt.I./25 the 9.SS D. 'Hohenstaufen' remained on the front longer than had originally been planned so that 'Wiking' might be given the chance to withdraw its troops. This precipitated heavy fighting with the Red Army in which many Soviet tanks were destroyed. Wöhler was not at all impressed by this stubborn operation of Stadler's. In the light of the commotion that had surrounded the delayed start of Bittrich's II.SS Pz. corps at the beginning of the 'Frühlingserwachen' operation, of which 'Hohenstaufen' had been a part, it was very easy to understand Wöhler's annoyance. Wöhler and Dietrich met each other at the headquarters of Bittrich's II.SS Pz. corps and the Army Group commandant immediately accused Stadler of insubordination and of having been slow off the mark. Dietrich quickly came to Stadler's rescue, the man whom he regarded as an 'excellent divisional commandant.' The truth of the matter was that the 9.SS was just not as fast as it used to be for the simple reason that it only had a mere 30% of the rolling vehicles it used to have.

At any rate, the atmosphere rapidly deteriorated. On 21st March, Varpalota fell into the hands of the Red Army, on 23rd March the Germans lost Veszprem and on 24th March Wöhler informed Guderian that he would deal remorselessly with any deserter he encountered. Behind the retreating front special units were set up for the express purpose of executing deserters under the motto: 'He who gives in to cowardice will die in shame.' Wöhler who had never dared to stand up to Hitler now showed no mercy towards his own soldiers.

In executing deserters no differentiation was made between army and Waffen-SS soldiers. According to Balck not all that many men were killed. The operation partly derived from a general feeling within the Army Group that people had really expected more of the Waffen-SS élite troops. The Waffen-SS, throughout the war the armed combat unit of Himmler's SS imperium, was now having to fight for its life like any other German army unit. With the fall of the Third Reich now clearly in view, a degree of respect for these 'political' soldiers which had perhaps even been combined with a certain amount of hidden fear was slowly disappearing. It was easy to understand why ordinary army officers were so averse to Waffen-SS soldiers who had always behaved in such a superior way, were equipped with the best weapons and who had generally established for themselves an aura of being 'the chosen few'. On the other hand, in being at the forefront of many of the battles the Waffen-SS had been forced to pay a heavy price for this image of theirs and in Hungary they had simply done their very best. It was partly because of the negative reports continually streaming in from Balck that Wöhler's criticism started to become harsher, thus, prompting him to be as direct and as personal as he was with Stadler for instance.

Dietrich was well aware of the fact that his units were no longer of the same calibre as those that he had commanded at Koersk in 1943. Dietrich told Otto Wöhler about the 8,500 soldiers lost in the Ardennes and about how a mere 3,500 men had subsequently been brought in to compensate the loss, the vast majority of whom came from the German navy and air force. Several hundred Ukrainian volunteers had also been brought in. After the war, Albert Stückler of the I.SS Pz. corps was able to verify the story told by Dietrich of the situation with his troops. The 6.SS Pz. army was not really a military élite anymore.

Papkeszi was nothing more than the mid point of what was to become a massive exodus. Barely a week later, at 14.30 on 30th March 1945, 'Wiking' reached the 'Reichsschutzstellung' - also sometimes known as the 'Raabstellung' - which formed a boundary between the German Reich (now Austria) and Hungary. 'What a return to the homeland', Jahnke bewailed in his diary. 'The roads are packed with refugees and units returning from battle. Amidst the chaos the gendarmes and officers do their best to create some semblance of order but wioth no succes. The 'Reichsschutzstellung' has been inadequately fortified and the reinforcements are guarded by poorly armed infantrymen of the 'Volkssturm'. At Jennersdorf, on our right flank, the Red Army has broken through the front lines. Our first job will therefore be to win back our fortifications.'

During these days of disorganized retreat, 'Wiking' lost one of its controversial officers, Fritz Vogt. He was badly wounded during a Red Army air raid on 2nd April 1945. When SS-Oberführer Karl Ullrich heard what had happened he rushed to the scene of the accident and pinned his own 'Eichenlaub' on Vogt's lapel because he knew that this was the award the dying officer had always wanted to receive. After Vogt's death the medal was returned to Ullrich who still has it in his possession. On the balcony of the old people's home in Bad Reichenhall where he now lives Ullrich showed me his glistening Ritterkreuz and Eichenlaub with ornamental shoulder-pieces which he keeps behind glass in a small show-case with a wooden frame. It was strange to think that for a day one of those medals had been worn by Fritz Vogt, the man so feared by his soldiers that they would have preferred the presence of Russian T-34 tanks to his presence. Behind Ullrich rose the Bavarian Alps. We were not far from Berghof and Hitler's eagle's nest, the place where Horthy had once been forced to listen for hours on end to Hitler's monologues and where Ullrich's sister had worked as a servant. 'Shall I drive you there?' asked Ullrich the eighty-three year old one-time divisional commandant of 'Wiking'.

Army Group war reports of events during this period confirm the situation sketched above. The Army Group South division was completely exhausted from the five different offensive operations carried out in Hungary during 1945. According to assessment reports of the time as many as twenty-four divisions were only fit for carrying out light defence activities. The list also included famous divisions such as 'Das Reich' which by then had only seven (!) tanks left. In the I.SS Pz. corps things were not much better. SS-Brigadeführer Otto Kumm, commandant of the 'Leibstandarte Adolf Hitler', once the crème de la crème of the German army, complained that his men were overtired and kept falling asleep while under artillery fire. Likewise, divisional officers often kept falling asleep during strategic talks.

In withdrawing towards Győr (Raab) Dietrich's panzer army had changed places with Balck's 6. army as if they had castled. The dream of making Hungary a stepping stone to the Romanian oil fields could now be definitely forgotten. Nor was it possible to hold on to the western bank of the Danube any longer in the vain hope to protecting the fields of Nagykanizsa. Furthermore, the oil refineries in the Székesfehérvár area had by now also been lost for good. All in all, the Germans viewed each one of these losses as a great strategic loss. More than once refineries like the one at Petfürdő were alluded to in the Army Group diary and termed 'vitally important'. In this respect, the Army Group had been completely swept up in Hitler's oil obsession. After 16th March the 2.Pz. army attacks went on for several days but eventually they petered out.

It was not only the southern attack of the Red Army that had ruined Hitler's oil plans but also the troops that were sweeping northwards. There the Army Group had concentrated most of its efforts on retaining the refineries around Komárom, Szöny and Füzitő. Again, there seemed to be little logic in the strategic plans. Already on 15th March, before the start of the Soviet offensive in the Vienna direction, 70% of the refining capacity had been lost. During the course of 1945, and at the request of the Russians the Western Allies had bombed the refineries and bridges at Komárom on several occasions. However, the Army Group still endeavoured to protect and fortify the city which was rapidly becoming threatened on two sides. The northern assault of the Red Army had reached the Naszály - Mocsa - Nagymand - Kisbér line by 19th March and was pushing the units of the 96.I.D., the 711.I.D. and the battle group Lenz (Gren.Brigade 92 (mot.) ever deeper into the defence. In the fighting that was taking place on the edge of the Gerecse and Pilis Heights, whole groups of Germans were rapidly getting closed in. On 21st March, Felsögalla and Alsógalla - places in the industrial area that the Germans had fought so hard for during the 'Konrad' I operations - fell into the hands of the Red Army.

On the Gran front, to the north of the Danube, things began to become unstable once again despite all the andeavours of operation 'Südwind'. At Tat the Red Army formed a bridgehead and transported a number of strong units to the western bank of the Gran in twenty ferry boats. After the I.SS Pz. corps had left to fight on the 'Frühlingserwachen' front the German front at Gran had once again been undermined. Three weak infantry divisions tried to hold but without success.

In the meantime, Komárom had quickly been turned into a fortified stronghold. For the purposes of construction the 8. army had offered up the Pz.D.'FHH'2 which was commanded by Günther Pape (formerly of the 'Gruppe Pape') and the newly drawn up 13.Pz.D. commanded by Dr. Bäke. These units came from the Pz. corps 'FHH' (of General Kleemann). A new Waffen-SS cavalry unit also sped to the front: the SS battle group 'Ameiser'. The majority of men in this unit came from the SS-Reiter Rgt.92 commanded by SS-Sturmbannführer Anton (Toni) Ameiser, a section of the 37.SS Freiw.Kav.D. 'Lützow' (of SS-Standartenführer Karl Gesele) that was being drawn up in Bratislava (Pressburg).

It was not for the first time in its history that Komárom was being made into a fortress. In 1849, during the Hungarian war of independence, the city had similarly been converted into an important stronghold. Even after the Hungarian forces capitulated, Komárom managed to hold out for months against the Austrian and Russian besiegers.

Even though it was well fortified, the present struggle for Komárom was destined to last for only a short time and the reason for this was simple. The Red Army was clearly the superior power so the German soldiers decided to take to their heels before the city was completely surrounded. On 22nd March, the Red Army made its first attempts to capture Komárom by descending on the city from an area to the north of the Danube. Though the German losses were heavy they managed to hold off the attack but on 24th and 25th March the situation rapidly deteriorated. The German infantry forces in the front line, the 211.V.G.D., 46.V.G.D. and the 357.I.D. were no longer able to stop the attack. Together with the 1. Romanian army the Soviet 57. army and the 7.G. army mounted a twenty or so division strong attack on the Gran front. However, the Red Army's sights were set on an objective that was much further away than Komárom. The target marked on the Stavka's maps was Bratislava, a destination far beyond the rear guard of the German army.

When it looked as though the enemy was going to penetrate the German lines directly to the east of Komárom and when the troops which had been defending the Gerecse and Pilis Heights fled to Komárom from the south, the Army Group realized that they had definitely lost Komárom. Between 27th and 29th March the Germans then evacuated their troops from the key position they had held at Komárom under the supervision of Dr. Bäke. No less than 20,000 troops descended from the Gerecse and Pilis Heights region and joined the retreating units which were withdrawing towards Bratislava along the Slovakian bank of the Danube.

Soldier Kliemchen of the FEB 54 (6. Pz.D) witnessed the dramatic retreat. Until then the soldiers of the small unit to which he belonged were being trained as snipers in Komárom. The long line of soldiers streaming across to the northern bank of the Danube was proof enough that the defeat in the Gerecse and Pilis Heights was absolute. 'We were camped on a peninsula in the Danube, close to the bridge crossing. At first, we were a little hopeful, mainly because the 'FHH' division was next to us, but when their tanks started to withdraw to the northern bank as well, we knew that the battle for Komárom really was lost.' The snipers of the FEB 54 linked up with the column of troops that was forming on Slovakian soil. Thirty-six tanks of the 13.Pz.D. created the steel fist of the army that was to lead the troops safely into Bratislava and following behind these tanks were long lines of soldiers such as those of the Rgt.283 (Oberstleutnant Von Boeltzig), Rgt.284 (Major Pipo) and Rgt.287 (Oberstleutnant Magawly) of the 96.I.D. While this grey column of soldiers slowly moved westwards the sound of heavy bombing could be heard behind them. Army engineers were blowing up the bridges at Komárom. The bridges were collapsing in heavy segments and plunging into the water of the Danube in much the same way that the bridges at Budapest had exploded and fallen into the same river not so very long before.

Vienna, the oil of Zisterdorf and the myth of the 'Alpenfestung'

When the 'Reichsschutzstellung' had been broken through, all German eyes turned westwards. Vienna was like a great magnet attracting not only all the German troops, but also the Red Army. By now the situation within Army Group South had stabilized a little. The defeat suffered between lake Balaton and the Danube had been devastating but at least the Germans been able to escape and save themselves just in time. The officers now hoped that in having gone a little further westwards they would be able to stand their ground.

The 'Reichsschutzstellung' was not the only fortified defence line. Just outside Vienna there was the 'Deutschmeisterstellung' and around Vienna another line of defence known as the 'Wienschutzstellung'. Further inland reinforcement work was being carried out on the defence works known as the 'Nibelungenstellung' and the 'Hagenstellung' which constituted the first defence line of the so-called 'Alpenfestung', the place to where, it was presumed, the Nazi top would retreat for the final battle. While the chaotic retreat was in progress arguments were continuing on both the German and the Soviet side about the battle's possible outcome. Balck accused the Waffen-SS of having fled from the Red Army whilst there had been 'material and man-power enough to deal with the crisis'. He also accused Stadler's 9.SS division of being responsible for the loss of the HuDm division. Naturally at this remove from events it is impossible to reconstruct the situation. We, therefore, have to rely on Wöhler and Dietrich's reports of what happened. However, the facts would lead one to doubt whether the 6. SS Pz. army really provided substantial opposition for the Red Army. In those days, Dietrich used to joke about the 'six' in 6. SS Panzer army standing for six tanks. Though a joke, it did more or less sum up the actual situation. Weekly German reports kept at the time which have been preserved and have come down to us give updates of the strength of the German army and would confirm that this was true.

There was also concern in the German camp about the continuing decrease in the number of Hungarian units. Now that the focal point of the war had moved away from Hungary the Hungarian soldiers were really not interested in fighting any longer. In the aftermath of 'Frühlingserwachen' and Budapest, three Hungarian divisions had been practically wiped out and those who had survived were not particularly keen to give up their lives for an already lost cause and homeland. By now, the Red Army was deploying more and more Hungarian units on its side so this only added to the confusion. The 2.Pz. army reported that every day some fifteen Hungarian soldiers were going over to the Soviet side. Walter Krüger of Nachrichten-Abteilung 12 in the 'Hitlerjugend' division confirmed after the war that great numbers of Hungarians had indeed been seen crossing over the enemy lines to join the Soviet ranks. 'They dropped their machine-guns on the roadside and we collected them.'

The Soviets were not entirely happy either. Tolbukhin was disappointed about the fact that even after having been almost completely surrounded the 6. SS Pz. army had still managed to escape, albeit with many casualties. He particularly blamed his 6.G. tank army for having been 'too slow off the mark' in moving into action. Tolbukhin could of course have also blamed himself for bringing in the corps too late. Both on the German side and on the Soviet side such minor human failings were all too apparent all of the time. Many claimed responsibility for success, but few were ever prepared to own up to defeat and ruin.

As far as the Red Army advance towards Vienna was concerned we can be brief. It has been described in detail by the Austrian historian Manfred Rauchensteiner. Between Neusiedlersee and Köseg and moving from north to south the 46. army, the 9.G. army and the 6.G.Pz army broke into the 'Ostmark'. Oberpullendorf fell on 29th March, Deutsch-Kreuz on 30th March and Sopron and Grimmenstein on 31st March. By 2nd April, the Red Army had reached the suburbs of Vienna by which time morale in the German ranks had sunk even lower and the only thing still driving the German soldiers on was the sheer terror of otherwise becoming Soviet prisoners of war. This fear was certainly grounded because during the first years of the war the Germans had let thousands of Soviet prisoners starve to death behind barbed wire. At this stage, even the most fervent National Socialist had to acknowledge that the war had definitely been lost. Volkssturm units stationed in the 'Reichsschutzstellung' and at other posts were jeered at by retreating soldiers for 'drawing out the war'. Rauchensteiner even reported that German units had plundered Austrian territory.

Sepp Dietrich and his staff arrived in Vienna, Germany's 'second capital', on 1st April 1945. Politically, the city was being controlled by Hitler's confidant Baldur von Schirach - the man also responsible for forming the Hitler Youth movement - who operated as Gauleiter (regional governor). In the grip of Nazism the city which had produced such inspired thinkers as Freud, Wittgenstein and Kraus was converted into a bastion of hardened reactionaries. The dream of Rudolf Habsburg, only son of Emperor Franz Joseph, to keep Vienna out of the grasp of Pan-Germanists and steer it in a pro Anglo-Saxon direction had been shattered. Nazism reigned supreme and had the city firmly in its grasp. On the streets that Mahler used to walk along and near to café-Central where intellectuals used to meet and talk Jewish citizens were later being forced to get down on their hands and knees and clean the flagstones with tooth-brushes. Rudolf Habsburg's failed mission ended in desperation and suicide. He died in Mayerling in the arms of his seventeen-year-old mistress and disciple, Baroness Mary Vetsera.
The opportunist Von Schirach watched the developments with concern. He knew what was expected of Gauleiters: utter dedication to the cause to the very end. Fritz Wächtler, the Gauleiter of Bayreuth, the place where

Wagner hailed from, was shot for defecting. Josef Bürckel (of Saarpfalz) had shot himself and Wilhelm Murr (in Stuttgart) later took a cyanide capsule. Joseph Goebbels set the example in Berlin. Together with his wife and children he was to follow Hitler's downfall. Von Schirach who was thirty-eight years old thought he was too young to die. He decided to evacuate his wife and children from the city. Von Schirach was disturbed about the irrational orders that kept coming in from Führer headquarters. On 1st April Hitler had telephoned Von Schirach to tell him personally that the 6.SS Pz. army was being sent to help defend the city: 'One of our best armies' Hitler commented.

Several hours later, Dietrich was able to inform Von Schirach first-hand of the state of affairs with the 6.SS Pz. army. Dietrich was perfectly honest about matters and told Von Schirach what bad shape his army was in. The two men knew each other well. Von Schirach had first met Dietrich when he was working for the 'Völkische Beobachter' newspaper in Munich, in the dispatching department. He found it all very incredible to learn that this same man was now the highest ranking Waffen-SS general. The two men discussed Hitler's order to immediately defend Vienna from the outskirts of the city. The next day Reichsführer-SS Heinrich Himmler arrived in Vienna in his special train. Himmler had come to personally assess the situation with his Waffen-SS troops. In recent times, the Army Group had been blaming the SS for more and more things and Himmler wanted to see if the SS still possessed its old fighting spirit. He called together a number of Waffen-SS officers and made a speech that was full of old clichés like 'stand your ground' and 'aim for victory'.

While Himmler was in Vienna, Hitler called again. On being alerted Himmler sped out of Von Schirach's room and rushed to the telephone. When he returned he was visibly shaken. Hitler had attacked Himmler for the 'diminishing' effectivity of the Waffen-SS and had made it clear that he was planning to take disciplinary action. To Hitler's mind the 'Leibstandarte Adolf Hitler' no longer deserved to bear his name. According to Von Schirach Himmler had retaliated more fiercely than ever before in his 'faithful Heinrich' (Treue Heinrich) career. 'If you want me to strip Waffen-SS men of their Eiserne Kreuzen and Ritterkreuzen then I shall also have to take medals away from those men who lie dead on the banks of lake Balaton. The soldiers cannot give more than their lives!'

Once back in the room with Von Schirach and Dietrich Himmler explained how Hitler had also ordered the Waffen-SS to take off their 'Aermelstreifen', armbands embellished with the name of the division. On hearing this Dietrich was absolutely furious; he hurled his medal adorned with diamonds into the corner of the room. 'If I tell this rubbish to my men they'll go straight home!' he yelled. Von Schirach and Himmler were of the same opinion, so together they resolved to keep Hitler's orders secret.

Hitler had decided to follow in the footsteps of Frederick the Great, his big hero, and he had not been afraid of disciplining his élite troops. This particular order of Hitler's precipitated several rumours that continued to circulate in post-war literature on the subject. There was, for example, the myth that certain Waffen-SS officers had ripped off their medals, put them in a chamber pot and sent them to Führer headquarters. Apparently part of the shot off arm of an SS soldier bearing the 'Aermelstreifen' had also been placed in the chamber pot. However, since Dietrich had decided to ignore orders this story could not have been true. The incident only served to reinforce the general feeling alive within the Waffen-SS that they were being abused and that they were misunderstood. Telegrams reporting the war's progress verified these sentiments. During the early days of the Soviet-Viennese operation, Stadler had sent word that the 9th SS division was being 'completely used up' by the army. There was a leadership crisis in the Army Group. The army felt that it was about time the Waffen-SS lived up to all that it claimed it was. After the war Gaedcke commented: 'The 6. army gained a certain satisfaction from the 'Aermelstreifenerlass' news. The SS units had not lived up to their reputation.' Balck was a little more guarded in what he wrote. He agreed that it had been necessary to take some sort of measures but wrote, 'as ever things were taken to extremes at Führer headquarters and they over-reacted'. The political decisions that had been made far away from the front were merciless. 'Dietrich is no strategist, he is at most a divisional commandant', was what Goebbels said about the man he had once described as the 'Blücher of National Socialism'. Martin Bormann maintained that the 6.SS Pz. army was 'abominable' ('Hundesschlecht').

The disciplinary action taken against the Waffen-SS was not unique. Hitler had once behaved similarly towards troops stationed at the garrison in the Crimea. On the Hungarian front the commandant of the 8.Pz.D, Generalmajor Frölich, had once been dealt with strictly for reacting 'too sluggishly' to the Soviet offensive on the Gran during the 'Konrad' I operations. He had been removed from office. Similarly, in 1944 the commandant of the 4.SS Polizei Panzergrenadierdivision, Fritz Schmedes, had been punished by Himmler when he had put in a request for his men to be given time to rest and refresh themselves a little. Himmler had transferred Schmedes to the 'Dirlewanger' SS Brigade, a penitentiary unit commanded by Dr. Oskar Dirlewanger with a petty officer's corps composed of thieves from prisons all over Europe, political prisoners, poachers and other offenders. After fighting against partisans and quashing the uprising in Warsaw in 1944, 'Dirlewanger' had earned itself the reputation of being a ruthless brigade. The Bratislava combat commandant, Oberleutnant Freiherr Von Ohlen und Adlerscron was sentenced to death for cowardice.

After the 'Aermelstreifenerlass' incident Hitler decided to prevent anyone within Dietrich's army being promoted. This was partly rectified when after Hitler's death and during the last days of the war a number of men did receive promotion and certain awards were handed out. One such person to receive a medal was Otto Weidinger, commandant of the 'Der Führer' regiment (within 'Das Reich'). He was given the

'Schwerter' award alongside of the Ritterkreuz he already had. The regiment saw this as a righting of wrongs for the unjustly meted out 'Aermelstreifenerlass'.

Schirach and Dietrich then quickly got down to the business of summoning up courage for the battle of Vienna. Notices ordering that women and children should be evacuated were posted throughout the city. 'Where to?' was the question that somebody had daubed across one of the posters.
In the 'Kleine Wiener Kriegszeitung' Von Schirach wrote on 3rd April: 'Vienna's time has come!' He regarded it as an honour to be able to welcome back his 'old friend' SS General Dietrich - together with his SS divisions - to Vienna where they would be fighting. Dietrich merely indicated that the fighting would be heavy and that he could promise nothing, only that the units would do their very best. 'It was obvious' wrote Von Schirach's post-war biographer, 'that neither of these men wanted to be buried under the ruins of the city'.

On the day when the Red Army reached the suburbs of Vienna, the General of the Infantry, Rudolf von Bünau, was appointed commandant of the Viennese defence system. At first, people were confused by the fact that Vienna was being termed a 'defence area' rather than being declared a stronghold, but it was obvious that the city's defences were too weak for it to be called a fortress. Apart from anything else the city had no natural geographical barriers or defences as did Budapest. From a decree issued on 30th January 1945 it is possible to deduce what was meant by a 'defended area'. In short, what it all amounted to was that Von Bünau was to do everything in his power to see that the city remained in German hands.
As second capital of the 'Reich' Vienna was a great prestige object. Since no further orders were received the matter of how exactly the defence system should be set up was left entirely to Von Bünau to decide. In one respect, Von Bünau was relieved. Hitler knew Vienna from his

youth and some were afraid that he might have decided to involve himself in every detail of the battle. On the other hand, though, the task ahead was one that Von Bünau found most awesome. He was a sombre man who easily gave in to despair. It was, therefore, not surprising to see that when the battle commenced Von Bünau straight away stumbled towards the Red Army in the hope of being killed. 'Das Reich' soldiers suddenly noticed what was going on and managed to save him just in the nick of time.

Matters improved slightly for Von Bünau and his men when, for the first time in ages, substantial reinforcements were sent to back up the Army Group. Hitler had always given high priority to the southern front, so he was more than willing to send his strong Führer Grenadier Division to fight for Vienna. Though the battle had been in full swing since 4th April and the last trains with units of men from the new division were still arriving on 8th April, the fighting forces were glad of the reinforcements. The new division was attached to Bittrich's II.SS Pz. corps that was waiting to defend the city. After the unfortunate events of 'Frühlingserwachen' Bittrich's corps was only a shadow of the corps it had once been. The three main units of the corps, the 6.Pz.D and the 2. and 3. SS Pz.D. 'Das Reich' and 'Totenkopf' had, when put together, as much tanks and equipment as the Führer Grenadier Division on its own. In practice Bittrich's corps was equivalent to two divisions augmented with Flak, Volkssturm and Hitlerjugend units and assault battalions.

On 4th April, the situation became more acute. At the points on the front where 'Totenkopf' and 'Das Reich' were fighting and where stationary Flak (24. Flak D. under the command of Generalmajor Grieshammer) formed the core of the defence line, the Red Army made some progress. Bittrich and Von Bünau decided to move the front further into the city and this they achieved without any Red Army breakthroughs which was strange when one considers how much stronger the Red Army was on the battlefield by this stage. The Red Army had brought in the I.G.mech. corps (4.G army) and the XVIII.G.S. corps (46. army) simply to tackle the 'Totenkopf' division. The explanation for the slowness of the operation was probably political. In Austria, just as had been the case in Warsaw, the Red Army had its underground resistance fighter contacts. They were obviously keen to deliver Vienna undamaged into the hands of the Soviets. The key figure in this whole plan was Major Szokoll who had organized an armed rebellion due to begin on 6th April at 12.30 hours in which the city would be freed and the way made open for the Red Army. However, the plans were leaked out and most of the underground rebels were rounded up before they had time to revolt. The II.SS Pz. corps dealt harshly with the rebels and disposed of them quickly: their bodies soon afterwards swung from lampposts in Florisdorf.

In retrospect one can only speculate on whether the uprising would have been a success, but what is certain is that the revolutionaries were serious. Szokoll had been depending on the support of several assault and infantry battalions and a Croatian 'Reserve and Training Brigade' in Stockerau. In total this amounted to several thousand soldiers. Szokoll was also relying on the support of 20,000 Viennese people some 6,000 of whom were armed. The situation somewhat resembled the rebellion led by General Bor in Warsaw. Even the Soviet attitude to it all was similar. Just as in Warsaw the Red Army seemed to hold back a while before mounting its assault, as though waiting for some kind of internal conflict to be thrashed out. The Soviets had probably been hoping that, in this way, they would be able to keep down their own losses while at the same time allowing the existing political infrastructures on the Nazi and resistance sides to completely collapse, thus enabling them to later effortlessly introduce a new regime.

Though the danger had been assuaged the rift between the army and the Waffen-SS had only widened. Bittrich felt that he could no longer trust the men of the 'Alarm' battalions who were dotted around the city. He was also shocked to see that the resistance movement had penetrated to such high levels - Szokoll who had been one of Von Bünau's confidants had been involved in defending the city. Bittrich was, therefore, keen to make it known that, as far as he was concerned the SS corps could not be extricated from Vienna fast enough. Von Bünau reported that this was not possible. As commandant in charge of defence works he had his responsibilities. Hitler appealed to the Army Group to take firm command in Vienna so that law and order could be re-established. The Reichsführer-SS, Himmler, threatened to send in units that would 'show how to restore order'.

On 7th April, army and Waffen-SS relationships hit rock bottom when Dietrich - possibly supported by Himmler - placed Von Bünau under Bittrich's command without any further explanation in the vain hope of restoring order. Officially Von Bünau was still in charge of defence operations, but in practice he had little more power than that of a divisional commandant. Von Bünau, thus, became Bittrich's subordinate officer and was left without any troops to command. As far as Vienna was concerned, this was perhaps the best arrangement. Von Bünau, a man lacking in imagination, tried at all times to follow Hitler's unreasonable orders as closely as possible. Dietrich and the other SS officers (notably Bittrich and Rudolf Lehmann, commandant of 'Das Reich') who had often been close to death were less inclined to take all the extreme orders issued by the OKW seriously. On 13th April, an order was received from the OKW which had been signed by the Chef OKW Keitel, Reichsführer SS Himmler and Bormann, Party Bureau Leader, which dictated that any army commandants venturing to disobey orders would be sentenced to death and their families imprisoned. On hearing this all the SS officers simply shrugged their shoulders and went their way, even more so than before. Dietrich sent word to Berlin that the situation in the city was becoming hopeless.

Von Bünau was by now virtually powerless and, therefore, hardly in a position to protest. On the very day when Dietrich 'reinstated' him, Otto Wöhler, the only man who could possibly have been of help to him (in his capacity as Army Group commandant) was replaced by Generaloberst Dr. Lothar Rendulic. Rendulic, himself an Austrian, had continually tried to protect Vienna from too much violence and had supported the policy that Vienna should slowly be surrendered. Next the German forces withdrew to the other side of the Danube canal and cleared away the final bridgeheads to the east. The next step, partly in the light of the Soviet victories on the western and eastern sides of Vienna, was to release the Führer Grenadier Division for deployment on the northwest Viennese front. This was the first indication so far given that the Germans were seriously planning to move out of Vienna. By 11th April, the Red Army had already assembled 45,000 soldiers and 138 4.G. army tanks on the western bank of the Danube canal. The main action of the battle then moved to the centre of Vienna where the historic Stefans-Church was seen to go up in flames. The Austrian resistance fighters and the Red Army blamed Sepp Dietrich for this dreadful act of destruction which according to them had arisen from Dietrich's pure frustration. In reality, much the reverse was true, Dietrich was not at all interested in becoming involved in a final battle for Vienna. The Waffen-SS was no longer a Napoleonic-style army that saw fighting to the death on the battlefield as the highest possible honour a soldier could aspire to. Escalating disagreement with the army and loss of confidence in Hitler were what had convinced Dietrich that he was not going to offer up his life and become a martyr. The SS started making preparations to break out of Vienna in a north-westward direction towards Korneuburg where the Führer Grenadier Division and parts of the 96.I.D. and the 37.SS 'Lützow' and several smaller units were stationed.

In the end, there was probably quite a different explanation for the fire in the Stefansdom. According to the historian Rauchensteiner what was most likely was that it had been started while large scale plundering was going on in the city. Such outbreaks of fire were common during spates of plundering and so, in the consternation, the Stefans-Church could easily have caught fire.

During these last days in Vienna, another scandal also developed. The Reichsbrücke over the Danube canal fell undamaged into the hands of the Soviets. The eastern front also had possession of the bridge at Remagen. Normally, the army commandant in charge would have had to pay for such a mistake but in this case it was not that simple. Von Bünau was answerable to Bittrich of the II.SS Pz. corps which meant that he could not be held fully responsible. The man who was, therefore, ultimately responsible was Rendulic, but he had only held his current position for a short while. It was at his command, though that the bombs beneath the bridge were armed and then disarmed three times over.

As soon as the bridge fell into Soviet hands, speculation again began. Had the members of the resistance movement handed it over to the Red Army? Had unclear orders (even the Führers headquarters had got involved in the dispute) led to a misunderstanding? In post-war literature on the matter it became the subject of much speculation. Ultimately, the answer can be found in 'Gekämpft, Gesiegt, Geschlagen', the obviously unread memoirs of Lothar Rendulic. Here Rendulic confesses that though the blowing up of the bridge was not his immediate domain (he was first answerable to OKW) he had made it explicitly clear that he was against destroying the bridge unnecessarily and had ordered that the bombs should be defused. A message sent on the 12th of April from the 6.SS Pz. army criticized the fact that the explosives under the bridge were not ready for instant detonation. No new order was issued to change the situation.

On 13th April the II.SS Pz. corps finally moved away in a north-westerly direction. They left a city in flames behind. The giant revolving wheel of the Prater could be seen burning like a massive torch and it somehow seemed to symbolize all the violence of the war. Still, the metropolis on the Danube could count itself lucky. Budapest, the other big city on the Danube, had been much harder hit than the Austrian capital. About 13% of

Vienna lay in ruins, by contrast 74% to 82% of Warsaw had been destroyed, 54% of Berlin and 60% of Dresden. Earlier on Von Schirach had said to Otto Skorzeny, when he had suddenly appeared in Vienna, that he would rather 'hold out and perish'. But when the Russians came he changed his mind. 'The Russians have broken through, it is high time for us to leave Hofburg', was what Schirach's second-in-command, Gauleiter Wieshofer, had said. 'Surely you do not intend to defend Hofburg with your pistol!' he had exclaimed. 'Well! The time has come! Let's go!' Von Schirach had replied, but he fled. The man who had knowingly sent Hitlerjugend battalions of young men to their certain death could now be seen fleeing to save his own skin. 'It was a biological crime', Von Schirach admitted after the war. Together with two VW-Schwimmwagen, a Mercedes-cabrio and two trucks from the Führer Grenadier Division packed full with food rations Von Schirach disappeared from the political arena. He fled towards St.Pölten, the place where Dietrich had set up his headquarters in a castle. Though there was no enemy to be seen for miles around a security unit watched over Dietrich: 'In case Hitler tries to get his revenge for the fall of Vienna', Dietrich explained. From then onwards, Von Schirach was the liaising officer of the 6.SS Pz. army. Obviously, Dietrich's fear was not totally unfounded. Towards the end of the war, SS units tried to arrest Göring, the war-time head of the Luftwaffe. It was thanks to his loyal body-guard, Fallschirmjäger, that Göring was saved from being arrested and possibly also from being executed.

Far away in Moscow 24 gun-shot salutes reverberated from 324 cannons on 13th April 1945. The Russians were celebrating the liberation of Vienna. The men of no less than 50 Red Army units were given honorary 'Vienna' awards. The second capital of Nazi Germany and the old capital of the Habsburg Empire had fallen.

The units which had made their way westwards via the northern bank of the Danube had not done any better than Dietrich's army. They left Komárom, the old fortified city on the Danube, burning behind them. 'The oil refineries have completely gone to rack and ruin and are no longer of economic interest', the Army Group noted.

The units, which were now a part of the 8. army, were confronted here also by the huge superior power of the Soviets. The Germans only had 50 soldiers to each kilometre of front! All hopes were pinned on the Bratislava stronghold (Pressburg). The commandant of the 'fortress' was Lieutenant Freiherr Von Ohlen und Adlerscron who was particularly hoping that the experienced soldiers of the 96.I.D. would be able to defend the city. Like Von Bünau, Von Ohlen had been given an impossible task. Already on 1st April, almost at the same time that the German units started to withdraw, General Sumilov's 7.G. army reached Bratislava. On 4th April, the 'fortress' was finally seized by the Red Army.

By then, most of the garrison, Von Ohlen included, had left the city. Van Ohlen had set the example himself by establishing his headquarters in a castle outside of the city, contrary to the wishes of his superiors. The last to leave the city were the troops of the 96.I.D. who fell under Major General Harrendorf and one of the Hitlerjugend battalions. In allowing the men to go, Von Ohlen had contravened OKH orders to defend Bratislava until the last moment and so it was that the city's commandant was sentenced to death for the crime of 'fleeing from the enemy'.

The German units withdrew to the Lower Carpathians or were pushed towards the front to the north of Vienna. The Hitlerjugend battalion that had fought with great élan in Bratislava marched on to Vienna and, on 6th April, began fighting at Hütteldorf with a unit of the Red Army. Three Soviet tanks were lost in the conflict. The next day, the battalion joined up with Bittrich's corps and later, together with a Pz.Jg.Commando, it was integrated into the 'Werwolf' battle group.

The struggle also eventually had to be given up at the front where the 2.Pz. army of the General of Artillery, De Angelis, was fighting, within whose territory the oil fields of Nagykanizsa fell. Already in January 1945, De Angelis had pleaded for changes to be made because his stretch of front was much too long. He wanted his army to be able to adopt better defensive positions. The request had been refused, the argument being that the front had to remain as far east as possible, away from the so strategically important oil fields. In March also, after 'Frühlingserwachen' had failed, De Angelis had repeated his request, but once again it had fallen on deaf men's ears. What was noted down in the Army Group diary was that Hitler had 'sharply rejected' the request.

Führer headquarters did, however, direct that De Angelis should be given extra units to reinforce his army and to protect the fields at Nagykanizsa. The units sent were: the infantry forces of the 297.I.D., the 117.Jg.D. and the 14.Waffen Grenadier Division of the SS (Galiz no.1) led by SS-commandant Fritz Freitag. At the same time, everything possible was done to boost oil production in the Hungarian fields. Führer headquarters even instructed that extra trains should be laid on so that the oil could be transported to other places for refining since most of the Hungarian refineries were out of action.

It would only be possible to hold on to the fields at Nagykanizsa, if De Angelis was able to keep the 'Margarethe line', which extended from lake Balaton to the river Drava (Ob.Southeast), intact. In practice, this was an impossible mission. Nevertheless, the Army Group received verbal orders to this effect from the Führer on 29th March which were confirmed in writing the next day. In his communiqué, Hitler called the oil reserves at Nagykanizsa 'decisive'. Only days later, the oil fields at Nagykanizsa came under Red Army artillery fire.

Still, as a military tool, oil was to play an important part one last time in these final days of the war and in a more contrived way than ever before. As Jean Boisson once said: 'Stubborn persistence almost always turns into persistent stubbornness' and with Hitler who prided himself in his ability to show great resolve such a develpment was more than evident. Whether his resolve

Freiherr Von Waldenfels, commandant of the 6.Pz.D. a unit that Hitler deployed no less than five different times to fight for oil reserves.

were manifested in the length of time he could hold his arm up in the Hitler salute position (i.e. much longer than Göring could!) or whether it pertained to winning the war through 'sheer will-power' was immaterial to Hitler.

After having lost all the Hungarian oil fields Hitler was now left with only the small Austrian fields of Zisterdorf, a place to the north-east of Vienna. Now that no more oil was coming from Nagykanizsa these were the last reserves of the Third Reich and despite low and falling production levels (due to all the war activities) these fields were still of very great importance. Already in November 1944, an Austrian 'Landwehr' battalion (no. 897) had been sent to guard the oil fields and on 13th April, the day when Vienna fell, Hitler issued orders to reinforce the defences there.

The division chosen for this job was the 6.Pz.D. which had that very same day made a narrow escape via the Reichsbrücke. For the 6.Pz.army it was the fifth time they were being deployed to protect oil fields. The unit which was commanded by General Von Waldenfels had taken part in the 'Konrad' operations (partly fighting with the 'Gruppe Pape' unit) and had been a part of the 'Frühlingserwachen's' main thrust. This new mission had to be completed within the 8. army's domain which extended roughly over the whole of the area to the north of Wetzleinsdorf where Dietrich's 6.SS Pz. army Führer Grenadier Division was operating. The Army Group was further ordered to defend the oil area with Flak (the 32/XVII Heimat-Flak battery) and instructed only to destroy the Vienna-Braclacv-Prorov (Prerau) railway line at the very last minute, so that oil could continue to be transported westwards for as long as possible.

Although the Zisterdorf oil area received some protection from the river Morova (March), the task was unrealistic, particularly in the light of developments in Vienna and now that the SS units had broken out in a north-westerly direction. Until the 6.Pz.D. arrived, the troops responsible for keeping up the front, alongside of the weak 'Landesschützen'-bataillions, had been: the 37.SS Freiwilligen Kav.D. 'Lützow' and units of the SS battle group 'Trabandt' which was led by Paul Trabandt, former commandant of the 18.SS Panzer Grenadier Division 'Horst Wessel'. Just to add to the confusion, local Gau Niederdonau politicians, who had caught up with the latest plans at Führer headquarters, began to involve themselves in the oil area defence policies. Dr. Jury, Gauleiter of the Lower Danube region, was of the opinion that with the Red Army drawing ever closer there was only one way to save the oil area. He immediately asked senior army officers if they could bring in German airborne troops to protect the area surrounding Zisterdorf. At the time, there were more important things for the Army Group to bother about than the requests of military laymen. Jury's argument that losing the oil fields would be 'fatal' did nothing to change matters. On 17th April, the Soviets started to surround Zisterdorf and the 8. army began to withdraw its troops. By this stage, the oil fields of Zisterdorf were no longer important. The oil towers that had been bombed and fired on by Soviet artillery were aflame. Before leaving the area the German army filled up all their tanks, vehicles and jerry-cans with fuel because they knew that after this there would be no more fuel to take them westwards. They also knew that ultimately they would be captured by the western Allied Forces which were already filtering into Austria from the west, but they found this preferable to an uncertain future in Soviet captivity.

The 8. army, commanded by General Kreysing, was not able to escape that easily from Hitler's oil obsession. When the Red Army suddenly and unexpectedly changed its angle of attack by directing the 6.G.Pz. army northwards, Hitler once again instructed that an offensive should be mounted in the direction of the Zisterdorf oil fields. Kreysing received the order on 18th April, two days before Hitler's 56th birthday. There had once been grand plans to present Hitler with the extensive oil fields of Ploesti on his birthday, now he was going to have to make do with the small and inadequate fields of Zisterdorf.

Kreysing protested but his objections were answered with further orders from the Führer which he decided to ignore. The 6.Pz.D. army that was supposed to be carrying out the offensive was sent off to the Mistelbachs area where the Red Army was threatening to break through.

A number of German units joined forces and in a combined effort, supported by a final desperate attack mounted by the German Luftwaffe, managed to halt the Red Army advance. This minor triumph gave Hitler reason enough to once again send troops to Zisterdorf. On 22nd April, the attack began. Together with units of the SS battle group 'Trabandt' the 6.Pz.D. attacked the Soviet units to the east of Zisterdorf on 23rd April. The battle lasted for about a day and surprisingly the Germans did gain some ground even though they were up against stiff opposition. When they started to lose the battle Kreysing decided to call off the offensive and send the 6.Pz.D. back to the northern flank where it looked as though coordination efforts between Army Group South and Army Group Centre might just go wrong.

Viewed in its broader context the oil operation in Austria looked even more ludicrous: on 16th April 1945 the Russians had initiated a massive offensive and Russian soldiers were now marching from the Oder towards Berlin. At the outset of this their final offensive the armies of Zhukov and Koniev were infinitely more powerful than the German forces. The Red Army had 270 pieces of artillery and grenade launchers per kilometre of front (!) General Gotthard Heinrici, commandant of Army Group 'Weichsel'(Vistula), had the awesome task of having to try and combat this massive onslaught. The 'Nibelungstellung' on the Oder was as ineffective as the 'Reichsschutzstellung' had been or the 'Margarethestellung' on the Hungarian front. On the day when the Soviet offensive began, Heinrici's soldiers received a special 'order of the day' from Hitler: they were spurred on to achieve an historic 'victory'.

Only a few days later, the front collapsed and the Red Army marched on to the Elbe. The Soviet advance then moved so quickly that OKH headquarters at Zossen had to be vacated at top speed. On 20th April, Hitler's 56th birthday, the first Soviet tanks appeared outside Berlin. It was partly because so many of the remaining troops were being deployed on the Hungarian front that the defence of Berlin was now left chiefly to poorly equipped reserves and units of the 'Volkssturm'. The German poet, Theodor Körner, had once said 'Nun Volk steh auf!', and in these final weeks this became the motto of the last reserves of the Third Reich as they went to meet their certain fate. By the end of 1944, the 'Volkssturm' consisted of no less than six million men, many of whom were either old or very young (often only sixteen years old: born in 1928). These troops had few weapons and most were expected to hold back Zhukov and Koniev's tanks and the western Allied invasion armed only with old guns and a few rounds of ammunition or, at best, Panzerfäusten.

The 'Volkssturm' had been created as part of a campaign launched by German leaders to make the war above all else a people's war. If men no longer had the incentive to fight for their country and their leaders, they would at least still want to fight to save their own lives. The whole conflict was turned into a kind of 'Weltuntergang' or fight for survival. The other army units linked to this campaign were: the 'Volks' grenadier divisions, the 'Volks' artillery corps and the 'Volks' launching brigades, all of which had been active on the Hungarian front. 'Heimat an die Front!' the propaganda minister Goebbels had chanted. Now that they had run out of aircraft fuel, even the air force had arrived on the battlefield with its Luftwaffe field divisions. Admiral Dönitz' navy supplied marine infantry soldiers and in an effort to raise morale new divisions were named after German heroes of the past such as: Theodor Körner, Albert Leo Schlageter, Scharnhorst, Ferdinand Schill and Clausewitz. In the very last days, the Germans even harked back to the free corps spirit of just after the First World War by establishing the so-called 'Freikorps Adolf Hitler'.

To remain in control during these final desperate days of the war the Third Reich ruled the people with a hand of iron. The State Minister of Justice, Otto Thierack, had ordered that a law should be intruduced stating that all who disobeyed orders would quickly be brought to justice and go before a firingsquad. On 9th March 1945, the law was amended and a 'special tribunal' was introduced so that people could be brought to justice without the intervention of a lawyer, only the permission of the honorary Lieutenant-General, Rudolf Hübner, was required. It was the task of this tribunal to execute Hitler's special orders. The first death sentences came very soon after the new ruling had been introduced. The men responsible for losing the bridge at Remagen had to pay for the mistake with their lives. During the last months of the war, some 500 Germans per month went before the firingsquad. This record number of executions constituted yet another black page in German history. In the days and weeks after the First World War when mutiny had been rife, 150 Germans had gone before German firingsquads each month.

Another useless idea to emerge from the catacombs in Berlin was the notion of the so-called 'Werwolf' action. 'The Werwolf is there, whoever surrenders will be shot!' With this propaganda Himmler and Goebbels tried to inspire sabotage actions deep in the heart of the 'Reich', in regions that had already surrendered to the Allies. On the whole, the people involved in these acts of sabotage - which were carried out in contravention of the war-time laws - were very young confirmed Nazis. The most spectacular of all the 'Werwolf' actions was the one that led to the murdering of the Hamburg major, Franz Oppenhoff on 25th March 1945. Oppenhoff had declared that he was prepared to cooperate with the Allied Forces, that is to say, with the Western Allies. As the final battle drew nigh, there was much talk of suicide actions. The Nazi leaders came up with a ghastly so-called 'Rammjäger' plan involving suicide air commandos, German-style 'kamikazes' which would be required to deliberately crash their aircraft into Allied air force planes flying over Germany. It was obvious that such desperate measures would do nothing to change the outcome of the war.

Hitler was only too well aware of the reality of the situation. It led him to the extremely depressing conclusion on 19th March, only three days after the failure of 'Frühlingserwachen', that he could no longer concern himself with the future of the German people. This was what he intimated to Albert Speer at the time. Now that it had become clear that the Slavic people would win the war the future was obviously theirs. Hitler therefore issued orders for his 'Nero' plan to be executed, a plan that would be detrimental to his own Reich. According to Hitler there was no longer any need to feel concern for those left behind in the German Reich because 'the good were already dead'. The Nero plan dictated that the entire German communication network, infrastructure system and all industrial activities within the German Reich should be destroyed. With all-out war raging in the east and west and devastating air raid attacks destroying some 25,000 German dwellings every month, the Third Reich had been turned into one big smouldering ruin.

During the last weeks of the Third Reich, a number of prominent Nazis made last-ditch attempts to secure safe futures for themselves. Himmler had got in touch with Count Bernadotte, cousin of the Swedish king and vice-chairman of the Swedish Red Cross. The Count had made a humanitarian visit to Germany and Himmler had hoped that in return for releasing Jewish hostages he might be able to 'buy' himself freedom. The plan did not work and neither did Von Ribbentrop's plan. He had tried to make a deal with the west at the end of the war. By now, Hitler disapproved of virtually every plan suggested to him and because most lines of communication had broken down it was becoming ever more difficult for negotiators to keep in touch with the authorities. At one stage, there were only two telephone lines left at Führer headquarters. On one occasion, when two people simultaneously tried to make calls, the lines got crossed. Hitler then came on the line and said: 'this is the Führer speaking'. The bookkeeper on the other end of the line shouted, 'have you gone mad'. Hitler instantly hung up and grumbled: 'now they are even saying that I'm mad as well'. In the Führer's bunker a last ray of hope was felt when word was received of the death of the American president, F.D. Roosevelt, on 12th April in Georgia. Goebbels immediately concluded that this must be pure providence and, for a short time, his hopes were raised. The Allied Powers did not change their political course. During the final days of the war, only the troops of the SS general Steiner and the German army general Wenck were able to offer any hope but only in theory. The units were by now too weak to launch any large-scale military operations and the fall of Berlin was inevitable.

Hiltler refused to flee to the Bavarian Alps and what happened next is common knowledge. On 29th April, Hitler signed a political testament in which he once again laid all blame for everything that had happened in the war on the Jews. The next day, he committed suicide. Up until the very last moment Hitler had held on stubbornly to his convictions. The future of Nazi-Germany was now in the hands of Vice-Admiral Dönitz who had worshipped Hitler. In his proclamation made the next day he said: 'Germany's greatest hero in the fight against Bolshevism has fallen'.

The months of April and May 1945 saw the fall of Nazi Germany as a political and military power: a hard reality that could not possibly be ignored by the Army Group South. During the last days of the war the only hopes alive within the German camp were hopes based on myths and lies. Germany had no last minute super-weapons or secret diplomatic solutions and the downfall that was coming to it was inevitable. Wöhler had been sadly mistaken when, around the end of February and the beginning of March 1945, he had agreed to go along with the 'Frühlingserwachen' offensive presuming that Hitler must have 'other tricks up his sleeve'.

Even the 'Vergeltungs' weapons, of which the V1 and V2 missiles were the most famous, were not enough to make the war go in favour of the Germans. There had been new technological weapons on the German side, such as the Me-262 jets, but all such opportunities had been completely ruined by bureaucratic slip-ups and by Hitler's sheer stubbornness. Even the last thread of hope, the so-called 'Alpenfestung' which was rumoured to be backing up the Army Group South, turned out to be a myth.

During and even after the war, there had a been a notion, particularly amongst the western Allies, that Hitler and his most loyal followers would probably entrench themselves somewhere at the time of the final conflict. It had, furthermore, been presumed that the Alps, an excellent natural fortress, would be, for Hitler, the perfect place to hide away in. This belief, which as mentioned persisted in post-war literature on the subject, was only reinforced by the incorrect information that had been passed on by the Allied military intelligence service.
An American 7. army report drawn up by Colonel William W. Quinn on 25th March 1945 gives some insight into the assumptions made at the time by the Allied Forces. Quinn contended that the German army élite, mostly composed of Waffen-SS soldiers and well trained mountaineer troops, would almost certainly gather in the 'Alpenfestung' for the final big battle. It was thought that Reichsführer-SS Heinrich Himmler had already accumulated 80 élite army groups in the area in small 1,000 to 4,000 man strong units ready for engagement in battle with the Allies. It was thought that the Third Reich had 200,000 to 300,000 soldiers hidden in this last bastion. As far as American intelligence was concerned the 'Alpenfestung', furthermore, had its own - partly subterranean - weapon-making industry where fighter planes (Messerschmidts) and other weapons were allegedly being manufactured. It was thought that part of the Czech Skoda weapon factory had been dismantled and transferred to the mountain stronghold.
It was clearly a notion that appealed to the imaginations of many because during the last months of the war a popular book outlining details of the whole 'top-secret' organization within the 'Alpenfestung' appeared on the American market.
In reality, there never had been such a stronghold in the Alps, though it was true that certain of the German

authorities had toyed with the idea of converting the region into a stronghold but each time such plans were put forward they were overshadowed by other more urgent military issues. The man who did return several times to the idea of constructing an 'Alpenfestung' was the Gauleiter of Tirol-Voralberg, Franz Hofer. He wrote to Martin Bormann on 6th November 1944 to ask when work was going to start on the construction of a natural fortress but he received no reply. At the Führers headquarters everyone had been busy preparing for the Ardennes offensive that was to be an overture to the planned offensive in the east and nobody had had time to look that far ahead into the future. Apart from anything else the 'Alpenfestung' plans were diametrically opposed to the 'Frühlingserwachen' concept which was designed to ensure that it never would be necessary to construct such a fortress.

Towards the end of 1944, the idea was once again brought up at OKW by Friedrich Von Boetticher, General of the Artillery, and passed on to Jodl. He, too, ignored the proposals for the simple reason that the developments in the Ardennes and on the Rhine had priority. Jodl hoped that the Rhine would form a natural defence line for the German homeland. On 9th April 1945, when Hofer visited Hitler, he finally had the chance to discuss his Alpine fortress construction plans with the Führer in person. The discussion was obviously fruitful because on 12th April orders were at last issued to the effect that the central stronghold in the Alps should be extended.

By now Hitler's Hungarian dream had been shattered and the proposed fortress in the Alps was commonly viewed as a last refuge for the units of the Ob.Southeast (Army Group E), Ob.Southwest (Army Group C) and Ob.West (Army Group G). An élitist group of the kind envisaged by the American intelligence service had never existed. On 28th April, two days before his death, Hitler instructed that the stronghold should be extended, but these plans were never realized.

The Army Group South capitulated in absolute isolation. Because communication was poor all kinds of misunderstandings arose on the German side. Rendulic was unable to establish contact with the OKW and decided to deal with matters himself. On 7th May, he arrived at the American 3. army where he was given a full military welcome. From there he went on to St. Martin from where he established radio contact with the American war-horse, General George S. Patton. Rendulic signed the capitulation of his army and afterwards went around the negotiation building together with Walker, the American General of the XX.Pz. corps. Rendulic tried to convince the Texan General of the importance of German-American relations. The American listened politely to what Rendulic had to say, but nothing ever came of the proposals. Neither Walker nor Patton, who as an anti-communist, might perhaps have been persuaded, really carried any weight. The main political decisions were all top-level ones made in Teheran, Yalta and later in Potsdam and the generals were what they had always been: mere tools of the political top men.

The main objective of the soldiers on the battlefield was to cross the demarcation line between East and West in a westerly direction. The western Allies and the Soviets had agreed that all Germans would be handed over to those against whom they had last fought. This precipitated a whole range of symbolic fights along the front line. For hundreds of thousands of German and Hungarian soldiers this meant release from years of imprisonment under harsh conditions in the Soviet Union. Not all the units reached the demarcation line though. The 6.Pz.D. of Von Waldenfels, deployed at the last moment at Zisterdorf, was one of the unfortunate units to fall into Soviet hands. A similar fate awaited the 3.SS Pz.Div. 'Totenkopf' which was commanded by SS-Brigadeführer Helmuth Becker. Unlike some other divisions this one had not engaged in symbolic battle with the Americans. Two American divisions which up until then had done nothing other than simply 'drive forwards' had thus got into great difficulties.

By way of punishment, 'Totenkopf' was handed over to the Red Army and few soldiers of that division survived the war. Helmuth Becker and the commandant of the pioneer unit of 'Totenkopf', SS-Hauptsturmführer Schwermann, were sent before a firingsquad on 28th February 1953, because of allegedly having sabotaged reconstruction work in Stalingrad (now known as Wolgograd).

The way in which the units were confined varied greatly. Some troops like the 'Der Führer' Rgt. of 'Das Reich', went into closed imprisonment. That unit had been deployed in Prague during the final stages of the war. The Army Group commandant, Ferdinand Schörner, had given special orders for Otto Weidinger's division to be detached to the Czech capital where they were to release the German garrison and thousands of Volksdeutschen there who were in difficulties. In Prague, an anti-German rebellion had broken out and the consequences were serious for ethnic Germans. Thousands of them were murdered. Part of the city had fallen into the hands of the Vlassov army, an army composed of a few thousand Russian soldiers who had fought on the German side, but who had now turned against Moscow and Berlin and were waging their own mini war. The 'Der Führer' Rgt. managed to penetrate through to the city centre and, packed and loaded with thousands of citizens piled into trucks and tanks, the regiment then turned on its heels and headed for the demarcation line.

With the 211.V.G.D. things were not so well organized. The commandant of this division, Lieutenant-General Eckhardt, got wounded and later died in Soviet captivity. In a letter written after the war Heinrich Pörtner, a soldier in the 211.V.G.D., described this final phase of the war as follows.

'On the afternoon of 8th May 1945 pamphlets informing soldiers that the German army had capitulated were dropped from Russian planes flying above the German troops stationed in southern Czechoslovakia. It was dark by the time what remained of the 4. company of the 365 Rgt. of the 211.V.G.D. had assembled at Moravske

Budejovice and had started discussing what would be the best route to take to reach the American front lines. We realized that it was not going to be easy. The river Moldau was at least 100 kilometres away.

Fear now started to spread and many of the men panicked. All the soldiers decided they were going to try to reach the lines of the western Allies under their own steam. After a quick conversation several comrades and I decided that we would join up with a few Russian Hiwis ('Hilfswilligen', i.e. Russian helpers in the German army) who possessed a horse-drawn cart. The Russians, who had been with us since 1942, were former prisoners of war. The cart was loaded with two sacks of oats and ratious other provisions for the journey. The horses badly needed the oats because they were so heavily loaded and the demands made of them were great. As soon as the roads, which were very bad, improved slightly the horses were made to gallop even though the cart was really too full to go at such speeds, but we were terrified of being caught by the Red Army. We expected to see T-34 tanks around every corner.

After a cold night of travelling through the woods and hoping to make good headway we reached a road that was blocked by thousands of vehicles and carriages all going westwards. Artillery soldiers started towing their cannons to the side of the road, unhitching their horses and carrying on without their artillery. Tanks were driven forwards until every bit of fuel had been used up and then they were set on fire. Trucks packed with food supplies came to a standstill for the same reason and local inhabitants plundered the deserted trucks.

By the early morning of 9th May 1945, we had passed the city of Neubistritz (Nová Bystrice) and shortly afterwards we stopped a while to rest. The stop was vital for the horses because they had not had a break since setting off the day before. Shortly after 14.00 hours, we reached Wittingau (Trebon). There armed Czech civilians lined the streets, red flags were flying and anti-German propaganda blared from the loudspeakers. We heard that they were expecting the first Soviet tanks to arrive in twenty minutes.

The rumour turned out to be true. At 16.00 hours, Red Army trucks caught up with our little cart. The Russian soldiers sitting in the trucks ordered us to immediately hand over all our cigarettes and watches. Those who did not cooperate straight away were beaten then the trucks accelerated and sped past us. We guessed that we might well be stopped again before reaching Budsweis and we resolved not to let ourselves be robbed so easily the next time. A little while later, we stopped the cart on the side of the road and unharnessed the horses. We then walked into the forest and waited for nightfall. From in between the trees we could see Soviet units passing by all the time. We were then joined by a few German soldiers. I had little food left and by then I had thrown away my pistol. When it was completely dark, the group split up once again and I joined up with two other soldiers. From then on we hid during the daytime and travelled by night.

On 11th May, we reached the Moldau river where the current was so strong that we did not dare to swim to the other side. The banks of the river were very overgrown which meant that we could easily search in daylight for a better place to cross over without being discovered. Eventually, we arrived at a house where a woman lived on her own. She gave us bread and then ferried us over to the other side of the river one by one in her rowing boat. Once again, we soon encountered armed Czech civilians on the streets. We carefully journeyed on. By now, the weather was beautiful. All along the route we kept meeting up with other groups of soldiers. One of the soldiers I met came from a place near to where I came from in Germany. We exchanged addresses and promised to contact each other's parents on arriving home and tell of our meeting for in case anything happened to either one of us. I later heard that the soldier in question had eventually reached his parental home after having made an 800 kilometre detour.

On 14th May, we met the first Americans and immediately gave ourselves up. We were put in a camp

The 'Das Reich' division in Prague, 1945. A 'Sturmgeschütz' bulldozes over a road block erected by anti-German demonstrators. 'Das Reich' endeavoured to save as many as possible German Czechs.

For thousands in Prague help came too late. This photo was taken on 5th May 1945. 'Volksdeutschern' lie murdered on the streets.

where I was reunited with other soldiers from my battalion. It was rumoured that the camp was going to be moved 100 kilometres westwards the next day so that we would be on German soil and the rumour was later confirmed by an American colonel. Joyfully we got into the trucks that were waiting for us and before long we were nearing the German border. When we were only ten kilometres away from the German border, the trucks suddenly made a sharp turn and started head due north and we became very apprehensive. At around 22.00 hours we reached Strakonice and fifteen kilometres further on the trucks suddenly drove into a field where Russian soldiers were waiting for us. We were chased out of the trucks with sticks and robbed of everything we had. An older German officer was unable to stand the humiliation of it all and so he shot himself in the head before my very eyes.

It was only when daytime came that I fully realized what was going on. Thousands of German soldiers had been herded together in that same field. In the afternoon the Russian trucks drove away. At the end of May, we were made to continue the journey on foot. People's faces grew ever more sombre because we were marching eastwards. At Slabings station we were loaded into freight trucks. We then travelled via Vienna and Bratislava to Budapest where we were left waiting at the station there for two days with very little food and drink. Then we were transported to Romania via Hungary. In the Carpathian Mountains two locomotives had to be put in front of the train. To pull the heavily loaded train through the mountains the locomotives had to be stoked to the hilt. The clouds of smoke produced by the locomotives penetrated into our wagons and everyone started to cough. I was frightened of choking. After stopping in Ploesti we were interned in a prison camp in Tocsani for one day. The journey then continued in an easterly direction for some days. We passed through Kiev and Orel and went on to Schekino, some one hundred and seventy kilometres to the south of Moscow, where we were detained in camp number 323/15. I was sent to work in a mine. After a short time, I was examined by a female Russian doctor and fortunately she found me too weak to do heavy work. Between then and the end of 1945, approximately twenty men died in the camp each week, some of them from pneumonia, but after 1946 no one else died.

In the summer of 1947, a rumour spread through the camp that German prisoners would be able to return to Germany in 1948. The Russians took advantage of the situation and to make us work harder told us that only the fittest labourers would be released. Every month throughout 1948 and into 1949 one person would be picked as 'best labourer' of the month. In April 1949, I was transferred from camp 7321/1 (Laptewo) to camp 7323/12 (Schekino) where I was required to do construction work. In all our conversations there was only one subject that preoccupied us: the date of our release. On 24th July 1949, I heard that I was one of the men listed to be freed with the next group of prisoners to be released and that night I could not sleep. Early in the afternoon clean clothes were issued and a Russian doctor carried out the final medical checks. They particularly checked people's left armpits for SS tattoos. On leaving every man was made to sign a document stating that he would never hold the Soviet Union responsible for damages.

Finally on 2nd September, we found ourselves in a train travelling west. We were transported in open goods wagons. We passed Orsha, Borisov and Minsk and on 6th September we reached Brest where the rail gauge widened and beneath us flowed the river Bug. We travelled on through Warsaw and Poznan until we reached the Oder and Frankfurt where we were first received in the Horn barracks. Afterwards we were sent on to the army barracks at Gronenfelde where we were attended to by Red Cross nurses. On 10th September, I found myself in a train travelling towards the western zone. After hours of waiting we were finally able to leave the Soviet zone behind us and once again we were assembled in a camp. That night nobody could sleep. We were all very excited and talkative. Family members were informed of our imminent return by telex. I travelled home by train via Göttingen and walked the last part of the journey to my parental home where my mother was waiting to greet me. It is impossible to describe how I felt after 1587 days in a prisoner of war camp. All people who have ever been prisoners of war pray that no one will ever again have to go through the pain and suffering of war.'

The last days of the Hungarian-Austrian conflict were imbued with an aura of military romance. Hitler's heavily hit Hungarian legions marched in the POW camps. The war which for many had commenced in 1939 had finally come to an end.

The Army Group South had now fought its final battle. What had started as an army and army corps offensive had degenerated, in the final days of the war, into a series of weak attacks mounted by depleted army groups. Right until the very last moment, Hitler had held on to what he maintained was strategically important on the eastern front: the oil fields within the area where the Army Group South was operating.

The Hungarian tragedy

'My last headquarters in Hungary was in a castle', recalled Balck after the war. 'When I looked out of the window I could see in the garden and on the terrace beautifully dressed ladies with glittering diamonds and plunging necklines and Hungarian magnates being waited on hand and foot by liveried personnel. It was an unforgettable vision of a bygone era and it somehow became engraved on my memory. My first impulse was to think: they have gone mad! The next day as we drew nearer to the border we caught up with an ox-drawn cart that was progressing slowly along the road. The count was seated on the box and perched uncomfortably in the cart were the ladies from the castle. The evening before they had bid the old world of magnificence and splendour a fond farewell, a world that had been destroyed in a red storm, never to return and I had found myself sitting at their deathbed.'

Indeed, the end of German military activity in Hungary heralded the beginning of a new communist era, a period that had begun when the Hungarian army officer, Bela Miklos, had introduced the 'opposition party' in Debrecen on 23rd December 1944. The Horthy era which had combined all that was good and bad in Hungarian feudal, puszta romanticism, was now gone for good. The last remnants of the Habsburg legacy had been buried when Budapest had fallen. To the Hungarians it had been yet one more traumatic experience in a series of negative experiences this century culminating in the 1956 uprising that was violently quashed by the Red Army. In the extraordinary events of 1989 Hungary was the first country in the east to raise the Iron Curtain.

The wounds inflicted in 1944 and 1945 had deeply affected all Hungarians. Raul Hilberg estimated that at least 180,000 members of the Hungarian Jewish population of originally roughly 800,000 people had been killed. Other estimates, like Eugene Levai's of 618,000 dead, remained considerably higher. Many of those who survived the Holocaust had moved to countries in the west. Hungary had thus lost a huge section of its traditional middle class community. From a total population of 14,699,128 (1941 census while the country was at its biggest) 3,765,299 men were eligible for conscription. No less than 300,000 of these servicemen died on the eastern front. As a result of Soviet occupation, a further 200,000 soldiers and 295,000 civilians (other sources quote 350,000 civilians and some sources 600,000 people in total) were interned by the Red Army. According to Hungarian estimates some 120,000 of these internees died from the hardships of imprisonment. In total it amounted to more than half a million dead and to this one must add the tens of thousands of Hungarians who died as a result of the various war atrocities and during bouts of plundering and raping.

There were also tens of thousands of 'Volksdeutschen' serving in Germany. Though 35,000 of them simply fought in the Hungarian army at least 22,125 were soldiers in the Waffen-SS (voluntarily or otherwise), almost 1,800 were serving in the German army and several thousand more were engaged as labourers by the German Reich. Some of these men died. Seventy to eighty thousand Hungarian 'Germans' (according to Hungarian statistics there were some 470,000 'Volksdeutschen' living in Hungary and twice this number according to German sources) joined the retreating German forces in 1944 and 1945 and left Hungary for good. If one bears in mind that during the course of the war, many Hungarian Germans had Germanized their names and had joined pro-German (SS) organizations one can understand why these soldiers were afraid of reprisals. 'Ninety percent of 'our' Schwaben were traitors', was what was written in the first editions of the press campaign launched by the communists that was published on 23rd August 1945.

Apart from all the killing and physical injury done to people, thousands of Hungarians who had suffered mentally and traumatically from the havoc wreaked by the Red Army in Hungary. The following entry taken from a diary kept by father Matyas of Pilisszentkereszt during the war indicates what the atmosphere was like:

'On the night of 26th December 1944 Pilisszentkereszt was liberated by the Soviets. Four thousand soldiers were billeted and after the sixth day the plundering began in which even officers took part. I was robbed three times... There was great suffering amongst the people. Soviet behaviour at night-time was abominable. Women and children between eleven and seventy years of age were raped. A certain captain by the name of Vladimir was the worst. A Russian general had moved into the parsonage and the chef from the Moskva hotel was made to cook for him.'

The Hungarian escapade was a disaster for the Germans as well. The fall of Budapest alone and the casualties from the 'Konrad' operations amounted (discounting the Hungarian losses) to a total loss (wounded and missing included) of almost 70,000 men. In addition there were the 'Frühlingserwachen' deaths and the casualties incurred during the 'Reichsschutzstellung' retreat and in Vienna so that the total number of German losses was well above the 100,000 men.

The Red Army losses were also tremendous. When, on 4th April 1945, the last area of Hungarian territory was liberated no less than 140,000 Russian soldiers had by then been slaughtered. Twenty thousand of them had died in the battle of Budapest. During the fighting in Austria a further 26,000 Red Army soldiers had lost their lives. All in all this made the final Hungarian conflict go down in history as having been more bloody and more violent than the final stages of the war in Berlin.

This meant that when Hungary was liberated by the Russians it had not only automatically become part of the communist regime but the virtually feudal Horthy era had also come to an abrupt end and fascism had been banished. Already in January 1945, when the 'Konrad'

Adolf Eichmann during his trial in Israel.

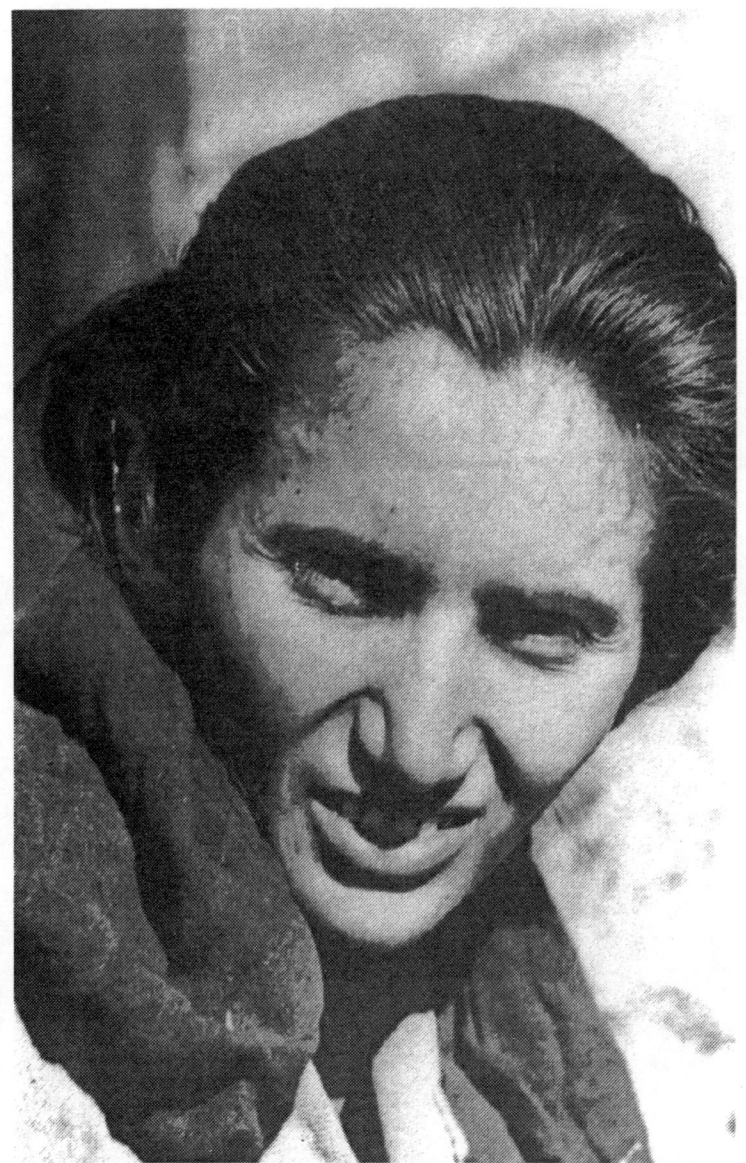

One of Eichmann's victims who survived the war. Many of the surviving Hungarian Jews decided not to return to Hungary but to seek refuge elsewhere.

Karl Ullrich, 1946, a prisoner of war in Regensburg. 'Wiking' and the Hungarian operations were history by now.

operations were in full swing, the anti-government faction was wanting to set up a people's tribunal so that Nazis could be brought to justice. The relevant trials did begin immediately after the war, in October 1945. They were held in the buildings of the music academy in Budapest. The leading Hungarian fascists, men such as Szálasi, Endre and Baky were sentenced to death and hanged. Hundreds of people turned up to witness Szálasi's execution. While two men in black coats and black hats lifted him up to the gallows with his hands tied behind his back a priest held a crucifix in front of him. Szálasi leaned forward to kiss the holy symbol then he was hanged by his executioners.
On 1st March 1948, no less than 39,514 Hungarian people were taken to court. Requests were made for death sentences to be passed 322 times and in 146 of these cases the sentence was also carried out. Around that time a number of court hearings relating to events that had taken place in Hungary were also continuing in Germany. Ribbentrop and Kaltenbrunner were held partly responsible for the tragedy that had befallen the Hungarian Jews and so too were a number of SS officers who had worked in the KZs. Curiously, Veesenmayer, without whose help the entire Hungarian Holocaust would not have been possible got off very lightly with merely a twenty year prison sentence. In 1951, his lawyer even managed to reduce the sentence by ten years and so it was that with remand Veesenmayer was released in 1952. Krumey and Hunsche, both part of the Eichmann commando team, were also given light sentences of only a couple of years. Wisliceny was extradited to Czechoslovakia and hanged in Bratislava. Speer, the driving force behind exploiting the country's economy, was given a twenty-year prison sentence.
Certain leading Nazis such as Kurt Becher, Otto Winkelmann and Adolf Eichmann escaped trials altogether by fleeing the country. Eichmann, though, was captured in Agentinia in 1960 from where he was abducted, taken to Israel, tried and hanged.

A number of officers were also made to pay for their part in the final conflict. General Von Hindy of the I. Hungarian army corps who, together with the IX.SS Geb. corps had defended Budapest, was sentenced to death and executed on 29th August 1945. His German colleague, Von Wildenbruch completed his term of imprisonment and returned to Germany many years later. Ernö Billnitzer of the army artillery unit in Budapest was imprisoned by the Soviets on 12th February 1945 and was released in 1948. In 1950, he was again arrested because of his 'hostile attitude to the State' and released again in the spring of 1956. He spent the rest of his days working as a hospital porter and died on 22nd December 1977. In the so-called OKW process which took place after the war Otto Wöhler was sentenced to eight years in prison but only had to complete half the sentence. Heinz Guderian and Sepp Dietrich received similar sentences and similar remands. A number of the veterans later wrote their memoirs: Guderian, Rendulic, Balck and Friessner. Guderian's book came to be recognized as a standard work. Balck's memoirs proved to be an interesting source of information on the army-Waffen-SS controversy. The Waffen-SS point of view was aired in a monumental book written by Georg Maier. After the war, Gille, Ullrich, and Jahnke started publishing a periodical entitled 'Wikingruf' which later changed its name to 'Der Freiwillige'. Ullrich, who had for a while served in the 'Totenkopf' division, went on to write a book on the divisional history of that particular unit. Felix Steiner, one of the founders of the 'Wiking' division, was buried in a graveyard in Munich. After the war, his humble grave became overgrown and unkempt and so Jahnke saw to it that a new headstone was erected there. 'When Herbert Gille died six men who had been decorated with the Ritterkreuz were standing at his bedside', Jahnke recalled. The old SS general had not been entitled to a pension, but his widow was supported financially by his circle of old comrades. In the post-war period Franz Hack worked on a book about the 'Westland' regiment which, during the 'Konrad II' operations, had got so close

to Budapest. In his latter years, he spent much of his time on the tennis court and preferred not to be reminded of the war too often. Once when a researcher had been pursuing a certain line of enquiry with him about a particular battle that had taken place in Hungary Hack had suddenly broken down and had started shouting: 'No more ... no more!'
During my years of research, the only 711.I.D. soldier that I was able to trace was Horst Lange. After the frontiers opened in 1989, he grasped the opportunity to travel to Hungary and look for the spot where he had almost lost his life and his youth in battle. He visited the place Dobogekö and concluded, 'it was here ...'

The Hungarian tragedy decribed here is now far behind us and today the new developments precipitated by the fall of communism in Eastern Europe are demanding all our attention. Now, fifty years on, the Hungarian tragedy may really be called history. On the other hand, though, we now have the chance to round off affairs which, because Europe was politically divided for so many years, were neglected for so long. The soldiers of then now often travel back, just one last time in their lives, to spots that were once battlefields. Holocaust survivors travel back to look at houses that once belonged to Jewish middle class citizens. The recent exhumation and reburial in Hungary of Horthy's remains is symptomatic of the present mood of wanting to 'rectify' the things of the past. Monuments have now also been erected to the Germans and Hungarians who fell in battle.

Hungarian oil, once the key strategic factor for the Germans, was no longer an important economic issue. In the early seventies the yearly oil production level was below the two million ton level which meant that Hungary was actually having to import fuel. Hungary now produces more than two million tons of bauxite per year and the annual aluminium production level exceeds 60,000 tons.

One thing that has not changed though is the importance of natural resources in the geopolitical planning of world leaders as was made only too clear during the recent war in Kuwait, in 1991.

Sources

The sources used for this book fall into one of two main categories; the material is either of a political or of a military nature. The political aspect derives chiefly from studies of the available literature and, thus, from secondary sources. The military information has been gathered partly from archive research.

When writing the chapter about the persecution of the Jews in Hungary the standard work written by Raul Hilberg was essential reading. The best sources for information on the political situation in Hungary were the Horthy memoirs and Macartney's standard book. The most valuable military source was the war diary of the Army Group South and all the relevant related documents. The diary which is virtually complete and covers events from the start of the 'Konrad' operations to the end of the war is kept in the State archive in Freiburg and in the Washington archive. It is not always easy to obtain literature on Hungary's military history. Gosztony's authoritative works on the subject are available in most university libraries. It was difficult to obtain certain of the self-published books and to gain access to the research material of the US Army War College. This latter material provided particularly good information about the final struggle on the eastern front. As far as the final battle on Austrian soil goes, the authoritative writings of Rauchensteiner were invaluable. If one shifts through the many divisional histories and military post-war memoirs one soon gains a good impression of what the atmosphere and people's frames of mind were like.

Finally, private diaries are available and eye-witness reports provided not only a valuable amount of oral history, but also a welcome break from the reading of dusty books and documents in archives and from what might otherwise have become a rather arduous task.

Select Bibliography

- Von Adony-Naredy, F., *Ungarns Armee im Zweiten Weltkrieg. Die Wehrmacht im Kampf Band 47* (1971).

- Von Ahlfen, H., *Der Kampf um Schlesien 1944/45* (Stuttgart 1980).

- Allen,W.E.D./Muratoff,P., *The Russian campaigns of 1944-45*. (London 1946).

- Andrassy,S., *Die Puszta brennt*. (Zürich 1948).

- Ardeleanu ea., *Horthyist-fascist terror in northwestern Romania. September 1940 - October 1944*. Bucharest. (1986).

- Arendt, H., *Eichmann in Jerusalem, a report on the banality of Evel*. (Middlesex 1983).

- Aschenhauer, Dr. R., (Hersg.) *Ich, Adolf Eichmann. Ein Historischer Zeugenbericht*. (Leoni am Starnberger see 1980).

- Barkai, A., *Das Wirtschaftssystem des Nationalsozialismus. Ideologie, Theorie, Politik 1933-1945* (Frankfurt am Main 1988).

- Bartalits, L.L.S., *Hongarije en de Anschluss 1918-1938*.

- Bayer, H., *Die Kavallerie der Waffen-SS*. (Heidelberg 1980).

- Beitter, G., *Die Rote Armee im 2. Weltkrieg. Eine bibliographie. Schriften der Bibliothek für Zeitgeschichte. Band 24*. (1984)

- Benz, W., *Die Vertreibung der Deutschen aus dem Osten. Ursachen, Ereignisse, Folgen*. [1985] (1995)

- Benz, W., *Antisemitismus in Deutschland*. (1995).

- Benz, W. (Hg.). *Dimension des Völkermords. Die Zahl der jüdischen Opfer des Nationalsozialismus*. [1991] (München 1996)

- Bierman, J., *Righteous gentile. The story of Raoul Wallenberg, missing hero of the Holocaust*. [1981] (1982).

- Biss, A., *Der Stopp der Endlösung. Kampf gegen Himmler und Eichmann in Budapest*. (Stuttgart 1966).

- Bloch,M., *Ribbentrop*. (1992).

- Bodolai, Z., *The Timeless Nation. The history, literature, music, art and folklore of the Hungarian Nation.* (Sydney 1978).

- Borcher, W., *Der Kessel von Budapest. 1944/45 Der Kampf um die ungarische Hauptstadt. Erlebnisberichte zur Geschichte des 2.Weltkrieges.*

- Borsody, S., (Ed.), *The Hungarians. A Divided Nation.* (1988).

- Bracher, K.D., *The German Dictatorship. The Origins, Structure, and Effects of National Socialism.* (New York 1970).

- Bracher / Funke / Jacobsen (Hersg.) *Schriftenreihe der Bundeszentrale für politsiche Bildung. Band 192. Nationalsozialistsiche Diktatur 1933-1945. Eine Bilanz.*

- Bradley, D., *Soldatenschicksale des 20.Jahrhunderts als Geschichtsquelle Band-II Hermann Balck, General der Pz Truppe a.D., Ordnung im Chaos. Erinnerungen 1893-1948.* (Osnabrück 1981).

- Braham, R.L., *The politics of genocide. The Holocaust in Hungary I,II.* (New York 1981).

- Broszat, M., / Heiber, H., (Hersg.) *DTV Weltgeschichte des 20.Jahrhunderts. Broszat, M., Der Staat Hitlers.* [1969] (1986)

- Buchheim, H., *Anatomie des SS-Staates band I. Die SS-das Herrschaftsinstument Befehl und Gehorsam. Gutachten des Instituts für Zeitgeschichte.* [1965] (1967).

- Budapester Stadtarchivs ed., *Budapest, die Geschichte einer Hauptstadt.* (Budapest 1974).

- Carp, M., *Holocaust in Rumania 1940-1944. Facts and Documents on the Annhilation of Rumania's Jews 1940-1944.* (1994).

- Carr, W, Hitler, *a Study in Personality and Politics.* (London 1978)

- Center For Land Warfare US Army War College. *Art of War Symposium 19-3 May 1986. From the Vistula to the Oder: Soviet Offensive Operations - October 1944 - March 1945. A Transcript of Proceedings.* (1986).

- Cerff, K., *Die Waffen-SS im Wehrmachtbericht.* (1971)

- Clarck, A., *Barbarossa, the Russian-German Conflict 1941-1945.* (New York 1966).

- Conner, A.Z. / Poirier, R. G., *Red Army Order of Battle in the Great Patriotic War. Including data from 1991 to the present.* (1985).

- Derogy, J., *De zaak Wallenberg. De meest tragische held van de Tweede Wereldoorlog.* (1981).

- Dettmer, F., *Die 44. Infantrie-Division Reichsgrenadier-Division Hoch und Deutschmeister 1939-1945.* (Friedberg).

- Dungan, J., / Stewart, C., *Ploesti. The spectacular ground-air battle of the 1st August 1943.* (London 1963).

- Dunnigan, J.F., *The Russian Front. Germany's War in the East, 1941-1945.* [1977] (London 1978).

- Favez, Jean-Claude, *Warum schwieg das Rote Kreuz. Eine internationale Organisation und das Dritte Reich.* [1988] (1994)

- Fekete, T., *Den Janzbach entlang. Beschreibung und Geschichte der Bergwerkgemeinde Csolnok.* (Budapest 1977).

- Fest.J., / Herrendoerfer, Chr., *Hitler eine Karriere.* (1977)

- Fischer, F., *Griff nach der Weltmacht. Die Kriegszielpolitik des kaiserlichen Deutschland 1914/18.* (Düsseldorf 1961)

- Fischer, F., *Hitler war kein Betriebsunfall.* München (1992)

- *Foreign Relations of the United States Diplomatic Papers 1944.* Vol. III. the British Commonwealth and Europe (1965).

- Friessner, H., *Verratene Schlachten. Die Tragödie der deutschen Wehrmacht in Rumänien und Ungarn.* (1956).

- Galland, A., *Die Erste und die Letzten. Jagdflieger im Zweiten Weltkrieg.* (München 198).

- *Geschichte des Grossen Vaterländischen Krieges der Sowjetunion. IV.* (Berlin 1965).

- Gilbert, M., *Auschwitz und die Alliierten.* (München [1981] (1982)

- Gladitz, N., / Lorenzo, P., *Der Fall Giorgio Perlasca. Dachauer Hefte 7, Solidartät und Widerstand.* [1991] (1995).

- Goebbels, J., *Dagboek 1945. 28 feb.-10 april 1945. De laatste veertig dagen van Hitlers propagandachef.* (1978).

- Goebbels, J., *The Goebbels Diaries 1942-1943. Edited, translated and with an introduction by Louis P.Lochner.* (1948).

- Gosztony, P., *Endkamp an der Donau.* (1969)

- Gosztony, P., *Ungarns militärische Rolle im Zweiten Weltkrieg. (Teil IV.) Wehrwissenschaftliche Rundschau 5/82.*

- Gosztony, P., *Hitlers fremde Heere. Das Schicksal der nichtdeutschen Armeen im Ostfeldzug.* (1976)

- Gosztony, P., *Unternehmen Margarethe.* (Die Zeit nr.12, 18 März 1994)

- Gosztony, P., *Miklos von Horthy, Admiral und Reichsverweser.*

- Gretschko, A. A., *Battle for the Caucasus.* (1971).

- Gretschko, A. A., *Uber die Karpaten.* (Moskou 1970).

- Grossman, A., *Nur das Gewissen, Carl Lutz und seine Budapester Aktion. Geschichte und Porträt.* (1986).

- Guderian, H., *Panzerleader.* [1957] (1980).

- Haffner, S., *Von Bismarck zu Hitler. Ein Rückblick.* [1987] (1989).

- Haffner, S., *Kanttekeningen bij Hitler.* (1975).

- Haffner, S., *Het duivelspact. De Duits-Russische betrekkingen van de eerste tot de tweede wereldoorlog.* [1988] (1989)

- Hallgarten, G. W. F. / Radkau, J., *Deutsche Industrie und Politik. Von Bismarck bis Heute.* (1974).

- Heeresgeschichtliches Museum (Militärwissenschaftliches Institut) *Militärhistorische Schriftenreihe Heft 14: Holzmann,G., Der Einsatz der Flakbatterien im Wiener Raum 1940-1945.* (1985).

- Heiber, H. (Hersg.) *Lagebesprechungen im Führerhauptquartier. Protokollfragmente aus Hitlers militärischen Konferenzen 1942-1945.* [1962] (1963).

- Henke, K. D. / Woller, H. (Hersg.), *Politische Säuberung in Europa. Die Abrechnung mit Faschismus und Kollaboration nach dem Zweiten Weltkrieg.* (München 1991).

- Hilberg, R., *Die Vernichtung der europäischen Juden.* Band I, II, III. [1961] (1990).

- Hillgruber, A., *Hitlers Tischgespräche.* [1963] (1968).

- Hillgruber. A., *Hitler. König Carol and Marschall Antonescu. Der deutsch-rumanische Beziehungen 1938-1944.* (Wiesbaden 1954).

- Hillgruber, A., *Der Zusammenbruch im Osten 44/45 als Problem der deutschen Nationalgeschichte und der Europäischen Geschichte.* (1985).

- Hillgruber, A. (Hersg.), *Probleme des Zweiten Weltkrieges. Neue wissenschaftliche Bibliothek Geschichte.* (Köln 1967).

- Hillgruber, A., *Sowjetische Aussenpolitik im Zweiten Weltkrieg.* [1972] (1979)

- Hillgruber, A., *Grossmachtpolitik und militarismus im 20.Jahrhunderts. 3 Beiträge zum Kontinuitätsproblem.* (Düsseldorf 1974)

- Hogg, I. V., *German Order of Battle 1944. The Regiments, Formations and Units of the German Ground Forces.* (1975)

- Von Horthy, M., *Ein Leben für Ungarn.* (Bonn 1953).

- *Hungarian Studies review, Vol.X Special Volume. Hungary and the Second World War* (1983).

- Institut für Zeitgeschichte Band. 35. (Oldenbourg) Szöllösi-Janze, M., *Die Pfeilkreuzler-Bewegung Ungarn. Historischer Kontext, Entwicklung und Herrschaft.* (1989).

- Irving, D., *Göring, a Biography.* [1989] (1990).

- Irving, D., *Hitlers War.* (New York 1990).

- Jäckel, E., *Hitlers Weltanschauung. Entwurf einer Herrschaft.* [1981] (1983).

- Jacobsen, H.A., *1939-1945. Der Zweite Weltkrieg in Chronik und Dokumenten.* (Darmstadt 1959)
- Jindra, Z., *Germany and the slavs in central europe.* (Prague 1961)

- Jordan, R., *Erlebt und Erlitten. Weg eines Gauleiters von München bis Moskau.* (1971).

- Juhasz, G., *Hungarian Foreign Policy 1919-1945.* (Budapest 1979).

- Jung, H., *Die Ardennenoffensive 1944/45.* (Frankfurt 1971).

- Kastner, R., *Der Kastner-Bericht.* (München 1961).

- Keegan, J., *Waffen-SS The asphalt soldiers.* The Pan/Ballantine illustrated History of World War-II. [1968] (1972).

- Kern, E., *Die Letzte Schlacht. Kampf in der Puszta zwischen Budapest und Plattensee.* (1972).

- Kerr, W., *The Russian Army, its Men, its Leaders and its Battles.* London (1944).

- Kissel, H., *Gefechte in Russland 1941-1944.* (1956)

- Kissel, H., *Die Panzerschlachten in der Puszta. Die Wehrmacht im Kampf 27.* (1960).

- Klapdor, E., *Mit dem Panzerregiment 5 'Wiking' im Osten.* (Siek 1981).

- Klee, E. / Dressen, W. (Hrsg.), *Gott mit uns. Der deutsche Vernichtungskrieg im Osten 1939-1945.* (Frankfurt am Main 1989)

- Klee, E., *Persilscheine und falsche Pässe. Wie die Kirchen den nazis halfen.* Geschichte Fischer. (1991)

- Kleine, E., / Kühn, V., Tiger. *Die Geschichte einer legendäre Waffe 1941-1945* (1981).

- Kuby, E., *Das Ende des schrecken. Dokumente des Untergangs Januar bis Mai 1945.* (München 1961).

- Landwehr, R., *Hungarian Volunteers of the Waffen-SS.* (1988).

- Lang, von, J., *Der Hitlerjunge, Baldur von Schirach. Der mann, der Deutschlands Jugend erzog.* (Hamburg 1991).

- Langer, W.C., *The Mind of Adolf Hitler. The Secret Wartime Report.* (1972).

- Laqueur, W., *Russia and Germany a century of conflict.* [1965] (1969).

- Laqueur,W., Weimar. *Die Kultur der Republik.* (1977)

- Lehmann, R., / Tieman, R., *Die Leibstandarte.IV/2* (1987).

- Leibbrandt, G., (Hersg.) *Die Bücherei des Ostraumes. Dr.I.Erhorn, Kaukasien.* (Berlin 1939).

- Lévai, E., Black *Book on the Martyrdom of Hungarian Jewry.* (Wenen 1948).

- Lévai, J. (Hersg.), *Eichmann in Ungarn. Dokumente.* (Budapest 1961)

- Littlejohn, D., *The Patriotic Traitors. A History of Collaboration in German Occupied Europe 1940/1945.* (1972)

- Loewy, H. (hg.) *Holocaust. Die Grenzen des Verstehens. Eine Debatte über die Besetzung der Geschichte.* (1992)

- Lewy, G., *De Rooms-Katholieke kerk en Nazi-Duitsland.* [1964] (1965) Polak&van gennip.

- Macartney, C. A., *October Fifteenth, a History of Modern Hungary 199-1945.* (Edinburgh 1957).

- Magenheimer, H., *Abwehrschlacht an der Weichsel 1945.* (Freiburg 1986).

- Magris, C., *Donau. Biographie eines Flusses.* [1986] (1991).

- Mammach, K., *Der Volkssturm. Das Letzte Aufgebot 1944/45. Kleine Bibliothek 233.*

- Marácz, L.K., *Hungarian Revival. Political Reflections on Central Europe.* (Nieuwegein 1996).

- Marton, K., *Wallenberg, de tragische levensloop van de Zweedse bevrijder van duizenden Joden in Boedapest die achter het ijzeren gordijn verdween.* [1982] (1983).

- Maser, W., *Der Wortbruch. Hitler-Stalin und der Zweite Weltkrieg.* (München 1995).

- Mayer, A.J., *Why did the Heavens not Darken? The Final Solution in History.* [1988] (1990).

- Maier, G., *Drama zwischen Budapest und Wien. Der Endkampf der 6.(SS) Panzerarmee 1945.* (Osnabrück 1985).

- Meyer, H., *Kriegsgeschichte der 12.SS Panzerdivision 'Hitlerjugend'. Band I, II* (1982).

- Minchinton, W.E. (ed.), *National Economic Histories., Hungary, a Century of economic Devolpment.* (New York 1974).

- Mitcham, S.W., *Hitlers Legions. German Army Order of Battle World War-II.* (London 1985).

- *Mitteilungen aus dem Jahrbuch der Kongl.ungarischen Geologischen Anstalt. XV. Band. Dr.Theodor Posewitz, Petroleum und asphalt in Ungarn.*

- Müller, R-D. / Ueberschar, G.R., *Kriegsende 1945. Die Zerstörung des deutschen Reiches.* Fischer (1994)

- Nagy, A., A *Cultural and Historical Review of Central Europe.* (Melbourne 1995).

- Palotás, Z., *A Trianoni Határok.* (Budapest 1990).

- Paul, W., *Brennpunkte, Die Geschichte der 6.Panzerdivision (1.Leichte) 1937-1945.* [1977] (1984).

- Pierik, P., *Strijd om Boedapest en Wenen 1945. (Militaire Spectator 1991/2).*

- Pierik, P., *Hongarije als wapenbroeder van Nazi-Duitsland. Hongarijes moeizame weg naar een eigen plaats in Midden-Europa. (Militaire Spectator 1991/5).*

- Pierik, P., *Van Leningrad tot Berlijn. Nederlandse vrijwilligers in dienst van de Duitse Waffen-SS 1941-1945.* (Nieuwegein 1995).

- Pohlmann, H., *Einsätze der 96.Infanterie-Division vom 4.8.1944-10.05.1945.*

- Pohlmann, H., *Geschichte der 96. Infanterie-Division 1939-1945.* (Bad nauheim 1959).

- Rahn, R., *Ruheloses Leben. Aufzeichnungen und Erinnerungen.* (Düsseldorf 1949).

- Ranki, G., *Unternehmen Margarethe. Die deutsche Besatzung Ungarns.* (Wenen 1984).

- Rehm, W., *Die Wehrmacht im Kampf, Band 21. Jassy, Schicksal einer Division oder einer Armee?* (1959)

- Rendulic, L., *Gekämpft, Gesiegt, Geschlagen.* (Heidelberg 1952).

- Riemenschneider, M., *Europäische Hochschulschriften Reihe III. Bd./Vol 316. Die deutsche Wirtschaftspolitik gegenüber Ungarn 1933-1944*. (Frankfurt am Main 1987).

- Rielau, H., *Geschichte der Nebeltruppe*. (1965).

- Ritgen, H., *Die Geschichte der Panzer Lehr Division im Westen 1944 - 1945*. (Stuttgart 1979)

- Reimann,V., *Goebbels*. (1971).

- Ros, M., *Bloednacht Mayerling. 1889-1945*. (Baarn 1989).

- Ros, M., *De jakhalsen van het Derde Rijk. De ondergang van de collabo's 44/45*. (1995).

- Safrian, H., *Eichmann und seine Gehilfen*. [1993] (1995)

- *(Der) Schicksalsweg der 13.Panzerdivision 1939-1945*. (1986)

- Schönfelder, M., *Einsatz der Verbänder der Waffen-SS auf dem Kriegsschauplatz in Ungarn in der Zeit vom 1.1.-31.3.1945*.

- Schramm, P.E. (Hersg.) *Kriegstagebuch des Oberkommandos der Wehrmacht (Wehrmachtführungsstab 1940-1945,* zusammengestellt und erläutert von Hans Adolf Jacobsen. Band I,II,III,IV,V,VI,VII.

- Schukow, G.K., *Erinnerungen und Gedanken*. (1969).

- Skorzeny, O., *Wir kämpften, wir verloren. Kriegsberichte der Waffen-SS*. (1962).

- Skorzeny, O., *Meine Kommando-unternehmen*. [1975] (1976).

- Speer, A., *Inside the Third Reich*. [1969] (1970).

- Speer, A., *Spandauer Tagebücher*. [1975] (1978).

- Speer, A., *Der Sklavenstaat. Meine Auseinandersetzungen mit der SS*. [1981] (1983).

- Spiel, H., *Glanz und Untergang. Wien 1866 bis 1938*. [1987] (1994).

- Stanton, S.L., *Order of battle, US Army World War-II*. (1984).

- Stein, G.H., *Geschichte der Waffen-SS*. [1966] (1978).

- Stoves, R.O.G., 1. *Paznzerdivison 1935-1945. Chronik einer der drei Stamm-Divisionen der deutschen Panzerwaffe.* (Bad Nauheim 1961).

- Stoves, R.O.G., *Die gepanzerten und motorisierten deutschen Grossverbände 1935-1945. Divisionen und selbständigen Brigaden - Aufstellung - Gliederung - Einsätze - Ende - Literatur.* (1986)

- Strassner, P., *Europäische Freiwillige. Die 5.SS Panzerdivision Wiking.* [1968] (1986).

- Sydnor, C.W., *Soldiers of destruction. The SS Death's Head Division 1933-1945.* [1977] (1990).

- Tieke, W., *Von Plattensee bis Osterreich. Die Heeresgruppe Süd 1945.* (Gümmersbach 1975).

- Tieke, W., *Der Kaukasus und das öl.* (1970).

- Tieke, W., *Das Ende zwischen Oder und Elbe. Der Kampf um Berlin 1945.* (Stuttgart 1981).

- Tilkovszky, L., *Acta Historica Academiae Scientiarum Hungaricae nr 20, Tilkovszky.L., Die Werbeaktionen der Waffen-SS in Ungarn* (1974).

- Tilkovszky, L., *Ungarn und die deutsche Volksgruppen Politik. 1938-1945* (Wien 1981).

- Tolstoy, N., *Die Verratenen von Jalta. Englands Schuld vor der Geschichte.* (1979)

- Toland, J., *The Last 100 Days.* [1966] (1967).

- Tremain, R., *Stalin.* [1975] (1978)

- Trevor-Roper, H.R., *Hitlers War Directives 1939-1945.* [1964] (1966).

- Trevor-Roper, H.R., *The Last Days of Hitler.* [1952] (1962).

- Truppenkamerdaschaft der 3.SS Pz.D. 'Totenkopf', W.Vopersal., *Soldaten Kämpfer, Kameraden.* Band 3 (1987), Band 5.a (1990), Band 5.b (1991).

- *United Restitution Organization. Judenverfolgung in Ungarn. Dokumentensammelung.* (Frankfurt am Main 1959).

- Venohr, W., *Aufstand in der Tatra. Der Kampf um die Slowakei 1939-1944* (1979)

- Waite, R.G.L., *Adolf Hitler als psychopaat.* [1977] (1978).

- Weidinger, O., *Kameraden bis zum Ende. Das SS-Panzergrenadier Regiment 4 'DF" 1938-1945.* [1962] (1978).

- Weidinger, O., *Division Das Reich. Der Weg der 2.SS Panzerdivision Das Reich Band V 1943-1945* (Osnabrück 1982).

- Wegner, B., *Hilters politische Soldaten: Die Waffen-SS 1933-1945.* (1983)

- Wieczynski, J.L., *The Modern Encyclopedia of Russian and Soviet History.* (1985).

- Wippermann, W., *Europäischer Faschismus im Vergleich 1922-1982.* (1983).

- Wistrich, R., *Wer war wer im Dritten Reich? Ein Biographisches Lexikon.* [1982] (1987).

Archive material

- Bundesarchiv Koblenz R4/835 fol.1/Die ungarische Industrie ab 1939. Statistisches Reichsamt, Zentralrat für die Auslandsstatistik und Auslandforschung September 1944.
- Bundesarchiv-Militärarchiv Freiburg, RH 60/V40
- Bundesarchiv-Militärarchiv Freiburg, RH 19V/45
- Bundesarchiv-Militärarchiv Freiburg, RH 19V/46
- Bundesarchiv-Militärarchiv Freiburg, RH 19V/58
- Bundesarchiv-Militärarchiv Freiburg, RH 19V/59
- National Archives, Washington D.C. Microfilm T-311, 162,163,165. (Army Group South)
- Rijksinstituut voor Oorlogsdocumentatie Amsterdam (RIOD).
- Privat archive Mirko Bayerl (Sweden), W. Vopersal (Germany), I.Heinrich (Germany), Perry Pierik (The Netherlands)

The photographs come from the State Archive in Koblenz, the National Institute of War Documentation in Amsterdam, Mirko Bayerl's private archive in Sweden and the private archive of Perry Pierik.

Verbal and written official statements/ available correspondence

- Adämmer, Reinhard (6. Pz. D.)
- Agte, Patrick (Chairman of the I.SS Pz. corps 'Comrade Circle')
- Antal, Dr. Saghy (inhabitant of Süttö)
- Banny, Leopold (writer)
- Bayerl, Mirko (Swedish researcher and authority on the 'Konrad' operations)
- Behnke, C. (4. SS. 'Polizei')
- Berwald (Chairman of the Society of Former 23.Pz.D. servicemen)
- Blume, E. (6. Pz. D.)
- Fdez-Solis (General Secretary Hermandad of the Azul/250.I.D. Division)
- Felgenhauer, Prof.Dr.Fritz (Vienna University)
- Fussen, J. (6 Pz. D.)
- Gaedcke, Heinz (Chief of Staff in the 6. army)
- Hack, Franz (5. SS 'Wiking')
- Hahl, Fritz (5. SS 'Wiking')
- Hausschildt, Werner (6. Pz. D.)
- Heinrich, Ingo (archive)
- Jahnke, Günter (01. 5. SS 'Wiking')
- Jakobs, Dr.N (3./4.Kav.Brigade/Division)
- Krűger, Walter (12. SS. 'Hitlerjugend')
- Lange, Horst (711. I. D.)
- Marácz, László, (Dutch researcher/Author)
- Menn, Waldemar (Treasurer of the 6.Pz.D. 'Comrade Alliance' (1. light))
- Meyer, Hubert (12.SS 'Hitlerjugend'/author)
- Müller, Conrad (3./4.Kav.Brigade/Division)
- Padua, A. (5. SS 'Wiking')
- Palotás,Z. (author/Budapest)
- Pohlman, Hartwig (Committee Chairman 96.I.D./author)
- Pőrtner, Heinrich (211. V. G. D.)
- Schmitz, Peter (Rgt.67/writer/researcher)
- Schmückle, Gerd (General a.D./author)
- Schraml, Franz (German-Croatian Legion Divisions)
- Siegel, Hans (12. SS. 'Hitlerjugend')
- Stahl, dr. Paul (6. Pz. D.)

- Stoves, Rolf (1.Pz.D. author)
- Stückler, Albert (I.SS Pz. corps)
- Ullrich, Karl (5.SS 'Wiking'/writer)
- Voigt, Horst (author/historian)
- Vopersal, Wolfgang (archive)
- Wanzenberg, Wilhelm (96. I. D.)

Abbreviations
(German and English explanations)

AA	(Reconnaissance unit)
Abt	(Unit)
aD	(off-duty)
AK	(Infantry corps)
AOK	(Army headquarters)
AR	(Artillery regiment)
art	(artillery)
Art	(Artillery)
AuEBtl	(training and reserve battalion)
Ob	(Commander)
B	(Observer)
BAMA	(State and Military Archives)
Btl	(Battalion)
D	(Division)
Div	(Division)
FAD	(division in training)
Flak	(anti-aircraft cannon)
Freiw	(volunteer)
G	(Guard)
Geb	(Mountain)
GefStd	(H.Q.)
Gen	(General)
Gren	(Grenadier)
Hgr	(army group)
HKL	(main front line)
I	(Infantry)
Jg	(fighter)
Kav	(Cavalry)
Kdr	(commandant)
Kgr	(combat group)
Kom	(company)
KTB	(war diary)
Lkw	(truck)
MG	(machine gun)
Mech	(mechanized)

mot	(motorized)	
O	(orderly)	
OKH	(Army High Command)	
OKW	(Supreme Command of the Armed Forces)	
Pak	(anti-tank gun)	
Pi	(engineer)	
Pol	(police)	
Pszt	(puszta)	
Pz	(panzer/armoured)	
Res	(reserve)	
Rgt	(regiment)	
s	(heavy)	
S	(infantry/grenadier)	
SD	(Security Service)	
Sfl	(mechanized artillery)	
SPW	(armoured truck)	
Szt	(saint)	
ung	(Hungarian)	
zbV	(for special employment)	
Ia	(command/leading)	
Ib	(supplies)	
Ic	(espionage)	
Id	(organization)	
O1	(of Ia)	
O2	(of Ib)	
O3	(of Ic)	

* As the reader perhaps will have noticed two different abbreviations are sometimes given for the same word (e.g. D and Div for 'division'). This is due to the fact that the abbreviations used in all the quotations have not been standardized.

Certain words or terms have not been translated because they are so typically and uniquely German.

The ranks of the SS and their British Army equivalents (1940)

Rank

SS	Wehrmacht	British Army
SS-Oberstgruppenführer	Generaloberst	General
SS-Obergruppenführer	General	Lt-General
SS-Gruppenführer	Generalleutnant	Maj-General
SS-Brigadeführer	Generalmajor	Brigadier
SS-Oberführer	Oberst	Colonel
SS-Standartenführer	" "	" "
SS-Obersturmbannführer	Oberstleutnant	Lt.Colonel
SS-Sturmbannführer	Major	Major
SS-Hauptsturmführer	Hauptmann	Captain
SS-Obersturmführer	Oberleutnant	Lieutenant
SS-Untersturmführer	Leutnant	2nd Lieutenant

Name index

Hitler is not included in the index of names

Allmendiger 47, 48
Abromeit 88
Ameiser 236
de Angelis 114, 175, 205, 214, 220, 252, 253
Antonescu 19, 27, 39, 40, 42, 43, 50, 53, 54, 55, 56, 61
Apor 98
Auguszt 94
Bach Zelewski 49, 66
Bäke 236, 237
Bakay 67
Balck 133, 135, 138, 159, 160, 168, 170, 175, 176, 185, 188, 203, 211, 214, 219, 222, 223, 225, 226, 230, 232, 233, 235, 239, 244, 273, 280
Barbie 99
Baum 214
Becher 103, 125, 279
Becker 153, 224, 264
Berlin 167
Bernadotte 103, 260
Bieber 161
Billnitzer 136, 148
Bittrich 203, 215, 216, 219, 220, 227, 232, 246, 247, 248, 250, 252
Boeltzig 238
Boetticher 263
Boosfeld 145
Bor 247
Bormann 17, 248, 263
Braham 94, 106, 108
Brand 101,102
Breith 114, 176, 181, 188, 220, 231, 232
Bullock 11
Bünau 245, 246, 248, 250
Bürckel 242
Burmeister 182
Carol II 42, 55
Chyczy 27

Conrad 149
Csatay 27
Dannecker 88
Darges 167, 170, 174
Dereser 39
Derogy 108
Dietrich 122, 201, 202, 205, 206, 207, 210, 216, 219, 225, 226, 227, 228, 232, 233, 235, 239, 241, 242, 244, 245, 248, 249, 251, 255
Dirlewanger 205, 244
Dönitz 132, 258, 261
Dörner 136
Dorr 151, 167, 182
Dorsch 123
Draganovic 99
Drakos 98
Drexler 149
Dumitrescu 55
Dülberg 149
Eckhardt 220
Ehrenpreis 106
Eichmann 15, 28, 34, 62, 74, 77, 78, 81, 88, 89, 90, 93, 94, 99,101, 102,103, 107, 108, 126, 179
Eicke 153
Eisenhower 35
Ekkesparre 145
Endre 78, 88, 92
Fegelein 103
Feine 88
Feketehalmy - Czeydner 87
Fischer 14
von Fölkersam 67
Franco 107
Franz Joseph 144, 241
Frederik the Great 117, 201
Freitag 241
Fretter Pico 61, 112, 116, 133
Freud 241
Friessner 44, 50, 53, 54, 55, 56, 57, 59, 60, 65, 70, 111, 113, 114,

115, 116, 132, 280
Fröhlich 176, 244
Gaedcke 133, 160, 161, 176, 179, 187, 189, 203, 206, 219, 226, 243
de Gaulle 48
Gehlen 120
Gercke 38
Gerstenberg 56
Gesele 236
Gilbert 94
Gille 151, 159, 179, 180, 181, 185, 231, 280
Gneisenau 19
Goebbels 40, 69, 96, 122, 201, 222, 242, 258, 261
Göring 56, 57, 123, 124, 151, 155
Gosztony 137
Gregner 146
Greiffenberg 31, 113
Greishammer 246
Grolmann 203
Grossman 107
Grothmann 176
Guderian 31, 115, 120, 127, 128, 132, 141, 179, 189, 190, 191, 216
Habsburg 241
Hack 179, 280
Haffner 12, 13
Hampel 203, 214,
Hansen 208
Harrendorf 167, 252
Harteneck 188, 216
Heiber 11
Heinrici 257
Hermani 180
Hilberg 80, 98, 103, 108, 109, 283
Hiller 85
Himmler 17, 18, 28, 32, 33, 34, 48, 85, 95, 102, 122, 135, 159, 160, 179, 180, 205, 232, 242, 243, 244, 248, 259, 260, 262
Hindy 145, 148, 280
Hintersatz 203, 205
Hofer 263
Hoffmann 230
Hoffmeyer 39, 56
Holste 185

Horthy 16, 18, 19, 20, 21, 22, 25, 26, 27, 28, 29, 31, 35, 39, 61, 62, 65, 66, 67, 68, 69, 70, 72, 79, 84, 87, 88, 91, 92, 104, 111, 144, 150, 234
Horváth 148
Hube 207
Hübner 259
Von Humboldt-Dachroeden 209
Hunsche 88, 89, 279
Jaekcel 11
Jaenecke 47
Jahnke 151, 153, 160, 168, 180, 189, 280
Janza 144, 146
Jeckeln 87
Jodl 17, 18, 39, 132, 191, 263
Jury 257
Jüttner 93
Kalandy 136
Kallay 18, 27, 29, 32, 35
Kaltenbrunner 102, 279
Kammler 92
Karoly 186
Kastner 101, 102, 103, 104, 105
Keitel 118, 127, 129, 248
Kern 72
Kernmayer 72
Kesselring 222
Kirchner 175
Klages 68
Klaus 146
Klee 99
Kleemann 235
Klein 137
Kleine 206
Kleist 18
Klement 99
Klett 147
Kliemchen 237
Kluge 48
Knoop 176
Koch 42
Koehler 221
Kokott 182
Komoloy 100
Koniev 257

König 220
Körner 258
Kostenbader 209
Krämer 206
Kraus 241
Krause 209
Kravschenko 171, 224
Kreutz 227
Kreysing 252, 253
Krüger 206, 215
Krumey 77, 88, 179
Kucklick 148
Kumm 209, 235
Kun 19, 22
Kündiger 136
Lakatos 67
Lange 178, 180, 281
Lanz 214
Lehmann 248
Lenin 12
Lentz 225, 235
Lévai 109, 273
Lewy 99
Ley 48
Liebisch 145
Lindenau 145
Lukacz 11
Lutz 107, 104
Mack 230
Magawly 234
Maier 280
Mainka 206
Manstein 18, 43
Maringgele 145
Martin 90
Marton 104
Marx 12
Michae 50, 55
Miklos 111
Malinovski 54
Mitzlaff 206
Molotov 41
Müller 102
Mussolini 61, 70
Napoleon 174
Ney 185, 186, 203
Novak 88, 86, 94

Ohlen 228
Ohlen und Adlerscron 244, 252
Oppeln Bronikowski 176
Oppenhoff 259
Ostendorf 227
Osztapenko 137
Pabst 148
Pape 161, 167, 169, 185, 236, 256
Patton 264
Peiper 208
Perlasca 107, 108
Philipp 178, 185, 186
Philipps 182
Phleps 59, 102
Phönix 147
Piepgras 207
Pipkorn 206
Pipo 238
Pius XII 97, 100
Plijew 115
Porsche 31
Pörtner 265
Portugall 146, 147
Priess 203, 207, 209, 227
Quinn 262
Quisling 104
Radowitz 61, 214, 230
Rahn 67, 68, 69, 70, 150
Rauchensteiner 241, 249, 283
Rauff 99
Rauschning 11
Reichert 170
Rendulic 249, 250, 270, 280
Reuter 207
Ribbentrop 18, 27, 41, 68, 69, 87, 88, 260, 279
Rietger 148
Roden 176
Rönnefarth 230
Roosevelt 100, 261
von Rost 207, 230
Rothe 137
Rotta 98
Rumohr 102, 129, 135, 137
Rundstedt 48, 118, 133, 222
Saur 31, 32, 124
von Schack 145

Scharnhorst 258
Schell 224
Schindler 105
Schirach 241, 242, 243, 245, 251
Schlageter 258
Schmedes 244
Schmidt 27
Schmidthuber 108, 109, 135, 144, 148
Schönfelder 146, 179
Schöning 147
Schörner 265
Schumilov 175
Schwermann 268
Seidl 88
Seredi 98
Siegel 208, 220
Siehl 230
Sipeki Balazs 79
Skorzeny 65, 66, 67, 68, 70, 111
Speer 31, 32, 39, 85, 86, 119, 123, 124, 125, 126, 210, 260, 279
Spielberg 105
Stadler 231, 232, 243
Stalin 41, 60, 185, 210
Stauffenberg 48
Steinbrenner 220
Steidl 134
Steiner 153, 280
Steinmetz 137
Stern 106
Streicher 96
Stückler 206, 216, 233
Szálasi 16, 62, 72, 73, 74, 86, 92, 93, 98, 279
Szokoll 247
Szombathelyi 27
Teleki 72, 84
Thierack 258
Thunert 185
Timoshenko 214, 215, 221, 223
Tito 27, 30, 65, 67, 221
Tittmann 97
Tolbukhin 54, 185, 228, 240
Trabandt 256, 257

Tucholsky 13, 14
Ullrich 153, 187, 231, 234, 280
Veesenmayer 29, 62, 67, 68, 69, 70, 72, 88, 93, 150, 279
Vetserab 241
Verres 111
Vertessy 132
Viktor 17
Vlassov 261
Vogel 230
Vogt 174, 187, 234
Vojacek 230
Vörös 65, 111
Wächtler 131
Wagner 242
Waldenfels 255, 264
Walker 264
Wallenberg 105, 106, 107, 108
Weichs 19
Weidemann 181
Weidinger 265
Weiss 105, 124
Wenck 116, 133
Wendrinsky 145
Westrick 85
Wieshofer 251
Wildenbruch 133, 134, 136, 137, 138, 141, 142, 179, 280
Wilson 62
Winkelmann 29, 62, 65, 133, 279
Winkler 57
Wisliceny 77, 78, 101, 279
Wittgenstein 241
Wöhler 60, 61, 112, 114, 115, 116, 133, 145, 159, 161, 165, 169, 174, 175, 177, 180, 207, 210, 211, 219, 221, 224, 226, 228, 232, 233, 239, 248, 261, 280
Wolf 135, 138
Zacharov 215
Zehender 102, 135
Zeitler 275
Zhukov 153, 257
Zimmerhackl 230
Zstojay 88